Contributors include: Sven Arne Bergmann, Donald L. Burnham, Louis Dupré, Maurice Friedman, Erich Heller, Walter Kaufmann, Theodore Lidz, Paul Ricoeur, Joseph H. Smith, Helm Stierlin, Erwin W. Straus.

"This inaugural volume is a disparate collection of 10 essays by 5 psychoanalysts and 6 humanists, the latter being professors of philosophy, religion, and the humanities. The papers span a wide range of topics, including art, literature, philosophy, language, ethics, mysticism, healing and creativity, and are arranged in three groups, relating psychiatry to art and literature, to philosophy and the development of thought, and to human affairs.

" A rich intellectual fare is offered by these papers for those who define psychoanalysis in terms of interpretation or hermeneutic activity and therefore as a discipline with more affinity for the humanities than for the natural sciences. . . . A stimulating adventure in ideas in the very important area of the relationship between the humanities and psychiatry."
—*American Journal of Psychiatry*

"A valuable contribution to the dialogue between psychoanalytic theory and humanist scholarship."—*Psychiatry*

Psychiatry and the Humanities, Volume 2

Thought, Consciousness, and Reality

Associate Editor
Harold A. Durfee, Ph.D.

Assistant Editor
Gloria H. Parloff

Editorial Aide
Katherine S. Henry

Published under the auspices of the
Forum on Psychiatry and the Humanities
The Washington School of Psychiatry

Psychiatry and the Humanities

VOLUME 2

Thought, Consciousness, and Reality

Editor
Joseph H. Smith, M.D.

New Haven and London   Yale University Press

1977

Library of Congress catalog card number: 76-640132
International standard book number: 0-300-02138-0

Designed by John O. C. McCrillis
and set in Baskerville type.
Printed in the United States of America by
The Vail-Ballou Press, Inc., Binghamton, New York.

Published in Great Britain, Europe, Africa, and
Asia (except Japan) by Yale University Press,
Ltd., London. Distributed in Latin America by
Kaiman & Polon, Inc., New York City; in
Australia and New Zealand by Book & Film
Services, Artarmon, N.S.W., Australia; and in
Japan by Harper & Row, Publishers, Tokyo
Office.

Contributors

Harold A. Durfee, Ph.D. William Frazer McDowell Professor of Philosophy, American University

Isaac Franck, Ph.D., A.C.S.W. Department of Philosophy, University of Maryland; formerly on the philosophy faculties at Catholic, Howard, and American Universities

Stuart Hampshire, F.B.A. Warden of Wadham College, Oxford

Albert Hofstadter, Ph.D. Professor of Philosophy, The Graduate Faculty, New School for Social Research, New York City

John S. Kafka, M.D. Clinical Professor of Psychiatry and Behavioral Sciences, George Washington University School of Medicine; Supervising and Training Analyst, Washington Psychoanalytic Institute; Consultant, National Institute of Mental Health

Wolfgang Loch, Dr. med. Professor of Psycho-Analysis, University of Tübingen, West Germany

W. W. Meissner, S.J., M.D. Chairman of Faculty, Boston Psychoanalytic Institute; Associate Clinical Professor of Psychiatry, Department of Psychiatry, Harvard Medical School; Staff Psychiatrist, Massachusetts Mental Health Center and the Cambridge Hospital

Stanley Palombo, M.D. Teaching Analyst, Washington Psychoanalytic Institute; has taught psychiatry and psychoanalysis at Harvard, Howard, Georgetown, and American Universities

Zeno Vendler, Ph.D. Professor of Philosophy, University of California, San Diego; author of *Linguistics in Philosophy* (Cornell University Press, 1967), *Adjectives and Nominalizations* (Mouton, 1968), and *Res Cogitans* (Cornell University Press, 1972)

Contents

Preface   ix

Introduction
  by Harold A. Durfee   xv

Thought and Consciousness
1 The Explanation of Thought
   by Stuart Hampshire   3
2 Words in Thoughts
   by Zeno Vendler   25
3 Dreams, Memory, and the Origin of Thought
   by Stanley R. Palombo   49
4 Consciousness, Thought, and Enownment
   by Albert Hofstadter   85
5 Analytic Philosophy, Phenomenology, and the
   Concept of Consciousness
   by Harold A. Durfee   111

The Construction of the Real
6 On Reality: An Examination of Object Constancy,
   Ambiguity, Paradox, and Time
   by John S. Kafka   133
7 Cognitive Aspects of the Paranoid Process—
   Prospectus
   by W. W. Meissner   159
8 Some Comments on the Subject of Psychoanalysis
   and Truth
   by Wolfgang Loch   217
9 Spinoza, Freud, and Hampshire on Psychic Freedom
   by Isaac Franck   257

Index   310

Preface

One source of Freud's creativity was sparked by conflict regarding his own philosophic bent. During the major part of his work he was regularly ready to derogate philosophic endeavor and to emphasize the differences between his own and philosophic methods. However, late in his life he wondered if, after all, psychoanalysis had perhaps in a roundabout way led him to philosophy.

In part, Freud's questions about philosophical thought were related to his view that a knowledge of the contributions of psychoanalysis would inevitably lead philosophers to change some of their formulations. For example, in 1913 he wrote:

> Philosophy, in so far as it is built on psychology, will be unable to avoid taking the psycho-analytic contributions to psychology fully into account and reacting to this new enrichment of our knowledge. . . . In particular, the setting up of the hypothesis of unconscious mental activities must compel philosophy to decide one way or the other and, if it accepts the idea, to modify its own views on the relation of mind to body. . . . It is true that philosophy has repeatedly dealt with the problem of the unconscious, but, with few exceptions, philosophers have taken up one or other of the two following positions. Either their unconscious has been something mystical, something intangible and undemonstrable, whose relation to the mind has remained obscure, or they have identified the mental with the conscious and have proceeded to infer from this definition that what

is unconscious cannot be mental or a subject for psy-chology.[1]

Currently, a growing number of philosophers are taking a serious interest in Freud's work, and psychoanalysts are becoming increasingly aware that basic points of difference within their own field often reflect unrecognized philosophic presuppositions. In this volume five philosophers and four psychoanalysts, while respecting the differences of fields and methods, offer mutually relevant reflections on a topic central to both fields—thought, consciousness, and reality.

To think is to represent. All thought is by a subject and of something. In broadest usage, what we mean by thinking is coextensive with what we mean by mind and the realm of the psychological. In these forms, sensation is also a mode of thought, as are drives and affects. (Drives are said to be represented by ideas and affects, but drives too are a level of representation, though not temporally prior to their embodiment in ideas and affects.) To think about thinking is to think of the nature of various modes of thought, each with its own mode of purposiveness or intentionality and each as a mode of representing the subject who thinks and that about which he thinks—the subject and his world. Human thought achieves awareness of this polarity in the passage from consciousness to self-consciousness.

Although in its broadest usage the term *thought* includes a hierarchy of modes, its meaning among both philosophers and psychoanalysts usually tends to be restricted, to refer to rational thought—in psychoanalytic terms, reality-oriented, conceptually organized, secondary-process thinking. Other modes of thinking in the broader use of the term tend to be qualified by special names—for example, primitive ideation,

1. Sigmund Freud, "The Philosophical Interest of Psycho-Analysis (1913)," *Standard Edition of the Complete Psychological Works* (London: Hogarth Press, 1955), 13 : 178.

drive-organized thought, primary-process thinking, fantasy thinking, affective modes of knowing, dreaming, special non-rational modes of thought that characterize creative and mystical experience, and special irrational modes of thought that characterize mental disorder.

One approach toward comprehending thought is to focus on its clearest and least ambiguous instance—the orderly, intentional, conscious thought of a rational person—as the proper realm in which to seek for a clear explanation of thought. Another approach toward comprehending thought is to seek for universals and interrelationships among the entire gamut of thought modes. However, in both approaches, rational, secondary-process thought is a clear point of reference.

Regarding thought as a point of reference, Paul Ricoeur wrote, in *Fallible Man* [2]:

> The strength of "transcendental" reflection is twofold. First, it lies in the choice of a beginning: it looks for this beginning in an examination of the power of knowing. We may reprove as much as we like this reduction of man to a knowing being, but this heroic reduction is by no means the result of a prejudgment. It is the decision to situate all of man's characteristics with reference to the one which a critique of knowledge brings into focus. This leaves everything to be worked out subsequently; but all the questions, those concerned with doing and those with feeling, if they are preceded by an investigation of the power of knowing, are placed in a specific light which is suitable for a reflection on man. The fundamental categories of anthropology, including and above all those which characterize action and feeling, would not be anthropological categories if they did

2. Paul Ricoeur, *Fallible Man,* trans. C. Kelbley (Chicago: Henry Regnery, 1965).

not first undergo the critical test of a "transcendental reflection," that is, an examination of the power of knowing. [pp. 26–27]

Perhaps the proudest title among psychoanalytic efforts to situate all of man's characteristics with reference to thought is David Rapaport's *Organization and Pathology of Thought*.[3] He closed the final chapter, "Toward a Theory of Thinking," by writing:

Thus a complex picture of thought-disorders emerges, which cannot be reduced to any single factor. Not even the powerful conception of regression to earlier phases of thought-development—which certainly is one aspect of most thought-disorders—can account by itself for these complex phenomena: much of what is automatized and autonomous remains unreversed by regression, and some may be irreversible in principle. It would seem that, after the many attempts to explain thought-disorders by a simple theory have proved partial or irrelevant, this complex phenomenon will finally exact a complex explanation. [p. 730]

The present volume, also toward a theory of thinking, considers various aspects of the theme set by Stuart Hampshire in the second Edith Weigert Lecture, "The Explanation of Thought." In explaining thought and in differentiating psychological explanation from the explanation of physical states and events, Hampshire seeks to establish the basis for his own and Spinoza's concept of human freedom. We find this theme recurring in Franck's article, "Spinoza, Freud, and Hampshire on Psychic Freedom," in Durfee's comments on the dialectic of consciousness and ontological powers, and in Hofstadter's concept of *enownment* as "liberation from and liberation into."

3. David Rapaport, *Organization and Pathology of Thought* (New York: Columbia University Press, 1951), p. 730.

Enownment, the process by which alienation is transformed into appropriation, is also discussed in other terms in several of the other papers. In the psychoanalytic terminology of externalization and internalization, the concept is the pivot of Meissner's study, "Cognitive Aspects of Paranoid Process." It is also related to Loch's consideration of the individual's construction of the "truth" of his own life; to Kafka's urging that both individual and communal alienation might be decreased by greater tolerance for (enownment of) multiple realities, along with the ambiguity and paradox they create; and to Palombo's suggestions on how new experience is integrated with long-term memory.

Vendler, in "Words in Thought," argues that thought is not simply suppressed speech. "Language is the means of expressing thoughts, not of having them." Durfee also touches on the issue of thought and language, questioning the search of analytic philosophers for meaning in the use of ordinary language—supposedly unambiguous—and, more broadly, questioning whether an explanation of consciousness can be given with clarity or must of necessity be ambiguous.

A line of tension between the search for clarity and the inevitability of ambiguity and paradox is maintained throughout the various points of views presented in these reflections on the genesis and nature of thinking. The polarity is correlative with the fact that all modes of thought other than sensation and perception reflect the structure of an original quest for the *absent* object. The object is given in sensation and perception; the object is constructed in ideation and thought. The object is received/constructed by a subject that comes into being and achieves (receives/constructs) selfhood and self-awareness by virtue of interaction with the object. A relatively stable self-object world is constructed but it endures not only by virtue of established structure but also by constant recurrence of the activity wherein self and object mutually constitute each other and a world.

A synthesis of perspectives into a unitary awareness of the object gives rise to a unitary awareness of the subject who has achieved the synthesis. To the first strength of Ricoeur's account of "transcendental" reflection, the second can now be added:

> reflection of a "transcendental" style . . . begins with the object, or to be more precise, with the *thing*. It is "upon" the *thing* that this reflection discerns the power of knowing, upon the thing that it discovers the specific disproportion of knowing, between receiving it and determining it. Upon the thing it apprehends the power of synthesis . . . reflection upon the object . . . brings into view . . . that in the subject which makes the synthesis possible. [p. 28]

J.H.S.

Introduction

HAROLD A. DURFEE

The central motifs that pervade these philosophic and psychoanalytic contributions extend the theoretical frontiers of both disciplines. The themes of ambiguity and paradox return time and again, as features of both the life of thought and the structure of reality. In addition, the Kantian concern with the real and the reconstructed past appears frequently. A third theme is one that permeates twentieth-century self-reflection, the freedom of man and the structure of reason. In the discussion of all of these concerns one finds an underlying tension or dialogue between classical rationalistic theory and the challenge to such rationalism arising from the phenomenological and existential borders of contemporary European self-understanding. Throughout the following essays this tension is evident in the intersection of the disciplines, for in the theoretical elaboration of modern issues in psychiatry as well as in philosophy, one will find considerations of the themes enunciated above: paradox and ambiguity, the real and the mind's constructions, freedom and reason, and rationalism and its limits.

Stuart Hampshire's Weigert Lecture, initiating this volume, continues the rethinking of Spinozism in the context of contemporary philosophy of mind, which he has pursued in previous publications. This lecture presents his most recent reflection on the ability of reason to influence our actions, and thus Hampshire provides a self-reflexive interpretation of human freedom. He develops extensively the uniqueness of psychological explanation and the limits of physical explanation for the interpretation of states of consciousness, thereby establishing the limits of psychology as a science in the explanation of mind. The very nature of thought, irreducible to discrete events, places strenuous limits on the scientific analysis of thought, for the laws of thought have their own unique character, neither identical with nor reducible to laws of physical nature.

In much Anglo-Saxon philosophy of mind and philosophy of language, thought is intimately associated, if not identified, with language. Zeno Vendler here analyzes the place of language in the life of thought, continuing thereby the careful investigation of thought that he initiated with *Res Cogitans,* and offering a fundamentally anti-Platonic interpretation of this relationship. Vendler associates thought specifically with man, as intrinsically related to man's linguistic ability, without succumbing to the modern temptation to reduce thinking to language. Thought is not "silent talk," and the philosophy of mind is not reducible to a philosophy of language.

Stanley R. Palombo's contribution returns attention to Freud and especially to the phenomenon of dreaming and memory in relationship to the interpretation of thought. Continuing his earlier work on dreams and memory, Palombo refines Freudian concerns with dreams, by use of information-processing models unavailable to Freud. He analyzes the way in which dreaming plays a central role in the processing of information to be accumulated as memory, as well as aiding in the development and evolution of reflective consciousness.

With Albert Hofstadter's essay on enownment, we turn more directly and explicitly to the concerns of Continental theory, which Hofstadter has regularly investigated, with special reference to the reflections of Martin Heidegger. Out of this European tradition Hofstadter offers a careful analysis of what it is for a thought to be owned. The doctrine of the intentionality of consciousness is clearly presupposed, while the essay concentrates upon the nature of the appropriation in the practice of therapy. Hofstadter distinguishes among consciousness, thinking, and practice, and explores the dialectic in which each of these features of mind appropriates its intended referent; for it is in such appropriation that what lies alien to the subject is made one's own.

It is especially fitting that after consideration of Anglo-Saxon philosophy of mind and philosophy of language, and after serious attention to Continental theories of thought and being, we turn to a consideration of the relationship between these two quite diverse traditions, for this division has dominated twentieth-century interpretations in both philosophical and psychiatric theory. In his essay, Harold A. Durfee continues his previous investigation into this relationship. He analyzes four areas of fundamental disagreement between them that demand attention if the modern mind is to establish productive conversation between traditions and cultures that have so seriously separated themselves from one another in this century. In the process of this analysis he proposes that the interpretation of the nature and status of consciousness—especially in regard to its clarity about the real and its relationship to being and language—is central to the overcoming of this deepest division of contemporary philosophy.

In John S. Kafka's essay, which explores some of the relationships between thought and reality, the focus is upon ambiguity and temporality. Kafka devotes special attention to cognitive relativity and the downfall of "commonsense reality." He draws upon Russell's "theory of types" for insight into ambiguity and levels of psychoanalytic explanation. The analysis of paradox is then applied to the temporal character of phenomena, especially in the psychoanalytic situation, focusing upon the role of changing time spans in the very presence and constancy of the object.

W. W. Meissner's essay develops further his research into the theory of the paranoid process. Beginning with the ambiguity of the internal-external distinction, of which Hampshire makes use, he notes its importance for the fantasy-reality distinction in psychiatry. By this analysis we have returned to one aspect of the problem of intentionality, and a rather detailed interpretation of how the process of intending an object arises or occurs. Meissner finds the psychoanalyst occupying a unique location for the investigation of this internal-external phenomenon. He then offers a careful analysis of the paranoid process with its use of introjection and projection, and a detailed elaboration of the fantasy-reality distinction, thereby providing a metapsychologic interpretation of the achievement of a sense of reality. He further analyzes the role of this dialectic in the development of self-identity as well as in the differentiation of the self from objects, allowing him to outline a program for the psychoanalytic investigation of one aspect of the cognitive process.

With Loch's essay on the concept of truth in psychoanalysis, we return again to the influence of Continental and existential philosophical theories upon psychoanalytic theory. The analysis is offered by a psychoanalyst quite conscious of most recent phenomenological and analytic philosophical reflection. Loch distinguishes between scientific and existential truth, emphasizing that in the psychiatric situation, the psychic world must make sense to all of the parties concerned; he thus introduces consideration of the modern attention to the problem of meaning since Frege. Truth must become the construction of meaning as "existence-carrying truth." Psychiatry seeks what the Hebrew contribution to Western civilization knew as "truth to live by," the analysis of which allows Loch to appropriate Wittgenstein's critique of private language.

It is particularly appropriate that a volume using Hampshire's Weigert Lecture as a point of departure should conclude with one of the few extended studies of Hampshire's thought in historical perspective—the essay by Isaac Franck.

It is also highly appropriate that a discussion between psychiatrists and philosophers should conclude with an exploration that serves as a bridge between them—a probing analysis of the relationship of Hampshire's thought to Freud as well as to Spinoza. There is no more central theme upon which to focus such exploration than that of freedom, and it is just such an investigation of historical and psychiatric theory as the context of Hampshire's thought that is offered by Franck. The analysis allows Franck to penetrate in some depth the intimacy of reason and human freedom, and to raise the serious question as to whether Hampshire's position is ultimately too rationalistic.

In these contributions centered around Hampshire's reflections, philosophers and psychiatrists have explored the latest developments in contemporary theory within and across both disciplines. While the mind is the ever-present focus of attention of both fields, each also intends to approach the real. These essays constitute an interdisciplinary consideration of these mutual concerns and of the theoretical issues implicit therein. They also exemplify that when psychiatry lives on the borderline of the humanistic disciplines, as this series of volumes strives to illustrate, it lives uniquely and authentically on its own most significant frontiers.

Thought and Consciousness

1

The Explanation of Thought

Stuart Hampshire

I have argued elsewhere [1] that psychological explanation has at least one peculiarity that distinguishes it from explanation of physical states and events: that a man's knowledge of, and his beliefs about, the factors determining his own states always modifies these states; and that a man's sentiments and attitudes are never independent of what he explicitly believes them to be. This is a complex subject that can be summarized under the heading of the reflexiveness of states of mind.

What a man believes about the nature and causes of a physical state of his does not always, or perhaps even generally, modify the state. If it does, we need to know how it does—that is, we need to know what the mechanism of the alteration is. But if I come to think that I love something or someone, my sentiment, whether it is love or not, is changed by my coming to believe that it is love.

This is *one* distinguishing feature of psychological explanation, which may be a good basis for saying that deterministic conceptions cannot finally be applied without restrictions to mental events: the subject's knowledge of the cause always, in his own case, to some degree modifies the effect.

The Edith Weigert Lecture, sponsored by the Forum on Psychiatry and the Humanities, Washington School of Psychiatry, Nov. 21, 1975.
1. Stuart Hampshire, *Freedom of Mind and Other Essays* (Princeton, N.J.: Princeton University Press, 1971), chap. 1.

All the human sciences have to work within this limiting condition—sociology and psychology particularly. In this respect, they must always be unlike the nonhuman natural sciences. Belief in sociological and psychological theories affects the subject matter to which these sciences are applied.

I shall here talk about different limitations or constraints on psychology as a science—constraints that also arise from the nature of thought, and that affect what can be considered as explaining a thought, as opposed to explaining a physical state or event. We conceive of persons (at least) as both thinking beings and as physical systems. As physical systems, persons are organisms that function in accordance with the laws of physics and of chemistry, some of the laws being known to us, many unknown. The outputs—that is, the behavior of the organisms described in physical terms—must be regularly correlated with physical inputs, even if the regularities are very complex relative to our intelligence, and even if they will always be difficult for us to discern. As thinking beings, severally, each man thinks of himself in the first person as a thinking subject, and, through dependence on the responses of others, thinks also of other persons as thinking beings.

Let us consider the first-person necessity first, and the way in which the question Why? as the demand for an explanation is naturally raised about my sentiments and attitudes. I have at any time desires, beliefs about my present situation, expectations about the future, fears about the future, plans and intentions linked to the expectations. I have a complex of propositional attitudes of these various kinds, and they explain what I am doing.

The question Why? asked about any of the thoughts, is always a challenge to connect the explicandum referred to with the network of thoughts of the same kind that the subject has, or has had: a belief with other beliefs, a fear with other fears and with beliefs, a want with other wants and with beliefs, and so on. A person is the locus of an immense store of beliefs, desires, and fears, and of many other propositional attitudes and sentiments that are all compounded of beliefs and desires.

I have elsewhere stressed a normative or quasi-normative element in the first-person questions and challenges about beliefs: Why do I believe this? I try to assure myself, if I can, that my beliefs, taken as a whole, are not incoherent and contradictory—that they do not cancel each other out and therefore become unacceptable.

Here I want to stress an essential feature of a person's desires and beliefs: that the immense store of his beliefs and desires is a store of which he is most of the time oblivious and unconscious. Under all normal conditions, we are totally unaware of the great majority of the vast variety of beliefs about the environment, and expectations of the future, that guide our actions and that enter into our plans and intentions. Most of them have never been formulated or expressed. There is no reason why they should be formulated or expressed, unless in response to an explicit inquiry; and in reply to explicit questions, only a tiny minority of our beliefs and desires and fears are expressed, whether the questions are self-addressed or other kinds.

The standard thought is one that has never been expressed in words or even brought into full, self-conscious awareness. A good example of a standard thought—an example taken from Wittgenstein, I think—is that expressed by the man who stumbles at the bottom of the stairs and says, to explain his stumble, "I thought there was another step." This kind of thought is more usual than the more elaborate thought expressed in the full sentence, I have been thinking about x and I have come to the conclusion that x is y. We do not know most of the inferences that we are making unless we are asked why we reached a certain conclusion; then we need to reconstruct the steps in our thought by which the conclusion was reached. A special ability may be required to recall and reconstruct the inferences and calculations that have been involved. The thought of skilled craftsmen and performers of all kinds, and also of game-players, is often particularly inaccessible to their own reflection; reflection is precisely the kind of thought, or topic of thought, in which they are not interested and in which their skill does not reside, unless they are also teachers. All of us, although sometimes to a much lesser degree, exercise analogous skills that we would have difficulty in expressing as thoughts.

The vast store of our collateral knowledge and beliefs is drawn upon in the day-to-day inferences that practical thought requires. In this respect, at least, a computer is a passable representation of a thinking creature, because when a question is put to it, it employs a store or bank of accepted propositions. Although as thinkers we are very much more versatile than the computer and also, in general, slower and more liable to interruption, we resemble the computer in our instantaneous use of a great number of stored propositions in responding to a problem presented. The light of consciousness illuminates only a small part of the store at any time. In contrast to this view of thinking, Descartes held that thinking depends on "ideas" and is associated with representation in consciousness. Spinoza, on the other hand, resisted this conceptualization of thought. To say of a creature that it is thinking is not to attribute any specific experience, or range of experiences, to it. It is to attribute to it a consistent tendency to more or less orderly and very complex responses, both linguistic and nonlinguistic, to very complex stimuli, including utterances in response to questions.

The orderliness and the connectedness of the complex responses, whether to situations or to questions, are necessary to thinking. A mental process may be day-dreaming, or musing, or the free indulgence of fantasy and imagination. But it will still have, as thought, a set of associative linkages when more rational ones are lacking. What free association in psychoanalysis reveals is always a connected process of thought, however concrete, metaphorical, and surprising. Insofar as orderliness and connectedness are lacking in an area of a person's behavior, we refuse to describe the process or performance as one manifesting thought in any strict sense. We sometimes speak of a mere *feeling* that something will happen as opposed to a *belief* that it will, just because there are insufficient connections and associations to justify the words *thought* or *belief* in this particular case.

To some degree, thoughts must be associated with other thoughts in order to count as thoughts; they come, as it were, in clumps, and the question Why? asked with reference to any particular thought is expected to elicit other thoughts that are associated with it, as evidence, as background, as occasioned by the same perception, or as in some way closely related to any of these three sources. In the philosophical literature, and particularly in Spinoza, the requirement of connectedness has been expressed by emphasizing the difference between the mere occurrence of images and the activity of thought, with the implication that a process of thought is not normally a succession of discrete events, as a succession of images is.

Certainly there are occasions when a single thought suddenly occurs to one—a thought, one might say, in isolation. This thought is usually of a specific kind: a hope, a wish, a belief, a fear, a doubt, a memory. But the thought that suddenly strikes one or drifts into one's mind has a wider context of thoughts, even though that context, and the connections within it, may not be known immediately to the subject, and may need to be searched for and uncovered. My argument does not require that there should be no unconnected and isolated thoughts, properly called thoughts, that come to mind and that are not parts of a continuous activity of thinking. Such thoughts certainly do occur. My argument does require that we look always for the contemporaneous thoughts, usually unconscious or preconscious ones, that form a context for the apparently isolated thought. When a possible context of contemporary thoughts has been found, however ragged and incomplete, it becomes possible to look for the connections within the clump. If the isolated thought remains entirely isolated from any context of thought immediately following or immediately preceding, conscious or unconscious, even when the subject has tried to find such a context, it would then seem that a mere string of words or a sentence had come into the subject's mind rather than a thought; or perhaps an image, if that was the medium of the so-called thought.

I have so far made three suggestions about thinking: first, that most of our thoughts, and particularly our beliefs and desires, are preconscious or unconscious or not fully conscious, and that we are not explicitly aware that we have them until a question, or perhaps a situation requiring action, leads us to reflect on them; secondly, that a process of thought is orderly, and is not normally represented as a succession of discrete events in a person's mind, as a succession of images is; thirdly, that for any given thought, whether belief or desire, there are connections with a clump of other beliefs or desires, many of them stored but forming a context within which the given belief or desire is placed. To these three features, we must add the equally important quality that I mentioned initially: thoughts, whether beliefs or desires, may always be made the object of second-order thoughts, beliefs about beliefs, desires about desires; and what a person believes about the nature and causes of his thoughts, including his beliefs, to some extent modifies the thoughts. If one puts these four features of thought together, and if one then inquires into the way in which the question Why? is answered in respect of thought, some negative conclusions appear immediately. First, that we should not expect to find explanations of thought that take the form of correlations, experimentally tested, between inputs of some specific kind and the outputs that are individual thoughts; for individual thoughts are not usually distinct and independently identifiable occurrences, in the sense that images and sensations are. Secondly, experimental observation of thoughts, by varying inputs in order to test variations in thoughts, is scarcely practicable as a consistent method of investigation, for several reasons; one of the reasons is that the reflection on thought is apt to modify and to complicate the original thought.

The question Why? asked about a particular person's past belief or desire, or about thoughts of other kinds, may be addressed to the thinking subject, as the person who is in the best position to know the answer. He may be self-deceived and he may make a mistake. But he is certainly in a privileged position in trying to trace the dependence of one belief upon another, and of the dependence of a desire on a combination of beliefs and other desires. A close observer may infer the dependences, having listened to the subject's reasonings and having watched his behavior, and sometimes he may even be able to convince the subject that he is deceived in his view of the connections in his own mind. But even if the subject is certainly not infallible, he is at least privileged in respect to conscious thought. He will modify his beliefs and desires, and they will change, as he reflects on their causal connections. He will even on occasion be ashamed of the causal dependences when he reflects on them, and he will consequently disavow and change what he has discovered to be his previous thinking.

The hypothesis that I present to you is that the explanation of thought, in the broadest sense of that word, will always be an explanation that links thought to thought by causal connections that are themselves explained by laws of thought, which are unlike the laws that govern physical processes in at least two respects: first, that they are in part normative, in the sense that they define a process of thought that is intelligible as thought; and *thought* is here a word that sets a standard or norm that distinguishes thought from a random sequence of images.

As it is natural, in our conception of things, that a physical change should occur in accordance with very general, quantitatively expressed laws of motion, so it is natural, in our conception of things, that a change in a belief, desire, or other propositional attitude should occur as the outcome of an argument of some kind, or of something that resembles an argument, or that could be erroneously taken for one, even though the steps of the argument are not represented as distinct events in the mind.

It is possible that a man can have in mind a good argument as the basis of a belief or desire that he has, whereas in fact his belief or desire is not, on this particular occasion, the outcome of that argument but rather of a much worse argument or pseudo-argument, and of a very low-grade inference. An extreme, but not freakish, case will illustrate the point: a man may be caused to believe by a hypnotist's suggestion that a cigarette will harm his lungs; at the same time, it may be true that he believes that cigarettes do harm his lungs because of what the doctor treating him for acute bronchitis has told him.

Another possibility is that a belief can be overdetermined, as, for example, most of our ordinary perceptual beliefs are, and that there are two or more independent, sufficient explanations of one's opinion. A person may know about himself that although some of the beliefs stored in his mind could constitute an argument for a certain conclusion, he in fact reached that conclusion in this instance by another, and perhaps inferior, train of thought. He would know this about himself if the second train of thought was entirely explicit and present to his consciousness, perhaps even expressed in speech or in writing at the time.

It is normally a condition of an acceptable explanation of a thought that the explanation should constitute a basis for a consequent transition of some kind, or that it could be taken as a basis for a consequent transition of some kind, as associations of ideas can be. An association of ideas is an inference that may be founded on some deceiving and superficial features of a thought, or rather of its expression; understanding the explanation entails perceiving either the connection to the thought, or the nature of the illusion of such a connection. One must distinguish the statement, He had a reason for thinking y, from a statement of the form, The association that made him think y, is a correct [or appropriate or reasonable] association. The singular causal judgment requires that a passage of connected thinking be referred to a particular occasion and the associations at that time, in the same way that a singular causal judgment about a physical change refers to a particular occasion, and to the instantiation of a law or correlation on that occasion.

An objection suggests itself: how can there be a causal relation, referred to a particular occasion, which is not a relation between entirely distinct and independently identifiable events? Have I not denied that the steps in a process of thought can normally be individuated as separate events? I have: on rare occasions the separate steps in a process of thought can occur in consciousness as distinguishable events, but this is the exception, not the rule. The causal connections are not established, as are causal connections between physical events, by referring to laws correlating independent events, but by laws referring to internal connections between thoughts, connections that make the thoughts seem intelligible. Yet the singular causal judgment, This belief that p made me believe that q, entails the singular hypothetical judgment, If I had been convinced, at that time, that p was false, then I would at least have reconsidered whether q was true, or been less confident about it. If there were no counterfactual implication of this kind in the judgment, it could not properly be called a judgment about causes; for the imputation of a cause entails a claim about the likely course of events if the initial conditions had been different. The question, therefore, is: in default of a method of experiment applicable to this range of cases, what evidence is available to justify the counterfactual judgments about thoughts, and what general statements take the place of natural laws in supporting the singular causal judgments? We cannot intelligibly make claims about what might have been without having something like a general principle to support the counterfactual claim when it is challenged.

To answer the counterfactual question, I need to ask myself what the order of my thinking was at the time referred to, recalling what some of my related beliefs and knowledge were at that time. The hypothetical counterfactual judgment is often uncertain and fallible. On the other hand, sometimes its nature is clear—that is, given knowledge of my standing beliefs and desires and habits, it is obvious that I would have thought so-and-so, and wanted so-and-so, if p had been false.

I do not think that there is a mystery or an anomaly in this unsystematic, perpetually unscientific method, in which one attempts to discern the causes of beliefs, desires, and other propositional attitudes as they existed on a particular occasion. Two types of generality are involved: first, there are the connections common to all thinkers because they set the limits of what counts as thinking: logic, and the rules of use of the language in which a particular person thinks and forms frameworks into which thinking processes can be fitted; second, there are the beliefs and desires and other mental attitudes of a particular person, which enter into his particular habits of thought. This second kind of knowledge of causes remains perpetually unsystematic.

I must protect myself against a misunderstanding. I am not trying to deny that we may find reliable correlations between physical inputs and mental phenomena, including beliefs and desires and other propositional attitudes. It is obvious that we often do. For example, we find that interference with the brain, whether chemical or surgical interference, may lessen a man's usual fears or destroy parts of his memory or produce an otherwise unexplained mood of elation. My claim is that we know in advance that we cannot find an adequate explanation of the specific nature of his fears, or of his beliefs about the past, or of the thoughts associated with his elation, without recourse to his standing beliefs and fears and hopes, and without recourse to standard connections of thought. I have used the word *thought* throughout in speaking of causes, because, as I indicated previously, I intend a contrast here with mental phenomena in a more general sense. To explain, by a thought I mean a mental event that, if it were conscious, or brought to consciousness, could be specified in a sentence of the *oratio obliqua* form: *X* believes that *p*, in which another propositional attitude, such as "hopes" or "fears," could be substituted for "believes." An adequate explanation of a thought shows why, in this man at this time, the thought took the form that it did, as formulated in the clause that follows the "that."

There are adequate explanations—adequate for some purposes—of why a man is less fearful than he was, or less elated, that do not mention what his fears were or what form his elation took—that is, the explanations do not relate the change in affect to his specific beliefs and desires. The associated phenomena of fear and elation can be abstracted and generalized without regard to particular fears and particular exalted thoughts. Abstracting from the content of the thought, which is the principal constituent of any fear or of any elation, one is left only with a very loose set of dispositions to behave in certain typical ways and perhaps also with some typical sensations. It is conceivable that without mentioning the beliefs and desires that affect the subject's thoughts, one can give a good partial explanation of his typical behavior in terms of some physical input or inputs that also lessen or remove the typical sensations.

The explanation will be only partial, however, because we distinguish fear and elation from cognate emotions, at least in human beings, principally by the subject's thoughts. Fear is fear of something, even if the object is a vague and indefinite one, and even if the object is not conceived or imagined with some specific description. Nevertheless, the physical inputs—for example, a chemical in the brain—may adequately explain, and constitute the cause of, a sudden change in a man's disposition to behave in a certain way and in a change in his actual behavior. We can test the correlation between input and outcome, and we may find that it is universal—that it is the same for all types, classes, and nations of men, no matter what their language and their customs and their habits of thought may be. The fact that the correlation is established by experiment, and that the input is invariably linked to the observable outcome, means that the causal connection is of a different kind from the causal connections between behavior and the beliefs, desires, and other propositional attitudes that are involved in a man's thinking. But the counterfactual implication holds in both cases.

The thesis is that there is nothing of a scientific character, corresponding to the natural laws of physics and chemistry, that supports singular causal judgments about thoughts in the way that tested laws of nature sometimes support singular causal judgments about physical changes; the prospect, therefore, for psychology is that either it must remain perpetually unsystematic or it must in a very circumscribed form become part of the physical sciences. As far as we can see into the future, the prospect for the physical sciences seems assured, in the sense that a roughly uniform method of explanation of physical phenomena is established in our thought and culture and is applied across all superficial barriers. Not only is there a uniform method of explanation, but also there is a roughly uniform technique of application of the physical sciences to practical problems, even though several of the physical sciences are only distantly linked to any technology, actual or projected. In general, one expects that theoretical understanding of the deep structure of physical systems will be followed by the practical control of physical states. Since we are living through a period of advance in biophysics and biochemistry, there is already both apprehension and exuberance at the thought of new power to change men's characters and dispositions by changing their genetic endowment and by chemical interference with the brain.

When the word *determinism* is used, one is thinking, at the least, of the possibility of accurate prediction of the immediate effects of actual or imagined interferences with the system under study; one has a vision of the precise dependence of observed outputs on controlled inputs, and of understanding coming through the range and generality of the laws stating these dependencies. Understanding of physical nature consists in the appreciation of this comprehensiveness, precision, and generality of explanation. When we think of the vast diversity of physical things whose surface aspects can be perceived in nature, and the apparent division of observed nature into largely distinct domains, the metaphor of a deep structure naturally imposes itself. Behind the changing manifold appearances, one expects the comparatively stable relationships that explain the surface phenomena; recognition of these relationships comes close to the Platonic account of understanding, which remains, I think, the best account.

But there is something to be added to the Platonism: the manipulative confirmation of the insights. Insight into deep structure, embodied in physical theory, would by itself be too abstract to constitute an understanding of physical reality. It would be open to the objections always made against Platonism—that it neglects the perceived, daily world in which we live. However strange and immaterial-seeming the entities referred to in physics may become, we shall always keep contact with material things through the manipulations of medium-sized objects, including the human body, manipulations that the theories suggest. With permission to exaggerate, one could say that the derived power to manipulate the medium-sized objects of ordinary perception, in accordance with the theories of physics, is the one necessary continuity in the science of physics through all conceptual changes that have occurred in the past and may occur in the future.

I am arguing that there is not now, and never will be, anything in psychology that resembles these dual aspects of physical theory: physical theory reveals a deep structure that underlies the diversity of physical things, whether living or nonliving, and it points the way to applications in the form of radically different methods of changing and improving the physical environment and the body. The project of a Newtonian science of thought began before Hume and continued as part of empiricist philosophy almost until the present day. In its classical phase, the theory implied that the association of ideas would exemplify fairly simple and very general laws, like the Newtonian laws of motion explaining celestial mechanics. Learning theory has perhaps developed in directions that, at least so far, are not contrary to this project.

But nothing in psychology corresponds to the discovery of the deep structure that underlies the superficial differentiations of the physical world. The improvement of thought always requires reflection, the formation of ideas of ideas, and a critical self-consciousness; there is no other method. From this standpoint, Freudian psychology is no more than an extension of reflection in order to bring to consciousness repressed wishes and beliefs; and free association reveals, not new laws of thought, or a deep structure, but familiar laws of association between ideas that are normally inaccessible.

This is the point at which Spinoza's double-aspect theory of mind becomes particularly relevant. If a man's thoughts are to be understood and, through a knowledge of the causes at work, controlled and altered, they have to be connected to a wider context of his thoughts, conscious and unconscious. When missing steps are supplied, a half-understood tract of thought becomes standard thought and therefore intelligible. But thought is always embodied in physical activity of the body and brain, and the activities of the brain, like those of any other part of the body, illustrate the general laws of physics. If you picked out a particular state of a man's brain, and asked how this came to be and how it might be changed, you would be referred to general relationships in biochemistry and physics, together with an indefinite and unfinished string of antecedent conditions of that brain state. The explanation would not be complete, because of the infinity of antecedent physical conditions in any particular case. But the explanation does give support to counterfactual judgments: If so-and-so had been done, such-and-such a bodily state would have resulted.

We must think of the brain as we think of the sense organs, such as the eye and the ear. (I add a little to Spinoza here, though I hope it is consistent with his main position.) The sense organs are the parts of the body that react most sensitively to the environment, registering the effects of external things and construing these effects as signals. But the whole body so reacts, and the exceptional powers of thought that human beings possess are the other aspect of an exceptional physical responsiveness; they are the other aspect of the complexity of the human body and brain as a living organism that is exceptionally active and exceptionally independent in relation to the environment. The improvement of health, vitality, energy, happiness—everything that contributes to a description of a person as being in a good state—depends upon the condition of the organism as a whole, not exclusively upon physical well-being nor exclusively upon rational discipline. Any state of mind has its physical embodiment and any bodily state is reflected in a mental disposition and capacity.

The correction of thought, and hence of philosophy and psychology, has a certain primacy when we have the improve-ment of men in view—improvement in the proper sense, which for Spinoza is a matter of sanity and of the exercise of free intelligence and of enjoyment in being alive. This pri-macy arises from the fact that medical knowledge, required for physical interference with the body, is itself a body of thought, and one that depends upon the larger theories of physics and upon scientific method; in order to improve med-ical knowledge, one has to have the rational thought of the idea of ordered improvement and the philosophy that sup-ports it. The thought of the possibility and desirability of correcting the intellect, and the formation of the resolve to do so, are necessary both for the correction of the mind and for the correction of the body. An understanding of the laws of thought, and of rational principles of argument, is neces-sary both to mental stability and to the correction of bodily ills—in the first case directly, in the second, indirectly.

But this is the only primacy of reason. If we consider the suffering and frustration of a person, whether that person is oneself or another, we need to remember that, in every case and without exception, we can try to understand and to ex-plain that suffering in two entirely distinct ways: as being em-bodied in a physical state, to be explained by prior physical states and inputs from external things, and also as being a state of mind, to be explained by associated states of mind, desires, and beliefs, in accordance with the laws of intelligible thought.

The common notion that if suffering or the frustration of desire is in question, the cause and true explanation must be *either* a thought *or* a physical state, is misguided. There never are, and never could be, two mutually exclusive possibilities. No state of a person is ever to be explained either as having only psychical causes or as having only physical causes. But when we have described the state under examination in terms of thoughts, or in terms of physical movements, then we are committed to looking for an explanation in matching terms, if we want an explanation that is clear and systematic.

Spinoza's double-aspect theory of personality, which is a consequence of his metaphysics, precludes the possibility of any competition in psychology between physical explanations and psychological—in the sense of mentalistic—explanations. The quarrels that have been known to occur in the last twenty years in clinical psychology, and even more in the popularization of psychology, are merely a misunderstanding, a consequence of bad philosophy and of a simplified Cartesianism. Confronted with miserable unhappiness and mental aberration of any kind, according to Spinoza's theory, one must look for the general laws of the association of thoughts that may explain the particular thoughts that constitute the unhappiness and the mental aberration in the particular case; and one must also investigate the physical condition of the unhappy man, for this physical condition, with its external physical causes, constitutes the bodily aspect of the unhappiness, just as the activity of eyes, nerves, and brain constitutes the bodily aspect of visual perception.

Whether at any particular time we have the necessary knowledge to change the physical state, perhaps by chemical means, is a contingent matter; whether we would do better, at any particular time, to try to change directly the thinking that has led to the gloomy thoughts, by tracing the fantasies that are associated with them, is also a contingent matter. One might try both approaches at the same time. We should be guided in practical policies by a comparison of our relative ignorance, at any particular time, in the two domains. For example, if we are considering the state that in terms of thought is described as anxiety, we may know that the physical aspect of this is changed by a certain drug. We might know this at a merely empirical level, knowing this singular causal judgment to be true: If this tranquilizing chemical is taken, the gloomy thoughts disappear. We might even be able to describe and to identify the type of bodily state in which the anxiety is embodied—the setting of the body, as it were, in which the thought is expressed. More usually the bodily state would have its own identity and description, and a general prescription for finding the relevant causal factor for this state, identified in physical terms, would be known.

There is an asymmetry, a lack of balance, between access to causal information about states identified under mentalistic descriptions—that is, in terms of thoughts—and the same states identified under physical descriptions. We have direct access to at least some of the order of our own thinking, and each man is, to some extent, the natural authority on what is making him believe, or want, or fear, whatever he does believe, want, or fear. To some extent only—for many of his beliefs, desires, and fears are preconscious or unconscious ones, and their causes will not be known to him except under very special conditions. He may even be self-deceived about his conscious mental attitudes, or he may make many other kinds of mistakes, when he picks out the causes. But at least with conscious attitudes he often knows directly certain negative propositions about what were *not* the causes of his beliefs, desires, or fears.

On the other hand, no one has any kind of privileged knowledge of the physical embodiment of his states; on the contrary, it will generally be rather easier for an external observer to watch and record bodily changes than for the subject himself to do so. Since man has direct access to some of the thinking that is related to his mental problems, there is a natural tendency for him to seek remedies for his own unhappiness by further thought. But the advisable policy must surely be to follow both the mental and physical paths toward a remedy simultaneously; there is no need for competition between them.

For some public purposes, and particularly for the mass treatment of problems of mental health, the deterministic explanation—that is, the physical one—is clearly to be preferred if it is available. It allows for exactly stated effects of exactly stated causes and therefore for exact control of any intervention made. The method of correction of bodily components of mental states must be general as well as precise, in that the remedies for unwanted conditions do not take account of cultural differences nor of any differences of language and habits of thought.

In correcting the thought that enters into a passion—which always includes a belief and a desire—one must consider carefully the particular concepts and descriptions occurring in the thought. All the variety and complexity of different conceptual schemes must also be considered. Perhaps partly with a view to meeting this problem, Spinoza proposed a highly speculative, oversimplified theory of the passions. For such a vocabulary to have authority, so that it might provide a common vocabulary for psychologists, we would need something like a completed theory of the passions, a systematic knowledge of connections between them. As things are, we do not even know whether such a theory would be possible. Meanwhile, we do know that men's desires, fantasies, and beliefs are to a very large degree culture-bound and language-bound; for their passions, constituted by their desires and beliefs or fantasies, are modified and formed by the conceptions that they themselves have of the objects and causes of their passions. As men's thoughts about their own passions change, the passions themselves change, and the changes are manifested in behavior. But when in the interests of mental health it seems desirable to institute such changes, one cannot have recourse to any general method for making them. The thoughts take local and individual forms, which need to be understood in their own terms before the reflective changes can be made.

There is an unchanging tendency for man to correct his own governing beliefs and desires by tracing their supporting grounds and setting them against a standard of clear thought. This is the ordinary use of intelligence, the natural and the sane tendency. There is also sometimes a desire or a need to look for uniform methods of changing the more destructive sentiments and desires. The demand for reflection and intellectual reform will continue alongside the demand for a deterministic science that uses general physical methods of cure and correction. These permanent demands, anticipated a priori, must function within the limits of the changing state of current knowledge. An empirical theory of knowledge must take note of the relative complexity of different techniques of physical treatment of the passions, given the starting-points in present knowledge. For example, the calculation might now be that the chemical transactions that are part of the bodily aspect of the passions are likely to become better known and more controllable, if research is pushed forward strongly enough, while research into the more fundamental bodily changes might be unprofitable given the present state of physiology.

It is utterly unnecessary, from the standpoint of Spinoza's theory, to be guided in medical research by anything other than an evaluation of the present state of the physical sciences. There is a sense in which disciplined thought about the body, as a branch of the physical sciences, is a modern development of thought, because, according to Spinoza's argument, false philosophies had separated the functioning of the mind and the functioning of the body to such an extent that the double effect of new discoveries in physics was not discerned. Not only can the discoveries be applied in changing desires and passions, but also they can constitute in themselves a modification of the passions in those who possess the new knowledge of how their passions are embodied.

I will end with a simple example that I have used elsewhere and that illustrates the double-aspect theory. Take the not unfamiliar case of a very young boy who has an overwhelming, even irresistible, desire to dress himself in women's clothes, and does so secretly, perhaps finding the clothes in his mother's wardrobe; he does not know why he has this desire, and certainly he has never heard of transvestism, or of any of the theories of personality associated with this concept. Suppose that the boy has been born into an entirely unsophisticated family, which also does not understand the phenomenon and knows nothing either of its name or of its nature. The interesting fact is that the boy acts out a desire which is highly specific and which manifests a fantasy he had without being able to articulate this fantasy. When he dresses up, he is acting under a very specific description—for example, he is governed by the idea of femininity, and not by the idea of maternity.

Such cases are, of course, very familiar to psychoanalysts, and they are analogous to cases of very young children who have very specific fantasies about birth which lead them to actions that have a very specific meaning for them. Such highly specific ideas, with their very strong emotional charge, are examples of thoughts that are culture-bound, at least to some degree, and that must be understood in their own terms if they are to be modified by reflection and self-consciousness. The interest in such cases is in the thought itself rather than in its physical embodiment. One might contrast such a case with that of a man who experiences a general anxiety that focuses upon changing and relative, unspecifically identified features of his environment. It would seem natural to look for a physicochemical remedy for the total state of which the various and unspecific anxious thoughts are the mental aspect. The problem would not be intolerably complex, too utterly remote from the knowledge that we actually possess.

2

Words in Thoughts

Zeno Vendler

Man is a thinking being; more than anything else, this feature sets apart this species of hairless apes from the rest of the world's inhabitants.

It may be argued, however, that we often use the verb *to think* in describing what some of the other higher animals do. "The dog thinks that I am his master," "The cat thinks that the mouse is still in the hole," and so forth. Since there is no reason to object that such locutions involve a misuse of the language, and since what we normally say determines the meaning of our words, the conclusion is inevitable: in some sense of the verb, at least, some other animals, too, can think.

What is that sense, and, on the other hand, what are the senses of the word that exclusively apply to humans, on the basis of which the definition of man as a thinking being still can be maintained?

The first suspicious feature that meets the eye in the examples just mentioned is the following: in these and similar cases, what the animal is supposed to think involves an error, or the possibility of error, at least according to the speaker's estimate: I am not the dog's master, and the mouse might not be in the hole. Thus, it seems, this kind of thinking is contrasted with knowing, and, of course, animals can know many things.

This article, prepared for this volume, has also appeared in *Philosophic Exchange,* Annual Proceedings of the Center for Philosophic Exchange, vol. 2, no. 2 (Summer 1976).

We often apply the verb *to think* to people, too, in the same sense. Somebody is about to cross a rickety bridge unconcerned. "He thinks it won't collapse," we say. And this may be true, even if the walker pays no attention to the bridge, has no conscious thoughts about it. Similarly, the prankster who has unscrewed the legs of my chair might say, as I am about to sit down: "He thinks it'll support him." The point here is precisely the lack of any suspicion or reflection on my part: *since* I have not noticed anything untoward, but go ahead unconcerned, I may be said to think that the chair will support me.

Now could it be said with equal ease in these situations that, for example, the cat *concluded* that the mouse was still in the hole, or that the walker *assumed* that the bridge would support him, or that I *hoped* that the chair would not collapse? Certainly not, unless there is some reason to think that the cat, as it were, weighed evidence, and that the walker and I noticed the weakness of those structures, but decided, on the basis of some considerations, to risk it anyway. Notice, however, that at this point the similarity between man and beast breaks down: cats, unlike people, cannot weigh evidence, consider reasons, make decisions, nurture hopes, and so forth. And the reason is simple: these actions and states imply mental events of which their subject is conscious—in other words, they involve having thoughts. Indeed, whereas, as we saw, there is no difficulty in saying that the cat, for example, thought that the mouse was in the hole, one would not say, without raising some eyebrows, that the cat had the thought that the mouse was in the hole, or that such a thought has occurred to the cat.[1]

What entitles us to say that cats and dogs know many things, or that they think this or that in the restricted sense

1. This distinction has been made clear to me by Professor Norman Malcolm. See his Presidential Address entitled "Thoughtless Brutes," *American Philosophical Association* (1972), pp. 5–20.

just explained? The observation of what they do is the obvious answer—of their behavior, in more pompous parlance. For neither knowing, nor being mistaken, nor thinking in the corresponding sense, need involve anything beyond that in either man or beast.

But how do we know that man, but not the beast, also has thoughts, in other words, that he is capable of a kind of activity that is not identical with overt behavior, and that need not even manifest itself in what he does? "Well, he can tell me what he thought, he can reveal in this way what went on in his mind." This, too, is an obvious answer, and the correct one at that. For, notice, what he says about his thoughts can be true or false, no less than what he says about other things. Thus the things that make what he says true or false in the first case are no less "real" than the things that make what he says true or false in the second. As one could not lie about dogs and cats if there were no dogs and cats, one could not lie about thoughts if thoughts did not exist. If Jim says, "I believe that Joe is innocent," then what he says can be wrong in two independent ways: either because Joe is guilty, or because Jim really thinks he is. In the former case Jim is mistaken, in the second he is lying.

Thus, there is a kind of thinking that is an exclusive prerogative of human beings. For if you say that, maybe, dogs, cats, and chimpanzees also have conscious thoughts, my answer is that there is no reason to think so, and so long as they are unable to tell us what they think, there cannot be such a reason. And when I say "tell" I mean *tell*—that is, convey to us, with set purpose and by the use of mutually comprehensible media, what they want us to come to believe about their thoughts as distinct from having those thoughts. And this is a tall order—even for Washoe and Co.[2]

Thus, to conclude with Descartes, "the word is the sole

2. R. A. Gardner, and B. T. Gardner, "Teaching Sign Language to a Chimpanzee," *Science* 165 (1969) : 664–72.

sign and the only certain mark of the presence of thought hidden and wrapped up in the body." [3] We know that man is a thinking being because he can talk and tell us what he thinks.

It is important to reflect upon the nature of the inference expressed in the last sentence. The *because* there marks an epistemological link, not a causal one. We know that the barn is on fire because of the smoke coming out. This does not mean, however, that the smoke causes the fire. In a similar way, although *our knowledge* that man thinks depends upon his ability to talk, it does not follow at all that his ability to think presupposes, or is a function of, his ability to talk. In other words, even though it is impossible for us to discover that a certain species of living beings have thoughts if they cannot talk, it is perfectly conceivable that there may be beings that can think without being able to talk. Unless, of course, the very ability to think, in the sense of having thoughts, presupposes the possession of a language.

This last relation is often taken for granted by many philosophers, psychologists, and linguists. Some of them even go as far as to assert that thinking is actually nothing but talking, albeit to oneself, silently. The classic passage making this claim is Plato's in *Theaetetus:*

> *Socr.* . . . And do you accept my description of the process of thinking?
>
> *Theaet.* How do you describe it?
>
> *Socr.* As a discourse that the mind carries on with itself about any subject it is considering. You must take this explanation as coming from an ignoramus; but I have a notion that, when the mind is thinking, it is simply talking to itself, asking questions and an-

3. R. Descartes, Letter (to Morus), February, 1649: AT v, 278, *Descartes Selections,* ed. R. M. Eaton (New York: Scribner's, 1927), p. 360.

swering them. . . . So I should describe thinking
as a discourse, and judgment as a statement pronounced, not aloud to someone else, but silently to
oneself.[4]

Plato, incidentally, is less sanguine about this view
(". . . ignoramus . . .") than some of its latter-day sponsors.
Gilbert Ryle echoes Plato in saying that "much of our ordinary thinking is conducted in internal monologues or silent
soliloquy, usually accompanied by an internal cinematograph-
show of visual imagery," and then goes on to explain the
origin of such an activity as follows:

This trick of talking to oneself in silence is acquired
neither quickly nor without effort; and it is a necessary
condition of our acquiring it that we should have previously learned to talk intelligently aloud and have heard
and understood other people doing so. Keeping our
thoughts to ourselves is a sophisticated accomplishment.[5]

Speech, we used to think, is the expression of thought. Now
Ryle tells us that it is, rather, thought that is the suppression
of speech. And he is by no means alone. Wittgenstein, too,
wonders about the possibility of deaf-mutes' thinking,[6] and
he says explicitly: "When I think in language, there aren't
'meanings' going through my mind in addition to the verbal
expression: the language is the vehicle of thought." [7] It would
follow, then, that in this case we think in a natural language,

4. 189e–190a. It is repeated with some changes in *Sophist* 263e–264a. I shall
call the view expressed in these passages "the Platonic theory," without making any historical claims about Plato's "real" theory of thinking. *Plato, The
Collected Dialogues,* ed. E. Hamilton and H. Cairns (New York: Random
House, 1961).

5. *The Concept of Mind* (New York: Barnes and Noble, 1949), p. 27. Again,
I do not claim that these passages represent Ryle's final word on thinking.

6. L. Wittgenstein, *Philosophical Investigations* (Oxford: Blackwell, 1953),
pt. 1, no. 342.

7. Ibid., no. 329.

whether English, German, or Chinese. At which point one
might wonder in what the understanding of something said
in a foreign tongue might consist: repeating it in that language, translating or paraphrasing it in our own, or what?

The contrary tradition, according to which thought does
not presuppose but is expressed in speech, also originates in
Greek philosophy. Here is a typical expression of Aristotle's
opinion:

> Spoken words are the symbols of mental experience and
> written words are the symbols of spoken words. Just as
> all men have not the same writing, so all men have not
> the same speech sounds, but the mental experiences,
> which these directly symbolize, are the same for all, as
> also are those things of which our experiences are the
> images.[8]

The Aristotelian tradition prevailed in the Middle Ages,
and the Rationalists, following Descartes, toed the same line.
The very influential Port Royal Grammar (*Grammaire
Général et Raisonnée*) insists that there is no similarity between the devices of language and the thoughts they are used
to express.[9]

Although there are some indications of reversion to the
Platonic tradition in the Empiricists' writings (in Hobbes
and Berkeley, for instance), its real revival is due to the rise
of behavioristic tendencies in the last hundred years. Although thought, in its very nature, is a private occurrence,
by viewing it as "suppressed" speech, one does not appear at
least to have trespassed too far into the forbidden preserve
of the mental.

I shall argue below that the Platonic view, according to
which thinking essentially or typically is talking to oneself

8. *De Interpretatione* 16a. *Aristotle, Selections,* ed. W. D. Ross (New York:
Scribner's, 1927).

9. C. Lancelot and A. Arnauld, *Grammaire Général et Raisonnée* (Paris:
Pierre le Petit, 1660; Merston, England: Scholar Press facsimile, 1969), p. 27.

silently, is mistaken. This conclusion does not exclude some lesser claims, however, of which I mention here two. The first one maintains that although the process of thinking is not the same as talking to oneself silently, nevertheless it essentially or typically involves the use of words, phrases, or sentences. The difference between the original Platonic theory and this watered-down version can be made clear by considering such word-games as Scrabble, crossword puzzles, and the like: in playing them, one uses words without saying anything. I shall claim that this version, too, is mistaken: although words may occur in thinking, their role is neither essential nor universal.

Finally, some contemporary philosophers maintain that the acquisition of a natural language is a necessary condition for having conceptual thoughts. This claim is based on the view that having a concept is nothing but knowing how to use a certain word. Again I disagree, but am willing to grant that the development and the refinement of our conceptual equipment are indeed greatly influenced by the language(s) we learn.[10]

I have restricted the sense of thinking that concerns me here to conscious thought. Our thoughts are some of the things of which we are or can become conscious. We are also conscious of sensations, feelings, emotions, moods, and so forth, and, of course, the play of our imaginations. These things, *pace* Descartes, are not thoughts per se. Having a headache is not having a thought—and the man on the rack may be unable to think, precisely because of the excruciating pain he is suffering. Similarly, daydreaming is not thinking but an escape from it, and the lascivious play of St. Antony's imagination did not add to, but rather interfered with, his holy meditations.

10. See my *Res Cogitans* (Ithaca, N.Y.: Cornell University Press, 1972), chap. 6.

What, then, are thoughts, and what is thinking? The word *thought* is normally used to denote the object of somebody's mental acts (for example, what one realizes, concludes, decides) or mental states (for example, what one believes, suspects, intends). These two groups differ in an important respect: a mental act occurs *in* a given moment, but a mental state lasts *for* a period of time. *"When* did you realize that *p?"* and *"For* how long did you believe that *p?"* we ask, and not the other way around. Similarly, it makes sense to say of a person that he still intends to do something, but not that he still decides to do it. In a mental act a thought is formed or conceived; in a mental state it is held and entertained. Indeed, we speak of beliefs, for instance, as if they were children: we conceive, nurture, and embrace them, hold them for a while, and if found misbegotten, abandon them or give them up. Moreover, whereas we are normally conscious of our mental acts, this is not true of our mental states. Their objects are ordinarily not in the foreground of our consciousness, yet they remain, as it were, at our beck and call: one can become conscious of them at will. Normally, again, people are able to say, when asked, what they believe, whom they suspect, and what they intend to do. We use the word *thought* in these senses when we offer "a penny for your thoughts" or when we say that, for example, the *Little Red Book* contains Chairman Mao's thoughts.

What one thinks, the thought, is conceived or entertained by the thinker: "Joe thinks (that is, believes, suspects, and so forth) that *p,"* "Then I thought (that is, assumed, realized, concluded) that *p."* The verb-object of *think* in these contexts is a nominalized sentence, in most cases a *that*-clause, which denotes the thought in question. Since there is a nearly perfect correspondence between the objects of mental acts and states on the one hand, and of speech-acts on the other—that is, between what one can think and what one can say—philosophers commonly refer to these common objects, usually expressed in *that*-clauses, as propositions. Thoughts, therefore, that can be expressed in speech are aptly called propositional thoughts.[11]

The verb *to think* used to attribute such thoughts to a person hardly admits progressive tenses: *I am thinking that p* or *He was thinking that p* are at best substandard sentences. There is, however, another context in which that verb is used progressively: *What are you thinking about?* and *Last night I was thinking about your theory for more than an hour,* and so forth. In these cases the thinking involved constitutes an activity that goes on in time, and can be pursued at will. Notice, the question *What are you doing?* may be answered by *I am thinking about Angola* but not by *I think that we should not get involved in Angola.* Similarly, whereas one might say of a man sound asleep that he thinks that Angola is not worth the effort, one could not say of him, while he is still asleep, that he is thinking about that place.

Nevertheless, the notion of thinking about involves the notion of thinking that. In order to show this relation, I propose to consider a related couple of concepts—namely, talking about something and saying something. Quite obviously, talking about something is a process that goes on in time, an activity in which a person may be engaged for a while. Now what does a person do when he is talking about a certain topic? Well, he says a few things about it. I cannot be talking about Angola, or anything else, without performing such speech-acts as stating and suggesting, arguing and concluding, guessing and predicting, accusing, blaming, condemning, and so forth. And what about thinking about Angola? The situation is analogous. I cannot be engaged in thinking about it without entertaining some thoughts (mainly of the propositional sort) about Angola and related matters. I may recall the facts, look for implications, realize connections, consider some possibilities, wonder about the consequences, decide to

11. Ibid., chaps. 2–4.

read more about the background, and so on. It would be
rather peculiar, indeed, if I were to assert that I was just
thinking about Angola, and yet, when asked what I thought
about it, could not answer a thing. Plato was right part of
the way: thinking is *like* talking, reasoning is *like* arguing;
they show a similarity of structure. This, however, does not
require identity. A word expressed in Morse code retains
some of its structure; yet saying a word does not consist in
uttering dots and dashes. What we think is normally expressed in words and sentences; but it does not follow that
we think in words and sentences.

I do not claim that all thought is propositional. The
painter may think intensely while staring at his canvas, the
composer while running his fingers over the keyboard, the
chess master while imagining the board two moves ahead.
They "see" lines, "hear" music, envisage a new setup, without being able to articulate in words, even if they wanted to,
what exactly they thought. But this kind of thinking seems
to be the exception rather than the rule. For otherwise the
Platonic temptation to view thought in general as an inner
monologue would not have the lure it generally has.

Having made the necessary distinctions and qualifications,
my first task is to show that thinking in the propositional
sense cannot consist in saying something internally, and consequently that thinking about something cannot be conceived
of in terms of talking to oneself silently.

Saying something is a specifically human act (*actus hu-
manus,* not merely *actus hominis*), and as such, is subject to
the will. This philosophical claim means that the agent performing an act of speech must be aware of what he is doing
and must intend to do it. This is not the case with all the
actions a man can perform. We are not aware of our digest-
ing of food, and we do not intend our heartbeat. Such ac-

tions, in fact, are normally not subject to the will. Some others, such as kicking somebody or breaking a window, may or may not be. That they often are is shown by the fact that, first, they *can* be performed intentionally, deliberately, on purpose; second the agent *can* have reasons for performing them; and third, he *may* be held responsible for having performed them. There are, finally, kinds of actions that by their very nature must be voluntary—that is, subject to the will: for example, robbing a bank, murdering the guard, and so forth. One can break a window, but not rob a bank, accidentally; and one can kill, but not murder somebody, unintentionally. Then it is clear that saying something belongs to this last category: one cannot state, promise, or order something, warn, accuse, or condemn somebody unintentionally either: the speaker must know what he is saying and must intend to say it.

This claim is not refuted by the fact that often the speaker does not "fully" know what he is saying or intend all the implications of it. Granted, one may betray a secret unwittingly, or identify somebody unintentionally (say, by addressing him, using his true name, in front of a detective), but even in these cases the speaker does intend to perform some speech-act or other: the "traitor" may just want to make an innocent remark, and the "identifier" just offer a friendly greeting. Such "double effects" are by no means peculiar to speech-situations. The child, by eating candy, may poison himself, and the soldier, by opening a door, may set off a booby-trap. They intend one thing, not the other.

If, therefore, thinking were talking to oneself, albeit silently, then it would follow that all thoughts were intentional—that is, subject to the will, since, according to the theory, to conceive a thought is to say something, albeit to oneself. And this is clearly false. It is false not only because of the obvious fact that thoughts often emerge ("crop up," "strike us," "dawn upon us") unasked for, and often keep bothering us to the point of obsession, but because of a deeper and more general reason.

In saying that a certain act (for example, smashing a window) was done intentionally, we do not merely mean that the agent knew what he was doing, but also that he could have done otherwise (if he had wanted to). Now, whereas it is certainly true that in thinking what I think I am aware of what I think, more often than not it is nonsensical to say that I could do otherwise (if I wanted to). Granted, there are certain forms of thought, such as decisions, assumptions, and the like, that are indeed subject to the will—that is, the agent is free to assume, or decide to do, something or other. There are, however, other forms of thought that by their very nature preclude such freedom. Think of noticing a similarity, realizing a connection, understanding a problem, discovering a solution, seeing an implication, recognizing a friend, and so forth. In what sense can these acts be intentional, free, or subject to the will? Does it make sense to say: "I suddenly saw the solution of the puzzle, but I could have done otherwise" or "Then I decided to realize the connection between the two aspects"? How unlike saying this is; in contrast, there is nothing wrong with such assertions as "I told him the solution but I could have done otherwise" and "Then I decided to state the connection between the two aspects."

Consequently, if the Platonic theory were true, then it would follow that in thinking, we "say" things to ourselves involuntarily, unintentionally—in such a way, that is, that we could not do otherwise. Moreover, as the previous argument about "unwelcome" thoughts shows, very often, as it were, we could not shut up to ourselves. We know, of course, that some people are "compulsive" talkers, cannot indeed shut up. But this is a pathological condition, compulsive behavior, or simply lack of self-control. No such explanation is applicable to normal thinkers.

To sum up: talking, saying things, are voluntary actions. Having certain common types of thoughts cannot be voluntary. Consequently, thinking in general cannot be talking to oneself, silently or aloud.[12]

I just said that the speaker must intend what he is doing, must "mean" what he says. What does such an intention actually consist of? Well, it depends on the type of speech-act he performs. In *stating*, for instance, that he was born in Ashtabula, Ohio, the speaker normally intends his audience to believe, through the recognition of his intention in saying those words, that he was born in Ashtabula, Ohio; in *ordering* someone to leave the room, he normally intends (via the same kind of recognition) the hearer to leave the room; in *promising* something, he intends (in the same way) to put himself under a specific obligation; and so forth.[13] In other words, he intends to be understood, not merely as to the content of his utterance, but also as to its illocutionary force.[14]

In the light of this, consider mental acts against the background of the Platonic hypothesis, namely, that thinking is talking to oneself silently, and having a thought is saying something to oneself. Quite obviously the result is absurd, and in this case, absurd with respect to any kind of mental act. For, to begin with the first aspect, how can I intend to be understood by myself in saying something to myself, when the very act of saying something presupposes that I understand what I am saying? Or, if I do not understand what I am saying, then what is the point of saying it to myself?

The second aspect leads to an equal absurdity. Consider such mental acts as coming to suspect, or coming to realize,

12. For the original idea behind this argument I am indebted to Tom Dimas.

13. Here I follow H. P. Grice's theory of meaning. See his "Meaning," *Philosophical Review* 66 (1957) : 377–88.

14. See J. L. Austin, *How to Do Things with Words* (Oxford: Clarendon, 1962).

something or other. If, for instance, my realization that p is the case consisted in my saying to myself that p, then I could not possibly intend myself to come to believe that p as a result of saying to myself that p, since in saying that p I would already have realized that p. To put it simply: what is the point of telling myself something that I know to be the case in the very act of telling? Or, to make it worse, what is the point of telling myself something that I have to know (if I am sincere) in order to be able to tell at all?

Then consider a mental act of another kind, a decision, for instance. I just decided to go to Paris next summer. What did I say to myself—"I'll go to Paris"? But then, what makes this inner speech-act into the carrier of a decision rather than a simple forecast or guess, or—to make it worse again—rather than just a sentence mentally rehearsed? "Well, you must intend it as a decision." But how can I accomplish that in talking to myself? By saying, perhaps, "I decide to go to Paris." This won't do, however, since this sentence is ungrammatical: except for the context of reporting a habit (for example, "I usually decide to . . ."), the verb-phrase *decide to* cannot be used in the first-person singular present tense. I can tell you what I decid*ed* to do, but the very grammar of the verb prevents me from making a decision by its use. For the same reason, such verbs as *realize, find out, discover,* and so forth, which are used to report the occurrence of some mental acts, cannot be employed in the very performance of those acts. It appears, therefore, that one cannot specify the form of one's thoughts by using verbal means. On the contrary, the principal means of marking the form of one's speech-acts is the use of the appropriate "performative" verbs (for example, *state, predict, promise, order, apologize*). This asymmetry alone is sufficient to show that thinking cannot be conceived of as talking to oneself silently.

Thus far we have considered the Platonic hypothesis in its full-blooded version, according to which having a thought consists in saying something to oneself in the strong sense of the word—that is, in performing a speech-act. The following arguments will demonstrate that even the watered-down version of the theory, which claims that at least the use of words is essential to propositional thought, is also untenable.

The freedom we enjoy in speech is not restricted to the mere option of talk versus silence. Even if we have decided to say something, further choices await us before we open our mouths: we have to decide, consciously or by mere routine, how to say what we have to say—that is, in what language, style, manner, and so forth. We talk differently to adults than we do to children, and we talk differently in the classroom, court of law, pub, or our own homes. In all of these cases one takes into consideration the audience's knowledge, standing, circumstances, presuppositions, and what not. For these reasons, people often are not satisfied with merely being told what somebody has said; they also want to know the exact words the speaker used. Accordingly, we have two distinct devices to reproduce what people said—namely, the indirect and the direct quotation. I might say, for instance, "All right, you told me that he had asked you to leave the premises, but I want to know exactly what he said, word by word." And such a request makes sense with respect to any kind of speech-act.

Now compare this situation with such mental acts as realizations, recognitions, decisions, and regrets. Suppose I tell you that last night I suddenly realized that it must have been Jones, the janitor, who opened my letters in the office. Would it make sense for you to ask for the exact words of my realizing this? And would it be possible for me to answer? Which of the following sentences "crossed my mind" in the act: "He must have done it," "It was done by Jones," "The janitor did it." Well, suppose I indeed "said to myself" (perhaps even aloud) "It was Jones!" What makes this into a realization? And what makes it into the realization of that particular thing? Surely it is not enough if that sentence merely crossed my mind. "No, you must have meant it," you say. But this would make it into an intentional act, which a realization is not. Then, perhaps, it was as if I heard somebody telling me "It was Jones." We indeed say things like "a little voice told me." But this would be the description of a hunch rather than of a realization. For one thing, did I believe the "little voice"? We feel that we are, once more, in the domain of the absurd—or the metaphorical.

I do not deny, of course, that that sentence, or some other, may have cropped up in my imagination, or may even have been (subvocally or vocally) articulated by me, in making that realization. I may have said to myself, "But of course!" or "How stupid of me not to have thought of that!" or what have you. Most of us, indeed, "think aloud" in unguarded moments, or even gesticulate and make faces. We must not forget that words are the natural means of expressing thoughts, so it is no wonder that thoughts and words are so closely associated that the occurrence of the former tends to evoke the latter. Some people cannot hum without beating the rhythm with hand or foot. So maybe some people cannot think without words crossing their minds. Nevertheless humming is not beating, and thinking is not imagining, or producing words, gestures, and the like.

The same thing applies, incidentally, to imagination in general, to Ryle's "cinematograph-show": images, too, may accompany thinking. In thinking about the law, one may visualize dusty tomes or a courtroom; in thinking about a mathematical problem one may see beads or numerals on the blackboard. This does not mean, however, that such imaginings are essential to thinking about these things.

Suppose that my realization that it was the janitor who had opened my letters was couched in the words, "He must have done it." Then the problem arises, how did the word *he* (mentally pronounced or heard) come to mean the janitor?

In normal speech we select referring devices (names, pro-
nouns, definite descriptions, together with accompanying gestures and the like), which, given the physical setup of the
situation and the course of the preceding conversation, enable
the audience to understand whom we have in mind. In doing
so, moreover, the speaker has to keep the particular audience
in mind: one would not rely on pointing, for instance, in
talking to a blind man, or on the use of a nickname in front
of an audience that may not be familiar with it. The encoding of the reference, therefore, is suitable or not, given those
circumstances and that audience. And this, of course, is the
source of possible mistakes: the speaker may misjudge the situation or the hearer's position, knowledge, condition, and so
forth. Correspondingly, even an objectively adequate reference may misfire due to inattention, mishearing, or mistaken
assumptions on the part of the audience—that is to say, mistakes can occur on the "decoding" end too. This feature—the
possibility of mistakes on both ends—is characteristic of and
essential to any use of a communicating device.

Yet no such mistakes are possible in thought, in the alleged
"silent conversation with myself." Who is the audience I have
to consider in picking the suitable medium? Myself, of course.
Is there, then, any possibility of selecting a word, a phrase,
an image, or what have you, which might be opaque, incom-
prehensible, or misleading to me? Or, on the receiving end,
can I fail to gather the identity of the thing or person I am
thinking about from the media thus provided? Of course not.
But then there are no media and no reference. What on
earth, indeed, would be the point of encoding a message to
myself, to be decoded—instantly and infallibly, mind you—
again by myself?

Thus, whereas in talking about the janitor I may have to
use such phrases as *he, that man, Jones,* or *the janitor* in
order to make you understand whom I have in mind, in
thinking about him I do not need any (subvocal) words,

(imagined) gestures, or what not, to determine, for myself, whom I have in mind. For, let it be the case that in making that realization I indeed said to myself, "He must have done it," silently, or even aloud. Then, if you like, the *he* referred to that man. But why? Because I had him in mind in saying that and for no other reason. But then my having him in mind cannot possibly consist in using *he* or any other phrase. It makes sense to say that I talked about that man in terms of his being the janitor, also that I referred to him by the words *the janitor;* it also makes sense to say that I thought about him in terms of his being the janitor—but it is nonsense to say that in my thought I referred to him by the words *the janitor.*[15]

A similar contrast between speech and thought arises in connection with ambiguous sentences, whether the ambiguity is due to semantic or syntactic factors. If I tell you that I am going to the bank, you will understand what I said one way (money) or another (river) from the circumstances—if you can decide at all. As to myself, I may "mean" it one way or the other. Now what does it mean to "mean" it, or understand it, in one particular way? Well, as to the first, it depends on what I intend you to come to believe, and—if I am honest—on what I really intend to do: go to the First National or to the riverbank. As to the second, it depends upon what you take my words to mean, and—if you think I am telling the truth—on what you come to think about my intentions. Now surely it is not believable that these mental acts (that is, my decision to go to the river, my intention to tell you the truth, *or to lie,* your understanding of what I said, or *your doubts about its truth,* and so forth) are all cast in unambiguous sentences—in sentences, that is, in which the word *bank* is replaced, or is accompanied by, an unambiguous paraphrase.

15. See my "Thinking of Individuals," *Nous* 10, no. 1 (1976) : 35–46.

Syntactical ambiguities raise the same problems. Think, for instance, of the mental flip-flop involved in the understanding of *Mary had a little lamb—and Jane a little pork*. Now why is it that my thought that Mary had (that is, ate) a little lamb is *not* ambiguous? Or can one say, "I thought 'Mary had a little lamb' and I meant it in the sense of eating"?

Then there are metaphors, allusions, ironic remarks, and so forth. "It was a very nice thing to do," I tell you, meaning that it was an awful thing to do. Is it possible to think that it was an awful thing to do in saying to oneself "It was a very nice thing to do"? "He must have hit the ceiling, I think." Can I ever be in doubt about what I just thought in this case? Yet the sentence *He must have hit the ceiling* is ambiguous.

To sum up, the use of language involves all sorts of ambiguities. It is up to the speaker, therefore, to prevent, and up to the listener to avoid, misunderstandings due to this source. In doing this both participants have to rely on the circumstances. Now if thought consisted in the use of language, then, first, there could be, and often would be, ambiguous thoughts (in the relevant sense of ambiguity); second, the thinker would frequently face the task of disambiguating (that is, finding the correct "reading" for) his thoughts; and third, he would have to rely on circumstantial clues in doing so. I submit that all these consequences are absurd.

People are not infallible; they commit errors in many things they do, and speech is no exception. They make mistakes of grammar, use the wrong word, and commit malapropisms and various slips of the tongue. Thus it often happens that they do not in fact say what they wanted to say, or even what they think they are saying. Of course, both the audience and the speaker may detect such errors, and then the speaker may come to correct himself. The audience, too, is liable to errors of its own. One may mishear the speaker, misunderstand him, and so forth. Errors can occur on both ends of the speaker-hearer relation.

This possibility casts a new pall on the Platonic theory, whether it be conceived actively, as talking to oneself, or passively, as hearing "voices" in the imagination. For, to take the first alternative, it would allow situations in which the speaker could be mistaken about what he actually thought. He might say things like, "I thought I thought that p, but then I realized that in fact I thought that q, so I corrected myself," or "I wanted to think that p, but in fact I thought that q," and so forth. I forego the pleasure of pointing out the various absurdities in such reports.

The second alternative, the passive one, fares no better. It leads to the possibility of misunderstanding, or failing to understand, one's own thoughts. "I am not sure what I thought"—the thinker could report—"it may be understood as p or as q"—as if trying to interpret an oracle.

Finally, having given the main arguments showing the implausibility and the falsity of the Platonic view, I shall sketch a few additional considerations to reinforce this conclusion.

Although we often ask the foreigner, "In what language do you think?" we do not take this question so seriously as to countenance such answers as, "I think in English now, but in bad English. I misuse words in my thoughts, I commit grammatical errors, and so forth. Moreover, owing to this handicap, I think rather slowly and in primitive sentences." I suppose "thinking in English" means nothing more than having the facility of expressing oneself in English directly without first formulating what one wants to say in another language, and then translating by means of some set procedure.

Very often we hear, "I can't think of the exact word for what I want to say." The most natural assumption is that the speaker does know what he wants to say. For after a while he might exclaim, "I have it! It is——." The word fits. Fits what? Fits into the sentence(s) the thinker entertains? Hardly, since many words could do that. But that word alone expresses his thought.

Similarly, in giving paraphrases or translations for a given sentence, one does not normally operate on a word-to-word basis. One gets the "sense" of the sentence, and then looks for another sentence (in the same language or another) that expresses the same sense. Now this sense is surely not grasped in terms of another sentence, since that is exactly what one hopes to find. Nor does one, like the foreigner who does not "think" in English yet, follow any set of rules—connecting words to words—in performing the task. Translating is not like projecting another picture from a given picture by some routine procedure leading from point to point, line to line, angle to angle, and so forth; it is rather like imagining the very thing the first picture depicts, and then drawing another picture, in another medium, of that thing.

Let us recall the kind of thinking chess players, painters, composers, and, for that matter, plumbers, repairmen, and so forth, are likely to be doing while performing their respective tasks. Their thinking, no doubt, is accompanied by a great deal of imagination representing colors, shapes, sounds, and various objects in a variety of configurations. Now compare these activities with the performance of such "verbal" tasks as writing a poem or a speech, playing Scrabble, solving crossword puzzles, translating, doing research in linguistics, and so on. Each of these activities involves thinking, often on a very high level. Yet, obviously, no less than in the previous cases, the help of the imagination is needed in the thinking process. The difference is that in these situations the imagination is enlisted to evoke not colors and sounds, chess pieces or pipes, but words, phrases, and sentences.

Then consider people who are natively blind or deaf. Quite obviously their handicaps will restrict the power of their imaginations: the blind man will be unable to imagine colors, the deaf man sounds. Moreover, unless specially trained, the deaf man will remain mute; consequently, no words at all will occur in the play of his imagination. Similarly, the blind person will not be able to think about color harmonies, and the deaf-mute will not be able to compose music or write poetry—at least not until their handicaps are compensated for in one way or another. There is no reason to believe, however, that such people cannot think about matters that do not require the kind of imagination they happen to lack.

The deaf-mute, of course, unlike the blind, also suffers the disadvantage of being unable to express the thoughts he has by the normal means—that is, by the use of language. But here again, the break between him and normal people is not so sharp as some philosophers want us to believe. There are many thoughts we are unable to express, either because the language itself fails to provide the facilities, or because our own command of the language is insufficient. As to the first point, I remind you, once more, of the kind of thinking done by composers, painters, and, often enough it seems, even by mathematicians and physicists—not to speak of the experiences and insights mystics claim to have. As to the second, think of inarticulate people (who may be very smart otherwise). Or think of yourself in a foreign country. You want very much to say something, and cannot. Then you try to say it in your native tongue—and fail again, because of disuse and confusion.

At the beginning of this discussion I remarked that there are certain forms of thought that we are unwilling to attribute to dumb beasts because these forms presuppose conscious thoughts in the agent. Since, moreover, thinking about something consists in having a series of such thoughts, we are equally reluctant to say that a certain dog or cat is at present engaged in "thinking" about something or other.

Now what about the deaf-mute? Are we equally unwilling

to say that often he wonders and guesses, assumes and concludes, deliberates and decides, pretends and hopes? Is it impossible for him to form beliefs, nurture suspicions, find out
that he was wrong, change his mind about the matter, and so
forth? And, accordingly, should we say that he is inherently
incapable of thinking about something or other for a while?
I do not see any reason to think so, since although such a
person cannot talk, we can communicate with him to some extent at least, via gestures, facial expressions, and pantomime,
*no less than with a person whose language is utterly unknown
to us.* I do not think that I would find a difference in kind
between the difficulty of communicating with a monolingual
Tibetan and the difficulty of communicating with a deaf-
mute. One can even mistake a weird-sounding language for
the mutterings of a deaf-mute, and vice versa, at least for a
while. Yet, given the hypothesis that the Tibetan can think
(since he can talk) and the deaf-mute cannot (since he cannot
talk), the difference should be categorical. For one cannot
really communicate with an unthinking being: communication with somebody consists in getting him to understand
what I think and what I want, and in coming to understand
what he thinks and wants, quite apart from appropriate overt
performance, if any.

Thus, as I said at the beginning, one cannot communicate
with a beast, but one can with a foreigner and with a deaf-
mute equally. For they both have, as St. Augustine puts it,
"the natural language of all peoples" at their disposal, to wit,
"the expression of the face, the play of the eyes, the movement of other parts of the body, and the tone of voice which
expresses our state of mind." [16] It is easy to imagine flattering
or embarrassing a *señorita* wordlessly—and whether or not
she is a deaf-mute makes no difference. Then think of flattering (or embarrassing) a dog. Thought, real conscious thought,

16. *Confessions,* 1. 8. As quoted by Wittgenstein, *Philosophical Investigations,* p. 2.

is required for the uptake of flattery or the response of embarrassment.

If so, then the Platonic account must be wrong. Language is the means of expressing thoughts, not of having them.

3

Dreams, Memory, and the Origin of Thought

STANLEY R. PALOMBO

Freud's remarkable early work, *The Interpretation of Dreams,* profoundly influenced both the behavioral sciences and the literary culture of this century. Beyond its importance to the psychoanalyst as a therapeutic tool, it opened up to scientific and philosophical investigation a stratum of human experience in which long-range motivational forces, effective on a scale of time comparable to the human lifespan, could be systematically observed in relative isolation from the immediate goal-seeking activity of everyday life.

In more recent years, however, Freud's theoretical explanation for the origin of dreams has become less compelling. In Freud's theory, a dream was the outcome of a fortuitous meeting between two very different mental phenomena, one the representation of an unconscious infantile wish, the other an innocuous fragment of the previous day's experience. The meeting was thought by Freud to come about in order to provide each of these phenomena with something it lacked but in some sense required—the infantile wish with a disguise that could make it acceptable for representation in consciousness, where it would achieve hallucinatory gratification; and the innocuous fragment with the emotional force of the repressed wish.

A large body of psychophysiological data has now been accumulated that demonstrates that dreaming is anything but a chance occurrence. For every subject it takes place in regular periods at fixed intervals over the course of each night. When dreaming time is missed during one night it is made up on subsequent nights. Deprivation of dreaming time causes a variety of disagreeable subjective effects and objective performance deficits (Greenberg and Pearlman, 1974). Infants spend a much greater proportion of their sleeping time dreaming than do adults. All mammals tested thus far, including the marsupials, exhibit the physiological concomitants of dreaming. Cerebral blood flow is higher in the dreaming state than it is during the most strenuous waking activity. In the dreaming state all voluntary muscular activity is inhibited (as it is not during nondreaming sleep).

Clearly, dreaming is an obligatory psychophysiological function of critical importance to higher organisms. A theory that stresses the hallucinatory gratification of infantile wishes will not account for everything we now know about dreams. Freud was working in what amounted to a scientific vacuum; for dreaming belongs to a class of higher-level biological activities that, astonishing as it may seem, remained scientifically unrecognized and unidentified throughout Freud's lifetime. I refer, of course, to the information-processing functions brought most forcefully to our attention by efforts to simulate with the digital computer complex human psychological processes and activities (Simon, 1969). Both the successes and the failures of these efforts have contributed to our growing understanding of the orders of complexity necessary for the performance of the basic operations of the human psychic apparatus.

It will be shown here that Freud's observations in 1900, and earlier, are sufficient to define the critical role played by the dreaming state in the processing and storage of new perceptual information. The results of new experimental work that supports and further elaborates this conclusion will also be presented.

In another article (Palombo, 1976) I have given a detailed

account of the series of steps (the memory cycle) through which a new sensory impression must pass on its way to a location or set of locations in the permanent memory structure. I will concentrate my attention here on the stage of the memory cycle that matches new experiences with past memories—that is, the stage of the dreaming state. In doing so I will suggest that, no less than in Freud's time, psychoanalytic observations are essential to the definition of a psychological model of sufficient scope to include the variety of phenomena now known to us. Such a model raises important questions about the evolution of the more advanced processes of reflective thought. In the concluding section I will explore the possibility that the memory cycle has a direct ancestral relation to conscious cognitive activity.

The Structure of Memory

Colby (1964, 1967, 1973) and Peterfreund (1971, 1973) have discussed the relevance to psychoanalysis of the information-processing model. Psychoanalysis is a problem-solving activity that makes extensive use of information-processing methods. I have described elsewhere (Palombo, 1973) how the technique of free association creates a unique opportunity for an exploration and examination of the patient's permanent memory structure.

Like the programmed associative memory structures that it resembles, the structure of the human permanent memory appears to have a number of features that present obstacles to any systematic procedure for searching out and locating a particular item of information. These obstacles exist prior to and independent of whatever additional difficulties may be created by the mechanisms of repression discovered by Freud. They must be dealt with by adaptive mechanisms specifically designed for this purpose. We shall see that in its adaptive functioning the dreaming state constitutes one of these mechanisms.

The inherent features of the permanent memory structure that interfere with the searching process are the following:

1. The large-scale structure of the long-term memory is a unilaterally directed graph with the properties of a tree growing from a point (Harary et al., 1965). Associations normally flow in one direction only, away from the origin and toward the periphery. The pathway leading from a superordinate nodal point is therefore inaccessible from the subordinate node that terminates the pathway. This restriction can be circumvented only by a special effort to trace the sequence of nodes traversed along the pathway leading to the particular nodal point in question.

2. Individual nodal points do not appear to be distinguished from one another as to type or quality of contents. Thus, the contents of any nodal point may be associated with the contents of any other. The basic unit of information appears to be the sensory image. Semantic information appears in nodal points that are subordinated to previously recorded sensory information.

3. Associations are unlabeled—that is, the fact that two associated memory units are linked tells nothing about the syntactic, semantic, or logical relationships between them.

A memory structure with these properties is designed for flexibility of storage rather than the instant availability of its contents for problem-solving activity. It is open to the introduction of new items of experience at any existing location in the structure, but it is notably lacking in rapid access to items already in storage. (This is one reason for the lengthy duration of psychoanalytic treatment.) The structure of the memory tree therefore maximizes the input of new information under the pressure of immediate events and affects, even when the ultimate significance and utility of this information are still uncertain. Lindsay refers to a simple structure of this kind (though not as simple as this one) as "the *ingenuous graph* for the given initial data set" (1973, p. 377; Lindsay's italics).

Once the pressure of events and affects has subsided, the ingenuous structure of the memory tree may be enhanced by the development of new linkages during the problem-solving activity of waking consciousness. In this way the more significant branches of the tree develop such features as reversible associations, nodal points addressable by content as well as by location, and a rich elaboration of semantic and logical relationships. These branches constitute what I would call the long-term *working* memory, as distinct from the passive or ingenuous structure of the long-term memory as a whole.[1]

How much of the passive memory structure is ordinarily incorporated into working memory is difficult to estimate, but it must differ considerably from person to person. In the case of the neurotic patient who consults a psychoanalyst, many critical elements of past experience are inaccessible. The presenting complaint and the initial history are drawn from his working memory; the analysis proper involves an extended exploration and activation of his passive memory.

Computer Simulations of Memory

Computer simulations of human memory described in the current literature tend to be simulations of the long-term *working* memory.[2] The success of these models in imitating the performance of human subjects in a limited-task environment is extremely impressive. Their generalizability to the human condition, however, remains to be determined.

One can see that the complexity of the output of an information-processing mechanism (C_o) depends on both its computational power (P) and the internal complexity of the information units which form its input (C_I):

1. Long-term working memory corresponds closely to the categories designated by Freud as "secondary process" and "preconscious." The passive or ingenuous image memory is the basis for Freud's "primary process" or "unconscious" in the developmental sense, but not his "dynamic unconscious," which results from the forceful repression of painful memories.

2. See Anderson and Bower, 1973; Schank, 1973; Wilks, 1973; Simmons, 1973.

$$C_O \sim (P)(C_I)$$

It is not surprising, therefore, that a mechanism of relatively limited computational power (a digital computer program in the current state of the art) can simulate the performance of a human subject if its information units are already highly elaborate at the time of input.

A successful program, like the Human Associative Memory of Anderson and Bower (1973), requires an input which is organized at the level of grammatical sentence or logical proposition. It assumes that perceptual information has been translated from sensory images into semantic structures, and that all associations are labeled and reversible. These conditions or their equivalent must certainly be achieved in local segments of the human long-term *working* memory, but they cannot be typical of the long-term memory as such.

A program that retrieves propositional statements from its memory and makes low-level logical inferences from those statements is a simulated student, not a simulated person. The human organism must find its way piecemeal and painfully through a universe stubbornly opaque.

I draw attention to this difference because the information-processing function performed by the human mind in the dreaming state, though in principle quite similar to analogous functions performed by intelligent computer programs, exists on a scale barely contemplated in the current literature of cognitive psychology.[3]

Dreams and Memory

The earliest suggestions that dreaming performs an information-processing function involved in the transfer of perceptual information from the short-term memory to the permanent memory were made independently by Greenberg and Leiderman (1966), Dewan (1970), and Breger (1967). Hawkins (1966) also pointed to the adaptive function of

3. For a view approaching my own, though stated in very different language, see Hunt, 1973.

dreaming by relating it to the memory system through Freud's metaphor of the "Mystic Writing Pad" (1925).

A terminological note is necessary here. To some experimental psychologists the "short-term memory" is a structure that can hold up to seven items of memory in full consciousness for about twenty seconds after immediate sensory registration. Information retained for longer than this period is considered to have been transferred to the "long-term memory."

What we are concerned with here is a short-term memory structure that accumulates the meaningful experience of a normal waking day, only a small portion of which will actually be transferred to the permanent memory. For example, a patient whose medial temporal lobes were removed in an effort to treat his intractable epilepsy was prevented from transferring new information into permanent storage, as described by Milner et al. (1968):

> During three of the nights at the Clinical Research Center, the patient rang for the night nurse, asking her, with many apologies, if she would tell him where he was and how he came to be there. He clearly realized that he was in a hospital but seemed unable to reconstruct any of the events of the previous day. On another occasion he remarked, "Every day is alone in itself, whatever enjoyment I've had, and whatever sorrow I've had." Our own impression is that many events fade for him long before the day is over. He often volunteers stereotyped descriptions of his own state, by saying that it is "like waking from a dream." His experience seems to be that of a person who is just becoming aware of his surroundings without fully comprehending the situation, because he does not remember what went before. [p. 217]

In addition to a deficiency in his short-term memory, this patient was unable to transfer the accumulated day residues into his permanent memory structure. The short-term memory referred to in this paper is the memory structure that stores the day's events. In the case example, this structure represented the outer limit of the patient's powers of retention. The long-term memory contains the items normally retained beyond this limit, items that can be recalled decades later without reinforcement during the interim.

Greenberg and Pearlman (1974) have reviewed the experimental literature and shown that, although routine learning in animals is not disrupted when followed by dream (REM) deprivation, the retention of a learning experience that requires adaptation to a new task environment is significantly disturbed. Their hypothesis suggests a generalized adaptive and integrative function for dreaming. However, in my opinion, a theory that specifies the information-processing nature of this function *in detail* is essential to further progress in dream research.

The Matching Process

The clues that lead to an understanding of the specific information-processing function of dreaming are contained in many of Freud's original dream reports in *The Interpretation of Dreams,* but most clearly in his descriptions of dreams that illustrate what he called the process of "condensation."

> [1] The face that I saw in the dream was at once my friend R.'s and my uncle's. It was like one of Galton's composite photographs. (In order to bring out family likenesses, Galton used to photograph several faces on the same plate.) So there could be no doubt that I really did mean that my friend R. was a simpleton—like my Uncle Josef. [vol. 4, p. 139]

> [2] None of these figures whom I lighted upon by following up 'Irma' appeared in the dream in bodily shape. They were concealed behind the dream figure of 'Irma',

which was thus turned into a collective image with, it must be admitted, a number of contradictory characteristics. Irma became the representative of all these other figures which had been sacrificed to the work of condensation, since I passed over to *her,* point by point, everything that reminded me of *them.*

There is another way in which a 'collective figure' can be produced for purposes of dream-condensation, namely by uniting the actual features of two or more people into a single dream-image. It was in this way that the Dr. M. of my dream was constructed. He bore the name of Dr. M., he spoke and acted like him; but his physical characteristics and his malady belonged to someone else, namely to my eldest brother. One single feature, his pale appearance, was doubly determined, since it was common to both of them in real life. [vol. 4, p. 293]

[3] If the objects which are to be condensed into a single unity are much too incongruous, the dream-work is often content with creating a composite structure with a comparatively distinct nucleus, accompanied by a number of less distinct features. In that case the process of unification into a single image may be said to have failed. The two representations are superimposed and produce something in the nature of a contest between the two visual images. One might arrive at similar representations in a drawing, if one tried to illustrate the way in which a general concept is formed from a number of individual perceptual images. [vol. 4, p. 324]

[4] I will therefore quote one more dream, which seems to be composed of two different and opposing phantasies which coincide with each other at a few points and of which one is superficial while the second is, as it were, an interpretation of the first. . . . Here there is no difficulty in separating the two components. The superficial

one was a *phantasy of arrest* which appears as though it had been freshly constructed by the dream-work. But behind it some material is visible which had been only slightly re-shaped by the dream-work: *a phantasy of marriage*. Those features which were common to both phantasies emerge with special clarity, in the same way as in one of Galton's composite photographs. [vol. 5, pp. 493–94]

The common theme here is the superimposition of images derived, on the one hand, from experiences of the day preceding the dream—"day residues" in Freud's language—and, on the other hand, from emotionally charged memories of the more distant past, often extending back to childhood.

The superimposition may involve not only static two-dimensional visual images as in Example 1, but also three-dimensional composite images of people represented in any or all sensory modalities, and by speech, behavioral, or other semantic indices as well (Example 2). These composite images are not static, but continue to change. Sequences of superimposed images changing over time may give the impression of superimposed fantasies or narrative structures (Example 4). The dream may also present what appears to be a struggle between opposing images from the recent and remote past, as in Example 3.

The process that brings about the superimposition of these images seemed to Freud to be directed toward a goal, the bringing into clear relief of elements common to both images or sets of images. This goal was achieved with varying degrees of success in Examples 1, 2, and 4, but was not achieved in Example 3.

Representations of current experience—the day residues ("my friend R.," Irma, Dr. M., the fantasy of arrest)—are being matched against representations of the historical past ("my uncle," the members of Freud's family represented by

Irma, "my eldest brother," the fantasy of marriage). The dream mechanism acts to determine whether the new and old experiences are linked to one another by common features or elements.

Example 3 is especially interesting, for it records an instance where the matching process has failed within the dream itself. The traditional psychoanalytic theory of dream construction implies the existence of a similar test situation in which a decision is made before the materials of the dream enter consciousness—that is, before they achieve representation in the sensory projection mechanisms. This test must determine the "suitability" of a given day residue to act as the vehicle for carrying a particular infantile impulse into consciousness.

Freud makes it plain that not every day residue is qualified to serve as the vehicle for every impulse. Therefore, a process of selection is necessary, during which any proposed combination of residue and impulse must be judged to be "suitable" or not. According to this theory, a positive outcome of the selection process will lead to the emergence into consciousness of the "suitable" combination. A negative outcome of this determination would have to mean that the mismatched dream materials could not enter consciousness at all—that is, they could not achieve representation in the sensory projection mechanisms if, in Freud's words, "the process of unification into a single image may be said to have failed." But this is exactly what has happened in Example 3.

For the model being presented here, the dream itself is the test situation in which the congruence between images of the present and the past is determined. Moreover, given the possibility of disruptive interventions by the censorship mechanisms, we would expect to find the full range of chaotic to coherent matchings appearing in the dreams that actually take place—as, in fact, we do.

An alternative explanation of the matching process is suggested by our knowledge (1) that dreaming is an obligatory biological activity of very high priority whose onset and duration are almost entirely unrelated to the content of particular dreams; and (2) that an enormous amount of computational effort is required to introduce each of the significant experiences of a single day's activity into suitable locations in the permanent memory, prior to and independent of the obstacles created by the mechanisms of defense. To discover a suitable location in the associative memory tree it is necessary to examine the contents of a potential superordinate nodal point already located in the memory structure and match them with the representation of the new experience. If the match is successful—that is, if relevant criteria of relationship are met—then a coded representation of the new experience is introduced into a new nodal point subordinate to the one containing the related older memory (Palombo, 1976).

This process is what Freud observed in dreams. The only method of comparison suggested by information-processing research that might be rapid and efficient enough for the processing of new experience for storage in the permanent memory is the method of comparison by superimposition. If the superimposed images reinforce each other in such a way that a coherent composite image results, the criteria of relatedness are satisfied and the match is successful. The dream is itself the test situation in which the match succeeds or fails.

Dreaming would therefore be a highly sophisticated version of one of the basic information procedures carried out by living organisms, the matching or equivalence testing of new experience against standards or expectations built up in the past (Miller et al., 1960). It differs from the typical biological testing situation in a number of ways, however. The quantity of information being processed is vastly greater. There may be no overt behavior of the organism accompanying a positive outcome of the test procedure—that is, insertion of the new experience into the permanent memory.

Further, the criteria for positive matching are flexible enough to validate marginal cases. In fact, they appear to be designed for maximum inclusiveness rather than for the fine discriminations we have learned to expect in simpler biological feedback systems. These unusual characteristics are, of course, precisely suited to the particular task at hand—the orderly expansion of a very large ingenuous image-based memory structure.

Dreaming and Consciousness

Once we have understood this information-processing function, some otherwise puzzling features of the dreaming state come more readily into focus. Let us examine, for example, the relationship of dreaming to consciousness. The data of experience are present in the psychic apparatus in two distinct forms. The more usual of these is a coded form that facilitates serial transmission and storage, much like the coding used to register data in the computer or on a videotape. Data in this form are not accessible to consciousness.

For most purposes coded data are satisfactory. When it is necessary to evaluate the significance of an experience in all its possible multiple meanings, however, the experience must be reconstructed in the sensory projection mechanisms in a form that reproduces as nearly as possible the subjective quality and impact of its original occurrence. It appears quite likely that the codes which record the information coming from different sensory modalities—visual and proprioceptive, for example—are not mutually translatable. In order to interpret the interaction of the information recorded in the various sensory modalities for a given experience it would then be necessary to reconstruct this information simultaneously, in all modalities, in the sensory projection mechanisms.

The evaluation of an experience depends to a considerable degree on the affective response it evokes in the experiencer, almost exclusively so in the infant and small child, but significantly so throughout life (Rapaport, 1961). A memory item stored in coded form includes an indication of the affective responses it has evoked when projected in the past, but in order to determine the affective value of a new experience or of an old experience in relation to a new one, the experiences in question must be displayed *at the time of the evaluation* in the sensory projection mechanisms.

There are two rather different situations in which a full affective response and consequently a full sensory reconstruction are required. One is the problem-solving activity of waking consciousness, in which the affective response is part of the evaluation preliminary to an action to be taken with respect to the outer world. Affect plays a double role here, as a source of evaluative information and as an impetus to action.

The other important situation in which affective response and sensory reconstruction are both required is the dreaming state, but here the action-initiating function of affect creates a problem, since no immediate action with respect to the outside world is required. It appears, in fact, that any activity in the usual sense would severely disrupt the concentrated effort required in dreaming. Accordingly, the voluntary muscular system is immobilized during dreaming. This allows the information-carrying or signal function of affect to be utilized without the inappropriate consequence of action.

There is also a major difference between the uses of the sensory projection mechanisms in waking problem-solving and in dreaming. In waking experience the sensory projection mechanisms produce a continuous monitoring of the outer and inner worlds. The complex current image of the actual world is maintained intact while components of it are examined and compared with internal exemplars of relevance and desirability. The activity of testing itself takes place within the perceptual context of the real world and is treated by the psychic apparatus as an actual experience in the world.

The situation is entirely different in dreaming. The determination to be made is a suitable location for the coded representation of a new experience in the memory structure. The reconstruction of the experience in the sensory projection mechanisms is only a means to this end. For the sake of speed and efficiency a method of comparison is employed (the method of superimposition) that distorts the appearance of the sensory imagery derived from the new experience by combining it with the representations of past memories. Once the existence (or nonexistence) of the match between the new experience and the older memory has been determined, no further use can be made of the double dream imagery that was created by the test procedure.

When its purpose has been served, the content of the sensory projection mechanisms—the double imagery of the dream—is then discarded, that is, prohibited from entry into the memory store. Unlike the record of the equivalence testing that takes place in waking consciousness, the dream contents do not constitute a representation of actual experience. What is preserved and introduced into the memory is the coded version of the new experience that provided the basis for the sensory reconstruction. This is the outcome toward which the memory cycle was aiming all along.

Such an arrangement may seem rather wasteful, for the dream contains information about the structure and contents of the permanent memory that, as Freud so aptly demonstrated, is directly accessible in no other way. Freud came to know this privileged information through the relatively small set of dreams during which the dreamer awakens, whether accidentally or when prompted by powerful affects. In the momentary consciousness of the awakening dream, the dream contents are transformed into a report on the permanent memory and its potential for matching new experience. In fact, in the nonaccidental awakening dream a mechanism exists that is capable of bringing the conscious waking attention of the dreamer to bear on something problematical that has been uncovered by the matching procedure.

The dream contents rescued from oblivion by the awakening dream may then become the nucleus of a new, expanded, and interpreted experience. The day residue that evolves from this experience will seek out in the next night's dreaming just those locations in the permanent memory from which the original problem arose. The feedback circuit thus established presents the psychoanalyst with an opportunity to direct his own interpretations to the specific locations in the patient's memory where new information concordant with current reality is most needed (Palombo, 1976).

Dreaming and Affects

Dreaming is the only natural state of mind in which the display of affect is free of the usual action consequences. To whatever extent this display is beneficial in and of itself, that benefit can be realized in the dreaming state most directly and with least risk, as Freud's original hypothesis would lead us to expect.

Nevertheless, affects must be displayed in dreams in order to recover critical information about the motivational states of the dreamer (past and present) that only reconstructed affects can convey. The possibility that the wish-fulfilling function of dreams might be secondary to such a prior adaptive purpose was anticipated by Freud in "Beyond the Pleasure Principle."

The dreaming state, then, is a natural precursor of developmentally more advanced states of mind in which the subject consciously and voluntarily promotes the occurrence of affect and simultaneously inhibits the action that would normally follow. The objective in these states of mind is the achievement of self-knowledge through an intelligent examination of feelings ordinarily beyond the range of casual introspection. It is this objective that distinguishes the Greek theater from Dionysiac revels, and psychoanalysis from abreactive versions of psychotherapy.

Freud's efforts to deal with the fact that dream imagery is not a report of actual experience are instructive. Lacking a clear conception of the adaptive purpose that might be served by a display in the sensory projection mechanisms that is not imitative of the real world, Freud assimilated all of the non-realistic aspects of the dream to the antirealistic distortions of neurotic defense mechanisms. But we now have evidence that the distortions of the dream content are due both to adaptive and defensive mechanisms acting in opposition to one another during dream construction.

Experimental Findings: The Correction Dream

The memory cycle model leads to a prediction unanticipated by earlier theories of dreaming. It suggests that when a failure of the matching process is exposed to consciousness by an anxiety-laden awakening dream, a new and more comprehensive day residue incorporating a representation of this dream is likely to be formed. This new day residue should then be matched successfully in the next night's dreaming with the identical experience of the past that contributed to the original anxiety dream.

Because the second dream would include new information about the anxiety dream gathered during the interval of waking consciousness, it would have the potentiality for correcting the difficulties that had caused the original mismatch. According to the memory cycle model, the correction dream should be directly observable. Lacking the anxiety that accompanied the mismatch in the initial dream, however, a successful correction dream would be unlikely to awaken the dreamer, to be remembered, or to be reported under ordinary circumstances.

The ideal experimental arrangement for observing the correction dream would be to monitor the sleep of a patient undergoing psychoanalysis and to awaken him after each period of REM sleep. If the correction dream hypothesis is correct, one should be able to discover by this method the correction dreams for the anxiety dreams reported in the previous analytic hour.

This experimental format, which has many research applications, was actually employed for another study several years ago by Greenberg and Pearlman (1975), who very generously made their data available to me. A full analysis of this material requires detailed attention to all of the patient's associations during the analytic hour in which the anxiety dreams were reported, and during the hour following the recording of his dreams in the sleep laboratory. This work is now being prepared for publication in monograph form (Palombo, manuscript).

The example below is taken from this study. For lack of space, a vast quantity of confirming associative material must be omitted, but the overall pattern of events as described here should be clear to the reader. The patient in this case was an unmarried man in his thirties whose father had recently died.

I will first give the text of an unsuccessfully matched awakening dream, which took place on a Tuesday night and was reported at the beginning of the next analytic hour, on the following Thursday. This is one of a pair of reported dreams, both of which were incorporated into correction dreams on the night following this hour.

> And then I dreamed that I married Kate Davis instead of Ellen Thornwald.[4] I decided something and I dropped her off because I made a mistake. I married one instead of the other. Now . . . a wife in here—I don't know what the hell she is doing in this dream, and I was in Fairfax in a local church. And I go there or to an antique shop or a garden—I am not sure what—and I was single when I went there. This is quite a dream. I was

4. Identifying data disguised.

making a film and I was also looking for girls at parties where I was making the film, and I was single. I had to get married in a church or a garden or an antique shop. And Ellen looked much better in the dream than she looks in reality.

This dream represents the typical Oedipal triangle, but with two modifications that blur the outlines of the conflict and reduce its intensity. The dreamer has himself taken the roles of the adult sexual partner, the father, and also that of the child-observer of the marital union between his parents. The rivalry for Mother has been minimized by the substitution of two women, neither of whom is in reality more than a casual acquaintance. The general atmosphere of uncertainty and indecision, and the suggestion that the marriage is somehow being forced on the dreamer, all add to the impression that he is trying at any cost to evade the responsibility for his own Oedipal wishes.

Perhaps the most striking aspect of the dream, from the psychodynamic point of view, is the absence of Father or of any adult male who might act as his surrogate in the triangular relationship. This suggests that the figure of Father has been deleted from the dream by the defensive operations of a censorlike mechanism.

At the time the dream occurred, the patient was preoccupied with deciding whether or not to marry his current girlfriend, Judith, a divorcée with several children. This preoccupation is clearly the source of the day residue concerned with the theme of marriage, although no specific experience relating to it was mentioned during the hour in which the dream was reported.

The Thursday hour did produce a memory of the past, though not of childhood, which had clearly been matched with the patient's present interest in the subject of marriage. It was in the same church where "all of my friends have gotten married—relatives, friends—a slew of them got married there." And he adds, "I am always running around taking pictures of everybody, everybody's family, and this and that—I am the historian, the photographer."

The major interpretive effort of the Thursday analytic hour began with the analyst's attribution of the lack of feeling in the reported dreams to the patient's fear of revealing himself. This brought forth an immediate response. The patient was afraid of seeming weak in relation to his father, whose overwhelming physical presence he referred to several times. His father was "a great bull of a man," enormously powerful and muscular. Even in death he seemed frightening to the patient, who described the "gray, ghostlike, stonish effect" his image produced. The transference of this feeling to the analyst was brought to the patient's attention repeatedly throughout the remainder of the hour.

By the time the hour had ended, it appeared that the patient's stereotyped image of his father had softened. The interpretations had provided him with an opportunity to compare his expectation that the analyst would react to his weakness as his rigid childhood representation of Father might have done, with the reality of the psychoanalytic situation. He could now attempt an identification with the analyst that permitted an exchange of feeling that would have been impossible when the hour began.

The following dream was reported when he was awakened in the sleep laboratory after an REM period on Thursday night:

> I dreamed about a police officer named Phil—a school bus—dreamed about running a ranch and Miss Iceland —a beauty queen—and the rancher, his name was King, I guess. The King Ranch. And he married Miss Iceland and I asked him how he met her and he said his cousin fixed him up in Iceland. And about the police officer—I

guess he was collecting furniture or something. Furniture? As I talk about this dream of a security member, mentioning furniture—I see an open casket, an image of an open casket.

The dreamer's relationship with Mr. King was more clearly defined in the report of the same dream at the beginning of the Friday hour:

> I was an owner of a ranch in Texas and my name was Mr. King— Robert King—King Ranch, and I married Miss Iceland, a beauty queen. This was a beautiful girl, this was a beauty queen. And then I stood back and then I became a third person. I asked King how he happened to meet this beautiful beauty queen. He said he had a cousin who lived in Iceland and he got fixed up. I said, hum, not bad.

This dream is unmistakably a reworking of the Tuesday night dream reported in the Thursday hour. The vagueness and aimless uncertainty of the original dream have been replaced by a quality of vividness in the imagery and assertiveness in the action. The patient's father, excluded from the earlier marriage dream, is represented here in his Oedipal majesty, replete with totemic attributes of horse and bull. (The King Ranch is famous for its breeding of these animals.) The mysterious antique shop has been transformed into the policeman's furniture collection. The school bus hints at a date during the Oedipal period or early latency.

Mother is also given royal status, and the intensity of her conflicting attractiveness and inaccessibility is graphically portrayed. The alternating identities of the women married by the dreamer in the original dream have been replaced by the contrasting feelings aroused by the single figure of Miss Iceland. The ambiguity between the roles of actor and observer is replicated in the new dream, but this time the role of the actor is clearly identified with Father.

In all major respects, then, the new dream reworks the conflictual issues presented in the original dream, and in so doing corrects a variety of omissions and indirections associated with the shallow and disorganized state of the historical material represented in the earlier dream. In the correction dream the issues are sharply focused, the connections with childhood memories of the dreamer's parents are deepened, and the glaring omission of Father's central role in the conflict is made good.

The associations to the King Ranch Dream, and to the other correction dream reported in the sleep laboratory on Thursday night (not described here), permit us to reconstruct a major portion of the process through which the original dream was formed, and the role played by the dream censor in this process. The following association to the King Ranch Dream during the Friday hour identifies the specific day residue of the original dream on *Tuesday* night, in which the dreamer was a photographer of weddings and families.

> Now this Icelandic beauty queen. I have seen her before. This is really a stunning girl, and Judith showed me a picture when she was married—an entirely different girl than she was now. She is very thin and sort of pale and emaciated looking. When she got married she was a very round-faced—not plump but an extremely blond, blond sort of a girl. If I saw her picture now, I mean, I still would say that is not you, absolutely not you. And there was some similarity between the beauty queen and what Judith used to look like. Maybe there is something there, I don't know—coming from Iceland there has got to be a relationship there. Mr. King is another one of those characters like Howard Hughes, you know, that I admire —immense wealth—a lot of power—doesn't seem to— well, from what I know just a recluse in a way. And he got married last in life I noted in the dream. I am sure

he would appreciate me marrying a . . . again—whatever it is.

The two Judiths of this fantasy were transformed into the two women of the Tuesday night dream and then into the double image of Miss Iceland in the correction dream. The parapraxis, "he got married last in life" brings us to another Tuesday residue that was excluded from both reported dreams but revived in both the King Ranch Correction Dream and in the second correction dream (not described here) of Thursday night. On Tuesday the patient's mother had asked him to remove some of his dead father's belongings from her house, including some articles stored in a bureau. The cryptic statement in the Photographer Dream that "I had to get married in a church or a garden or an antique shop," can now be explained. The *single* object that shares the properties of a church, a garden, and an antique shop is a cemetery.

At issue is an unconscious fantasy that marriage leads to an immediate death. Mr. King was married *last* in life. In the second correction dream, Mother is represented as a refrigerator from which Father's "effects" are being removed by the patient and two other men, who clearly stand for the analyst and the director of the sleep laboratory. This refrigerator evokes a memory from puberty of a refrigerator that made unpleasant noises during the night, preventing the patient from sleeping.

Father's death in the fantasy is the result of engulfment by a frigid Mother during sexual intercourse. The bigger they are the harder they fall. The patient's efforts to identify with Father's power will lead to his own downfall. Safety lies in the seclusion of the observer, who can close the door to the noisy refrigerator or turn off the camera when he chooses. Toward the end of the Friday hour a very early memory connected with this fantasy emerges:

I see a street-corner curb, a washed street, red sidewalk, black street all wet. I could be in Ocean City. The only time I went to Ocean City was—not the only time—but most of the times with my parents as a young kid. I was looking, you know, seeing an Ocean City scene—the Burgundy Hotel I stayed at, and then a floor scene and open box. The open box turns into a smaller box, and suddenly the smaller box turns into a big box of beetles, and they were slithering across the floor and disappearing in the crevices—huge bugs.

This appears to be the memory of a fantasy or dream originally experienced during the Oedipal period, perhaps at age three or four. It is a crude representation of the primal scene, parental sexual intercourse, through images derived from anal excretory functioning. The setting at a summer hotel suggests crowded quarters and an unusual opportunity for observing parental sexual activity. During the Thursday hour the patient had associated the themes "looking for girls" and "taking a film" with dreams of the past involving a beach house.

Because so many elements enter into the construction of this pair of dreams, we cannot give an exact description of the sequence of steps through which they were produced. But we can reconstruct a very useful approximation of this sequence, with a clear distinction between the defensive activity of the dream censor and the adaptive functioning of the memory cycle.

1. The sequence began on Tuesday with Mother's request to the patient that he remove Father's belongings from her house. This request gave rise to the fantasy that Father had been destroyed through his sexual involvement with Mother, with concomitant feelings of gratification at Father's demise and fear of a similar fate if he should allow himself to identify with Father.

2. This fantasy (which is unlikely to have been fully conscious) created a feeling of anxiety about the prospect of his own marriage to Judith. This anxiety was concretized in the comparison between Judith's present appearance and her appearance in the photograph taken at the time of her earlier marriage. A day residue was formed in which the two marriages were linked—his parents' marriage, which had destroyed or castrated Father, and his own prospective marriage, which might do the same to him.

3. In the process of dream construction on Tuesday night, a series of past memories was selected for matching with the day residues. These memories were related either to the theme of parental sexual activity as observed from a distance by the patient, or the theme of Father's death (both real and as imagined in Oedipal fantasies since early childhood). As revealed in the other dreams and the associations of these two analytic hours, enclosures of every kind were implicated in the death fantasies, including bathtubs, bathrooms, rooming houses, buckets, baskets, air tunnels, bus terminals, boxes, ice boxes, refrigerators, bureaus, desks, furniture in general, rolled-up rugs, and so on—each of these images carrying the double connotation of Mother's womb and Father's tomb.

4. Before the matching could take place on Tuesday night, however, the dream censor intervened and deleted all *overt* references to Father's death. The remaining material was then matched by the process of superimposition described above. Two dreams resulted, one in which the Burgundy Hotel memory of early childhood was superimposed on some current enclosure imagery relating to Judith; the other—the original dream described here—in which the patient's role as family photographer was superimposed on the current fantasy generated by the changes in Judith since her wedding photograph was taken.

5. After the Photographer Dream had been reported during the Thursday analytic hour, a considerable amount of

work on the frightening aspects of the patient's internalized image of his father was accomplished. The more human (though still highly idealized) image of Father that resulted from this analytic work was combined with the Photographer Dream report in a new day residue presented to the dream construction mechanism on Thursday night.

6. This new day residue, in which the revised image of Father had been introduced into the Oedipal configuration of the Photographer Dream, was not interfered with by the dream censor, whose objection had apparently been neutralized by the work of the Thursday hour. The new residue, therefore, was able to participate in the matching process without significant modification. In the process of superimposition it was successfully matched with the new material from the permanent memory structure relating to powerful men who had (in the patient's fantasies, at least) come to a bad end because of their involvement with women. The composite image formed by this superimposition was the marriage scene of the King Ranch Dream.

7. The original Photographer Dream had included the triad of *church, garden* and *antique shop,* which contained a reference to the cemetery where Father was buried that was sufficiently obscure to pass the scrutiny of the censor. In the new dream these elements were matched (or rematched) with some of the enclosure memories previously referred to, producing the images of the furniture collection, the school bus, and finally the casket itself.

This sequence of events confirms the novel assumptions of the memory-cycle model of dream construction, particularly with respect to the continuity and cumulativeness of dreaming and to the feedback function of the correction dream. In addition, it demonstrates the action of the censorship mechanisms in their interference with the adaptive purpose of the matching process. This finding in turn suggests that the most frequent cause of the mismatched dream that tends to awaken the dreamer—the kind of dream that is remembered and reported in analysis—is the obscuring action of the dream censor itself. We have seen how this action can be neutralized by the analytic process and successfully circumvented in the correction dream that results.

I suggest that the events described here could have taken place only through the action of an adaptive information-processing mechanism whose purpose is to integrate significant current experience with the deepest layers of the permanent memory structure. Freud taught us how dreams can provide us in the present with a powerful source of information about the past.[5] Our experimental observations confirm the hypothesis of the memory-cycle model—that dreams also serve to convey *new* information into the structure of the psychic apparatus that contains the accumulated record of the past.

Through the mechanism of the correction dream it is possible to introduce some of the elements missing from that record in such a way that what were previously disconnected bits and pieces may be reorganized into a coherent picture of past events. This finding does much to explain how, for a patient who is successfully analyzed, it is not merely his understanding of the past that seems to change, but the past itself.

The Psychic Apparatus

A theory of dreams leads inevitably to a theoretical model of the psychic apparatus as a whole. This is so because dreaming is the only psychic process that makes use of the sensory projection mechanisms in order to fulfill its adaptive function without at the same time transforming its contents through an output program into the logical and grammatical narrative structures familiar to waking thought.

The absence of output programming in dreams gives us an

5. See Breger et al., 1971, for a further discussion of Freud's view.

opportunity to observe the psychic apparatus at work at an organizational level that is much nearer to the more general structures appropriate for internal processing than is the conscious problem-solving activity of which we are usually aware. What we can now learn from these observations is that nonconscious information-processing is organized in its own way for adaptive purposes that are complementary to those approached through different methods in waking consciousness.

If we take the adaptive mechanisms of the memory cycle to be typical of the nonconscious psychic apparatus, we find ourselves thinking in terms of an interactional model of mental activity. The mind becomes an instrument for the comparison and evaluation of past experiences in the light of current needs. We have seen that in dreams the adaptive mechanism of condensation brings together the representations of distinct experiences in order to join them in the more comprehensive structure of the permanent memory. The defensive mechanism of displacement acts to prevent such an adaptive union by unilaterally splitting off one element before the evaluation can take place. The isolated "impulses" associated with neurotic symptoms appear to be constructed by and modeled after this unilateral defensive activity, and to be quite distinct from the impulse representations normally processed by the adaptive mechanisms of the ego in an interactive process that relates present needs with past experience.

This suggests that there are fundamental differences between the adaptive and defensive mechanisms of the psychic apparatus that have not been sufficiently emphasized in traditional psychoanalytic theory. The memory cycle is a primitive mechanism of the ego that must be present from birth or very shortly after. Otherwise, it would be difficult to account for the maturation of the ego or the development of object constancy during the first year of life.

Defensive interference with this adaptive sequence must begin very early, but not until the adaptive sequence itself becomes functional. The defensive operations of the dream censor cannot begin to work until the adaptive function of the memory cycle exists to be interfered with. It seems likely to me that defense mechanisms in general are designed to interfere with specific preexisting adaptive mechanisms of the ego. If this is so, then the traditional psychoanalytic picture of the psychic apparatus as a whole is modeled far too closely on the phenomenology of the mechanisms of defense.

Dreams and the Origin of Thought

The reflective quality of secondary-process thought, on which Hampshire and other philosophers rightly place so much emphasis, must have had an evolutionary history before reaching its present level of elaboration in the species *Homo sapiens.* I would imagine that this history began when the sensory projection mechanisms were withdrawn from direct contact with the external world and first became available for reproductive rather than merely receptive activity.

This reproductive activity would have acquired adaptive value to the extent that it could bring the record of relevant past experience into the arena of current issues. This could not have been done in a single step. The reproduction of a past event must initially have involved the reproduction of an action indissolubly linked with affect and sensory imagery. The fact that the entire skeletal muscle system is incapacitated in the dreaming state indicates both the importance and the difficulty of separating the imagery and information content of a reproduced memory from the action program associated with it. Unless and until this separation was made, there could be no possibility of *comparing* the present and the past without *confusing* them.

The crudity of the means by which the separation between

imagery and action is achieved in dreaming suggests to me that the mechanism of dream construction may have been the first step in the evolution of reflective consciousness. The ability to maintain simultaneously the imagery of present and past in the sensory projection mechanisms during waking consciousness, while at the same time performing the actions appropriate only to *the present,* must have been a much later development.

Information processing is an activity of all living systems. It takes place at the molecular level in viruses and at the electrochemical level in the protozoa. At what point does the evolutionary track along which information processing becomes progressively more complex branch off in the direction of reflective thought? The answer to this question must be somewhat arbitrary, but I find it useful to locate this point where the sensory projection mechanisms take on an information-processing function in addition to their role at the interface between organism and environment. (Perhaps this is what Freud had in mind when he suggested that the Ego originates as the integument of the Id.)

If, as I believe, dreaming was the earliest state of mind in which this development took place, then comparison by superimposition would be the precursor of cognitive thought in general, and the compartmentalized consciousness of dreaming would be the antecedent of all problem-solving activity during waking consciousness. I do not find these conjectures to be terribly far-fetched. Comparison by superimposition, or *condensation* in Freud's terminology, seems on logical grounds to be the simplest cognitive operation that could make use of the vast quantity of information that can be accommodated in the sensory projection mechanisms at one time.

I would also expect the uses of the sensory projection mechanisms for receptive contact with the outside world and for reproductive comparison of internal imagery to have developed separately before being combined in reflective thought processes during waking consciousness. If we accept this simple schema, we are well on our way toward a unified conception of mental activity at all levels.

A system for updating the contents of the permanent memory without the loss of previously stored information would be a necessary prerequisite for any cognitive activity that links the present to the past. The development of higher-level techniques for utilizing the information in storage does not, of course, eliminate the need for continued acquisition of new information. The mechanism of dream construction could therefore continue to perform its primordial function while serving as a model for higher-level processes, including the most general aspect of problem-solving, in which a new and unresolved situation is compared with earlier experiences for which a suitable program of action has been found.

Dreaming may be unique among the more primitive information-processing mechanisms of the adaptive ego in its employment of the sensory projection systems. But it resembles these other archaic mechanisms in its automatic, mechanical, and repetitive qualities. We have good reason to believe, from psychoanalytic data and from elsewhere, that conscious reflective thought occupies the apex of a vast pyramid of adaptive mental activity. The function of reflective thought in the economy of the psychic apparatus appears to be primarily a supervisory one, which is not surprising in view of its complexity and informational cost.

Although we are not generally aware of it, most of our adaptive functioning is carried on by automatic lower-level processes. As long as our interaction with the environment consists of routine and repetitive activity, these nonreflective information-processing mechanisms are sufficient. It is only when a new or novel response is required that the problem-solving mechanisms of waking consciousness intervene and take command. This is what happens when a car approaches suddenly while we are crossing the street. It is also what happens when we are awakened from a mismatched or unexpectedly affect-laden dream.

If the mechanisms of waking consciousness are prevented from monitoring the programmed activity of the archaic ego, as they are when this activity is concealed by neurotic repression, then they are unable to perform their supervisory role. The result is that the repressed automatisms of the archaic ego continue to operate as if all new experience were a repetition of the infantile experience for which the automatisms had been originally programmed. The aim of psychoanalytic treatment is to restore the supervisory capacities of the higher-level mechanisms, while at the same time permitting the more primitive mechanisms to be reprogrammed in the light of current experience.

Philosophers have tended to emphasize the discontinuities between reflective thought and the nonconscious supporting structures that form the basis of mental activity. Very few have resisted the temptation to sit in judgment between them, or to become the advocate of one at the expense of the other. The present divergence between the Anglo-American "school," represented by Hampshire and many others who follow the British empiricist tradition, and the Continental philosophers, who have been influenced primarily by the Romantic tradition of Rousseau and Schopenhauer, is a case in point.

Freud's sympathies were clearly with the Romantics. He was impressed through his clinical work with the helplessness of the supervisory functions of the ego when their sources of information about unconscious mental activity were cut off by repression. Following the Romantic tradition, he attributed the power of the primitive mechanisms of the archaic ego to their collusion with an irrational, impulse-ridden, nonpurposive psychic entity, which he called the Id. In doing so he was forced to deny the origin of pleasure-seeking biological impulses in earlier and more primitive states of adaptation.

At the opposite pole, we find a philosophical position that tries to enhance the value of reflective thought by isolating it from its supervisory role and attributing to it an essence that places it apart, scientifically and epistemologically, from the solid flesh of which dreams are made.

The raging disorganization of the Id and the sublimity of reflective consciousness in isolation from biological motivations are both authentic representations of subjective experience at times when the continuity of the hierarchical structure of the psychic apparatus has been disrupted. Beneath these subjective appearances, however, we must look for the adaptive structure in its entirety, and for the specific pathological influences that so often dissociate it into conflicting fragments.

REFERENCES

Anderson, J. R., and Bower, G. H. *Human Associative Memory.* Washington, D.C.: Winston, 1973.

Breger, L. "Function of Dreams." *Journal of Abnormal Psychology Monograph* 72, no. 5, pt. 2 (1967) : 1–28.

Breger, L.; Hunter, I.; and Lane, R. W. *The Effect of Stress on Dreams.* New York: International Universities Press, 1971.

Colby, K. M. "Experimental Treatment of Neurotic Computer Programs." *Archives of General Psychiatry* 10 (1964) : 220–27.

———. "Computer Simulation of Change in Personal Belief Systems." *Behavioral Science* 12 (1967) : 248–53.

———. "Simulations of Belief Systems." In *Computer Models of Thought and Language,* edited by R. C. Schank and K. M. Colby. San Francisco: W. H. Freeman, 1973.

Dewan, E. M. "The Programing (P) Hypothesis for REM Sleep." *International Psychiatric Clinics* 7 (1970): 295–307.

Freud, S. *Standard Edition of the Complete Psychological Works.* London: Hogarth, 1953–61:

  The Interpretation of Dreams (1900–01), vols. 4, 5.

"Beyond the Pleasure Principle (1920)," vol. 18.

"A Note upon the 'Mystic Writing-Pad' (1925)," vol. 19.

Greenberg, R., and Leiderman, P. M. "Perceptions, the Dream Process and Memory: An Up-to-Date Version of Notes on a Mystic Writing Pad." *Comprehensive Psychiatry* 7 (1966) : 517–23.

Greenberg, R., and Pearlman, C. "Cutting the REM Nerve." *Perspectives in Biology and Medicine* 17 (1974) : 513–21.

———. "REM Sleep and the Analytic Process: A Psychophysiologic Bridge." *Psychoanalytic Quarterly* 44 (1975) : 392–403.

Harary, F.; Norman, R. Z.; and Catrwright, D. *Structural Models.* New York: Wiley, 1965.

Hawkins, D. R. "A Review of Psychoanalytic Dream Theory in the Light of Recent Psycho-physiological Studies of Sleep and Dreaming." *British Journal of Medical Psychology* 39 (1966) : 85–104.

Hunt, E. "The Memory We Must Have." In *Computer Models of Thought and Language,* edited by R. C. Schank and K. M. Colby. San Francisco: W. H. Freeman, 1973.

Lindsay, R. K. "In Defense of Ad Hoc Systems." In *Computer Models of Thought and Language,* edited by R. C. Schank and K. M. Colby. San Francisco: W. H. Freeman, 1973.

Miller, G. A.; Galanter, E.; and Pribram, K. H. *Plans and the Structure of Behavior.* New York: Holt, 1960.

Milner, B.; Corkin, S.; and Teuber, H. L. "Further Analysis of the Hippocampal Amnesic Syndrome: 14-Year Follow-Up Study of H.M." *Neuropsychologia* 6 (1968) : 215–34.

Palombo, S. R. "The Associative Memory Tree." In *Psychoanalysis and Contemporary Science,* vol. 2, edited by B. Rubinstein. New York: Macmillan, 1973.

———. "The Dream and the Memory Cycle." *International Review of Psycho-analysis* 3 (1976) : 65–83.

———. "Dreaming and Memory: A New Psychoanalytic Interpretation." Manuscript.

Peterfreund, E. *Information, Systems, and Psychoanalysis.* New York: International Universities Press, 1971.

Peterfreund, E., and Franceschini, E. "On Information, Motivation and Meaning." In *Psychoanalysis and Contemporary*

Science, vol. 2, edited by B. Rubinstein. New York: Macmillan, 1973.

Rapaport, D. *Emotions and Memory.* New York: Science Editions, 1961.

Schank, R. C. "Identification of Conceptualizations Underlying Natural Language." In *Computer Models of Thought and Language,* edited by R. C. Schank and K. M. Colby. San Francisco: W. H. Freeman, 1973.

Simmons, R. F. "Semantic Networks: Their Computation and Use for Understanding English Sentences." In *Computer Models of Thought and Language,* edited by R. C. Schank and K. M. Colby. San Francisco: W. H. Freeman, 1973.

Simon, H. A. *The Sciences of the Artificial.* Cambridge, Mass.: MIT Press, 1969.

Wilks, Y. "An Artificial Intelligence Approach to Machine Translation." In *Computer Models of Thought and Language,* edited by R. C. Schank and K. M. Colby. San Francisco: W. H. Freeman, 1973.

4

Consciousness, Thought, and Enownment

ALBERT HOFSTADTER

As I sit here now quietly pondering, there is suddenly a snarling, piercing, head-splitting roar outside. It swoops in swiftly, increases in intensity, then subsides into a low, regular purr; it starts up again, more deafening than before, but though intrinsically as turbulent as ever, it relents, moves off, dies away into the distance, and vanishes within the encompassing sea of sound that constitutes the day's ordinary silence.

At first, having been absorbed in contemplation, I was startled by the clamor into vivid awareness of it. It called upon me for my attention, calling me away from my engrossment in the subject of this essay. It stunned me momentarily with its vehement self-insistence. I focused on that noisy din as though there were nothing else in the world to be concerned with. It filled the sphere of my consciousness as the central predominating object. I was startled into dealing with it on an emergency basis.

I managed. I was able to cope with it by means of a simple thought. "Why that's Bobby McCann on his motor bike dusting up the roads again, letting us all know that he's around!" The snarl of the throttle, the rider's rattle—these are his trademarks, with which he loves to take the center of the

The research behind the writing of this essay was carried on with the aid of a Senior Fellowship from the National Endowment for the Humanities and a special grant from the Research Committee of the University of California at Santa Cruz.

stage when school hours are over. One is never fully prepared for the assault. It always comes as a shock, waking one into awareness, challenging one to identify it and to say to oneself, precisely, "Why that's Bobby McCann!"

That sudden awareness is a piece of consciousness. This recognition is a piece of thinking. The function of consciousness is to present an object in its otherness. The function of thinking is to appropriate that alien object into ownness. Consciousness gives the mind something alien; by thinking, the mind domesticates the stranger. Thinking assimilates what is at first foreign to the mind and makes it something natural and familiar.

If we put together the two functions, those of consciousness and of thinking, into a single one, it may be formulated as the appropriation of otherness. The otherness comes through consciousness and the appropriation through thinking.

Consciousness itself is already a piece of thinking. When I am invaded by the clamor of the motor bike, I am aware of it as that clamor. I do not think the judgment, "This is a clamor," by an explicit reflection. Rather, I have a direct awareness of the clamor. In this directness it comes to me as clamor—not, for example, as a sweet taste or a blue color, but as this horrendous assault of sound. Although it startles me into a momentary loss of composure, this startling embodies an insight: clamor is here. I appropriate the alien in the fact of its alienness. That is the first mode of appropriation of the alien, a primitive act of thinking in which thinking and consciousness are one and the same without having differentiated into a process.

Thinking, in its turn, is also consciousness. It is consciousness which has moved from the function of presenting otherness to the specific function of assimilating it as such. Consciousness and thinking are not two separate activities. Thinking is a specific mode of consciousness, which is developed by consciousness at the point at which the task of appropriation is in order.

Identifying Bobby McCann is a rather simple piece of the thinking appropriation of otherness. Achievement of a successful science—for instance, a science of criminology—would be a somewhat more complicated piece of thinking appropriation. There are many differences, in principle as well as in practice, between a simple identification and the creation of a science. But in the most fundamental dimension of principle the two are basically alike. The scientist must first develop his awareness of data—phenomena—that are startling and do not fit into preconceived schemes. He must then develop the conceptual apparatus by means of which a workable interpretation of the phenomena can be achieved. The scientist will make use of investigative methods, ways of registering and arranging data, and schemes of explanatory analysis, in order to arrive at the judgments he seeks. Those judgments, however, will have the same basic function as the judgment about the boy on the motorcycle: they will serve to identify what is there. In them, the scientist's categories and schemata for thinking will capture the data, holding them in a form appropriate to the mind's needs: statistical arrays, causal orders, schemes for managing institutions, projects for restoring human beings to the mainstream of social life.

Thinking is not the only mode of appropriating otherness. Practice is more fundamental than thinking as a way of appropriating otherness. Practice is action. Bobby McCann was practicing. With his motorcycle he was putting his imprint on the world. I was one of the victims he chose to work on. He knew that he could startle me by pushing his way into my consciousness with the uproar of the bike. He uses the bike to gain recognition of himself in the neighborhood. He is realizing a purpose by employing means well calculated to attain the end.

In practice we take something and transform it so that it reflects what we wish it to be. This transformation changes it from being something just other than ourselves, and in that sense alien, into something that exhibits something belonging to us, something of our own. So Bobby practiced on my consciousness in such a way as to make my consciousness, which was not recognizing him, recognize him. He planted his image in my mind for the moment. He took over, appropriated my mind for his own immediate purpose.

Bobby's practice is a bit of triviality. But in principle it exemplifies all of practice, even to the extent of the kind of practice that takes hold of a whole human world and transforms it in a revolutionary way. Hitler and Lenin are Bobby McCann writ large. With differences, of course! All of what we know as industrial process and its technology is practical appropriation of what nature originally affords in the way of raw materials for the sake of impressing human purposes on them, exploiting them for human purposes, and assimilating them to man's life activities. Therapy is practice. It works on the subject, assimilating him to an ideal purpose, which is the therapist's—and presumably the subject's—notion of a more or less healthy human condition. However much the therapist may wish not to interfere in the subject's self-realization, his activity is nevertheless the appropriating of the subject to his, the therapist's, notion of what a human being should be.

Thinking itself is a form of practice. In it we practice on our own consciousness, transforming it into something we wish it to be. Before we have succeeded in comprehending something by thought, we stand in a relationship of ignorance to it. That is to say, insofar as we are conscious of it, it stands over against us as something other which has not been assimilated. Cancer has not yet been assimilated. It stands over against us in the most startling way, refusing itself, yielding only here and there by dint of persistent efforts to take hold of it. We are in a state of intellectual alienation from it.

When we try to comprehend it, what we are trying to do is to change the relationship from one of intellectual alienation to one of intellectual assimilation. We are changing our brains. When we come to know, we are different from what we were before; we have transformed the way in which our mind apprehends the other. By appropriating the object in knowledge, the mind at the same time appropriates itself to the nature of the object.

In the beginning was the deed. Even the Word was a deed —a deed practiced on the self as on the world.

The deed of practice is by its very nature an appropriation of otherness. The deed of thinking is a specific form of the human deed in general. It is the deed of transforming consciousness from the stage of alienation to the stage of appropriation as consciousness. In it the other becomes own to the self and the self becomes own to the other in the specific mode of consciousness, and thus consciousness itself becomes own to the self. By thinking, consciousness heals itself. It heals the breach it has originally instituted in letting the other appear as other, alien, foreign.

This is the basic function of thinking in the human economy: the transformation of consciousness from alienation to assimilation, as consciousness.

Thinking is not only itself a mode of practice. It also exists within a wider context of practice. Even when thinking is taken in its most subtle, refined, and isolated form—as in the pure thinking of the abstract mathematical theorist, the metaphysical philosopher, or the mystical religious contemplator —it is a form of practice and operates within a practical context. Carrying on the business of theoretical mathematics is part of the process of the construction of human knowledge. It comes out of the past and moves into the future. There is a tradition of mathematical thinking which is part of the intellectual tradition of mankind. The mathematician is early introduced into this tradition, beginning with his learning to count while an infant at home. He is supported by his culture, which lets him do the thinking it needs, gives him the language by means of which he articulates it, nurtures his mind over a long period of preparation, and, when and if requisite, makes this or that use of his discoveries. So in analogous ways metaphysics and mystical contemplation are embedded in the context of human practice and are themselves forms of that practice, developed at given stages for given ends.

Turning the viewpoint around, we notice that every form of human practice incorporates its own mode of thinking. This is a point of cardinal significance. Too often we associate with the word *thought* only certain salient kinds of thought. So if we speak of someone as a thinker we usually think of him as a philosopher or a theoretical scientist, perhaps a mathematician or a physicist, somewhat less a chemist or biologist, even less a psychologist, sociologist, jurist, legislator, artist, minister, mountain climber, automobile mechanic, physician—is the street cleaner a thinker? To be sure, the street cleaner doesn't spend most of his time thinking through the principles of his occupation, whereas the philosopher is supposed to spend most of his working time doing so. The theoretical mathematician, the physicist, and the scientist in general are likewise supposed to spend most of their time doing principled thinking. But since the judge, for example, sits on the bench, works in his office, presides over the trial, conducts the hearing, instructs the jury, and determines the sentence, we think of him more in terms of practice than in terms of theory.

Nevertheless, while he is doing all these practical things he is surely thinking practically and expressing practical thoughts. When he says to the defendant, "You are sentenced to a term of five to twelve years of imprisonment," he is not only performing a function and doing something to the defendant in the name of the law; he is also thinking of that defendant as one who is convicted and subjected to punishment relating to the conviction. This is as much an intellectual identification of the defendant as my thought about Bobby McCann was an intellectual identification of the hubbub he created. Jurisprudence as a science is the development of the corpus of thinking in which such a sentencing is embedded, just as theoretical physics is the development of the corpus of thinking in which is embedded a judgment in spectroscopy identifying a given gas. Jurisprudence does not have an identical character to physics; its categories differ, as do specific purposes and consequences. Notions such as private, personal, and public property, or obligations and their performance, restitution and reparation, or judicial enforcement, procedure, action, judgment, review, and execution—all such notions involve considerations of a kind alien to the apparently value-neutral objectivities of mathematico-physical thinking and to the allegedly value-neutral objectivities of behavioral thinking in the human sciences.

When we imagine the painter in his studio working actively at a canvas we tend not to think of him as being, at the same time, a thinker. He himself will often object vigorously to that idea, for his aim is not—or not merely—to declare a thought, but to create a work. Sometimes, even, he will say that his main effort is to express a feeling where thought would only become an obstruction. That happens usually in periods of artistic expressionism, when the expression of feeling becomes the dominant aim.

But whatever the spirit of the time and the artist, there can be no question but that he does vigorous artistic thinking that is intrinsic to his work as such. He is thinking painting all through the process of painting. At every moment he makes decisions: that area up in the left-hand corner needs to be toned down, this shape needs to give a vague impression of a biological form, that line needs to be broken, etc.,

etc. He is always aware, with intense consciousness, of the pigmented canvas before him in its alienated state, the state in which it is not yet as it should be. The empty canvas that stares him in the face in the beginning is at that moment in an extreme state of alienation. Therefore it is a challenge that has to be met. Or, in other moods, it is an opportunity to be exploited while the time is ripe. Seeing it as such is already an act of thought. It is an intuitive thinking, an immediate cognitive identification of something other as own in the shape of an immediate cognitive apprehension of the alien *qua* alien. To appropriate the other as challenge, threat, opportunity, or possibility is already—even in the very identifying of it as alien and estranged—an insightful appropriation of it as such.

As the artist proceeds, working out the design, determining the subjects and the materials, pulling them together, developing their tensions, searching for a resolution, his mind is ever actively alive, ever identifying, seeking out the other in its otherness and appropriating it in the specific aesthetic-artistic way that belongs to him as this individual artist—this practitioner of romanticism, realism, dadaism, surrealism, or superrealism. There is an essential intelligence involved without which art would be impossible. Picasso was as much a thinker as Einstein, Schönberg as much as Whitehead. Indeed, the question could be raised as to who of these was more concretely a thinker.

The street cleaner acts in an analogous way. All the time he is wending his way up and down the street he is making immediate perceptual identifications of dirt, rubbish, cleanliness, objects lost and found, having as constant mental horizon the notion of the street that has to be maintained in its tidiness and order. His problems may be small and the effort of thinking coordinately small. But as the judge is involved in the process of clearing up social disorder, so the street cleaner is involved in the process of clearing up the disorder of the street. There is no elaborate science of street cleaning, but there is a developing science of urbanistics, in which street cleaning has its due role. The street cleaner's thinking is a fragment of the context of urbanistics and eventually of our total thinking about human destiny.

So, to repeat, every form of human practice incorporates its own mode of thinking. That is to say also that man, throughout his entire existence and in every side and dimension of it, is a thinking being. Some thought may occur in other animals as well. But for man thought is especially significant because the structure of life in society and culture that he builds so far exceeds in complexity, depth, and possibility of value what any other animal we know about is capable of achieving, and because this structure rests for its possibility on intelligent insights, on the capacity to attain a thinking appropriation of the othernesses of man's world.

Consciousness, in coming to think, comes to its own appropriation of otherness. It is itself a mode of practice—namely, a practice whose object is our own consciousness, transporting it from a stage of alienation to a stage of assimilation or intelligent union with its object. It also occurs in a context of other practice in which we are in process of transforming objective matter, and its function within that practical context is to do the kind of intelligent assimilating of the alien that is there specifically required. That much has been uncovered about thought and consciousness in what has already been said.

What is the meaning of this phenomenon of thinking? What drive or impulse is at work in it, leading it to be and do what it is and does? What does this business of the intelligent assimilation of the alien come to? What part does it play in the totality of life? What are its importance and its power?

In order to be able to speak about these matters it is necessary to have a terminology. I have so far made do with what is most readily available. So I have spoken about the function of thinking as being to appropriate the alien object of consciousness into ownness, to domesticate or assimilate what is at first foreign to the mind and to make it into something natural and familiar, to appropriate and assimilate otherness in the specific manner of intelligence, to achieve intelligent union with consciousness' object. The chief words here are: first, the negative ones that represent the categories of difference—namely, otherness, strangeness, foreignness, estrangement, alienation; and second, the positive ones that represent categories of unity or identity—namely, ownness, familiarity, domesticity, appropriation, assimilation, unification, identification.

We readily recognize that these are various instances of the language of dialectic. They were not first introduced into language by philosophers, but they were first made into a technical terminology by the philosophers who created modern dialectic, and above all by Hegel, who made the dialectical process into the basic process of the total reality. I do not need to discuss his thought here. My purpose is different: it is to answer the questions raised in terms of what we ourselves can observe about the process of thinking and its operation in the wider contexts of life. I mention Hegel only because historical justice requires that the reference be made, just as reference to Newton has to be made when the discussion of theoretical mechanics begins, or reference to Freud when the discussion of psychoanalysis begins.

At the focus of my attention stands the process that is described as the becoming own of what is alien, the becoming domestic and familiar of what is strange and foreign, the reconciliation of what has been estranged and alienated, the appropriation and assimilation of what has been insistently other, unification and identification of and with the different.

These are diverse ways of referring to something that shows

itself continuously in all the domains and dimensions of human existence. Hegel believed that it was continuous through all existence whatsoever. Post-Hegelian thinkers—naturalist, Marxist, existentialist, and others—who have in some way taken up a dialectical manner of thinking, have been of two minds about the extent of its application—whether it is specifically restricted to human or animal existence, or whether it holds more widely of nature as a whole. Again, this question is not directly of concern to us here, where we are attending to the specific meaning of thinking consciousness in the context of human life. The reference to Hegel, however, is useful at this point, because in his writing about the total sphere of human life we can see how the dialectical principle operates continuously throughout its vast range while yet exhibiting essential differences in each area and at each stage of its process.

Starting from the most primitive biological dimensions of sensibility, irritability, and reproduction, and moving through the immediacies of the human being's embodiment in the natural environment, his feeling, habit, and behavioral mastery of the body; then through consciousness and knowledge, appetite, desire, interpersonal struggle and reconciliation, the search for comprehension and the search for happiness; then again through the construction of a social reality in law, morality, the family, civil society, the state, and history; and reaching finally the realms of human relationship to the infinite in art, religion, and thought, Hegel traced a development—not in time but in order of logical-ontological validity—in which there became evident an ever-renewed alienation and an ever-renewed resolution. Whatever be the critical judgment passed on the quality of his achievement, this much has to be said out of simple necessity: he showed that it was both possible and desirable to try to penetrate the meaning of all forms of human existence, from the most elemental biological to the most transcendental spiritual, by means of a suitable way of grasping them in dialectical terms. A hint of the nature of a critical negation of Hegel's dialectical doctrine can be gathered from my article, "Ownness and Identity: Rethinking Hegel" (Hofstadter, 1975).

Moreover, there is not the slightest importance to be attached to a word like *dialectical* for describing the kind of thinking that is called for. It is not the name that counts but the practice of thinking itself. To call it "dialectical" could even be a disadvantage because it invites people to bring in every relevant or irrelevant notion they think of, since the word *dialectic* attaches in their minds to something they have heard or read about Hegel, Marx, and other thinkers and their doctrines. This word *dialectic* has to be mentioned specifically in order to deprive it of its sting. What is of concern to us, and what alone is of concern, is the matter of the processes of alienation and reconciliation, estrangement and union, division, rupture, and breach on the one hand, and appropriation, assimilation, and identification on the other. Words like these must immediately stir the most active thoughts in the minds of psychological investigators of human experience. In them they can recognize the names of the processes with which they are constantly occupied.

If consciousness functions to present an object in its rupture from the self, in its otherness, so that it may be attended to as something calling for potential reunion, then unconsciousness functions to prevent that kind of presentation from occurring, because for one reason or another the stress of facing the assimilative, appropriative process is too great to bear.

On the other hand, it is exactly in reconciliation, union, appropriation, assimilation, and identification that the high points in human experience and existence are reached. Division and rupture have their essential functions, and human nature exhibits its potentialities for good and evil as it enters into the phase of difference. Difference can be destructive and creative. Experiences of difference can be among the headiest we have, and at some point or another every human being, even the saintliest and most self-liberated, finds himself within an ultimate difference. The negative—courageous, venturesome, aggressive, fearful, anxious, demonic—is always with us, in us, accompanying us to our end. But fullness of meaning comes only with dialectical fullness itself—that is to say, only with whatever momentary finality of affirmation we can attain.

These are all quite abstract remarks but their reference is to everything concrete in our experience.

If we are to answer the question of the meaning of thinking, then, it must be in terms of the place of thinking in the dialectical process by which alienation is transformed into appropriation. I call that process *enownment*.

The meaning and aptness of this term are immediately obvious. If A and B are alien to one another, then the process by which the alienation is resolved requires that A and B should become "own" to one another, in exactly the respect in which they are alien. If A and B are neighbors who have come to a breach of their neighborliness because of a dispute over the boundaries of their land, then the process of healing the breach requires that they should become reconciled precisely regarding the question of the boundaries. This might happen in different ways, more or less adequate and more or less satisfactory for one or the other of the pair— say, by a fight in which the vanquished gives way to the victor, or by a legal proceeding in which an adjudication is made to which the two are compelled to agree by the force of the state's law, or by a more friendly discussion and agreement in which the two try to come up with a result both will consider more or less fair. In ruder states of being, A might solve the problem by killing B, a solution typical of conditions that have sometimes been called the state of nature and under which nation-states for the most part still live. In this instance, all of the land would become A's own, but at the expense of his giving up the possibility of reaching an ownness-relationship of some kind with B—for example, slavery, mutual suspicion toleration, cocitizenship, neighborliness, friendship, kinship.

In both of the cases just considered an enownment comes about. If A and B fight and A is the victor, then B, by admitting defeat and giving way on the boundary question, has let what was his own become A's own, and he has let himself become A's own to do with as A pleases, to the extent of the victory. If they go to court and A's case is sustained, then the boundary is drawn according to A's own specification and both A and B agree to observe the legal rights and duties involved, both of them in this instance assuming the status of being legal persons respecting one another's legal personality, thus accepting each other as members of the same legal order, belonging together as own with own in this common legal order. What had before been "en-othered" has now been "en-owned." What had before existed in rupture and mutual rejection exists now in mutual embrace, reunited, enowned.

Beings that are enowned, having come into enownment, exist together as belonging together. Beings that have not come into enownment exist apart as split from one another, refusing each other, remaining in their isolation as alien and estranged. Enownment is the resolution of estrangement.

It is necessary to introduce a word of this nature because the English language doesn't otherwise contain one. Without it we have to make do with words like union, identification, reconciliation, appropriation, and assimilation. Union is too broad; identification suggests identity, which is too strong; reconciliation emphasizes peace and harmony, which is too smooth and limited; appropriation is too much associated with the active taking of something to be one's property; and assimilation tends to limit thinking to likeness and sameness and therefore to underrate the importance of the retention and development of difference. *Enownment* is strange enough to avoid these pitfalls. It suffers from the presence of the element *own* within it, which sometimes tends to make us think of property too, like appropriation. But when lovers promise to be "own" to each other, or when a people makes the cause of liberty its "own," or when a man vows to die for his "own" convictions if necessary, we understand what *own* is doing here quite apart from any accidental association with the notion of property. When we see *own* in this context it gives a new vitality to the word and lets it become an instrument for fresh thinking.

It is interesting that in his later thinking, in his search for the meaning of Being, Heidegger was led to introduce an ordinary word in an extraordinary sense in order to speak about the mutual belonging that occurs between man and Being, man and Time, things and their world, and other such relationships. His word is *das Ereignen, das Ereignis,* which ordinarily means event, occurrence, happening, but which (by a peculiar oblique etymology) can be read also as enowning, enownment. Despite the fact that he differentiates himself strongly from Hegel and the Hegelian dialectic, his thinking here nevertheless belongs to a process of alienating the Hegelian thinking and then transforming it into something own again, relevant to present conditions—an enownment. My present use of *enownment* is not the same as Heidegger's *Ereignis,* but the fact that he has been forced to find it is a warrant that something of the kind is needed (cf. Hofstadter, 1976).

The answer to the questions raised above regarding the meaning of thinking, and specifically regarding the drive at work in it, is to be given by speaking of enownment. The basic drive that extends throughout the spheres and stages of human existence, from the elemental biological to the transcendental spiritual, is the drive toward enownment: the enownment drive. Consciousness is a special phase of it (a phase of differentiation, alienation). We comprehend the

meaning of consciousness and its thinking as we comprehend
how they function in the process of enowning.

If it was possible to say above that throughout his existence, and in every side and dimension of it, man is a think-
thing being, it is now possible to say with the same uni-
versality that man is an enowning being. His thinking is part
of his enowning; it plays its specific role in the process.

Consider as elemental a phenomenon as appetite or desire.
This phenomenon has its specific quality and meaning, and
at the same time it incorporates its specific kind of consciousness, unconsciousness, thinking, and unthinking. Appetite for
food is developed out of bodily need. In the state of hunger
we tend to be alerted to (conscious of) inner bodily lack, and
to the significance of outer things for alleviation of the need.
Our consciousness is at once an awareness of the need and
of the possibility of its relief. What we are called on to do
here is first and foremost to think food. We search around
for food, develop means of obtaining it (from primitive gathering to technologized agriculture and husbandry), and invent means of preparing it and consuming it. There is a
whole corpus of thinking that structures itself around the
practice of the eating of foods.

My thought of food and eating is not a value-neutral, anti-
septically scientific, logicized conceptual construct. Food has
a complex meaning for me, at once emotive, conative, aesthetic, and religious, as well as logically cognitive, and it is
pervaded by social significance. When I perceive something
that I recognize as food, I am thinking a highly charged,
value-laden thought. It belongs to that facet of my life in
which I am concerned with maintaining and fulfilling my
being.

In this sphere of life the world confronts me at first as the
material field of my existence, in which I have to find material fragments which are fit for consumption. Consuming

them is enowning them in the most literal physical sense: ingesting them and assimilating suitable parts of them into my own body. Part of the chicken I eat becomes part of me. I enown that. The rest I disown in the usual way.

I am practically concerned with enowning matter as food. In my thinking, I try to differentiate out, in the material world, what is food and what isn't, how to acquire what is food and reject what isn't, how to make the right kind of matter into matter directly consumable as food. But also, my thinking is not only practical in this narrow sense. I dream about a belly full of meat, or about a dainty soufflé, or whatever else it is that delights me. I praise the cook's genius, admire the culinary creation almost as I would an achieved work of art. The food becomes a symbolical focus for other drives and emotions, and eating fulfills other needs; it fulfills my ego-needs while my belly is being filled. My thought processes include the many ways of relating thought content with thought content that are germane to fantasy and valuation, as well as to practice and logical inference. They stretch all the way to cannibalism or to the eucharist as sacramental participation in the divine power of being.

I am a food thinker in a manner similar to the way in which the painter is an art thinker or the judge a law thinker. In this thinking, I appropriate the material world by differentiating out within it those things which are food and food-related from those which are not, and I appropriate my consciousness to their difference. Those which are not are relegated to the far side of consciousness. The world appears to me in this thinking in the guise of food, just as the hubbub in the street outside appears to me as Bobby McCann on his motor bike. As part of the enterprise of enowning matter as food, my thinking enowns the world of matter as object of thought, appropriating what at first is alien in it so as to differentiate out in it what I can grasp as food, as food-related. Farmer, cow, milk and milking, corn, wheat, truck, delivery, store—the whole complex of production and distribution is invented by man's thinking practice in order to bring into articulation the interconnected system of food-relatedness. The practice of food production, distribution, and consumption gives a comprehensible shape to the world in this dimension. It is a shape which is genuinely comprehensible by its specific mode of thinking, food thinking. And by this thinking—logical and nonlogical, practical, aesthetic, social, economic, legal, industrial, political, religious, philosophical—the world is appropriated by the human mind and the human mind appropriated to the world. The two are enowned by means of the form of the mind's action.

The general business of human life is the dialectic of the development of alienation and its resolution by enownment. If anything is the meaning of life, it is this process. I say "human" here to set aside the question of other modes of life. In a more broadly philosophical context I would maintain that, with the requisite systematic ambiguity that changes meaning with changing subject matter, what is said here about enownment holds true of nonhuman life, and indeed of natural existence throughout. As a process, human life is the continuing flow of differentiation into difference, estrangement, foreignness, and of unification into assimilation, adaptation, appropriation. It is the continuing process of enowning. It is like a symphonic poem built of variations on this central theme, like Strauss's *Don Quixote,* or like a piece constructed out of a tone-row that continuously modifies its presentation, always turning up in new shapes, like a quartet by Schönberg.

We can discern this fact in its most general outlines if we look at the generic forms of life. These forms are basically three: conative or practical, cognitive or theoretical, and—the English language fails again, for while it has words like *affective, religious, contemplative,* it does not have a single good word for life in its concrete character of wholeness and unity; it only has abstract words like *integral, unitive, consummative, free,* or else one-sided words like *harmonizing, reconciling,* or *healing.*

As was pointed out above, the meaning of practice lies in its specific character as a mode of appropriation or, as we can now say, enownment. Practice consists in developing first a differentiation between what exists in a given situation, and what the agent of practice has in mind as an aim, end, ideal concept of will, as being what the situation ought to be. Practice is in the first place the differentiation between *ought* and *is.* If I weed my garden, then first I differentiate between the weed-ridden soil as it is and the idea I have in mind of its weed-free condition as it ought to be. The rest of practice consists in transforming the situation in such a way that what it is will conform with my concept of what it ought to be. In this way the differentiation, which is at first an alienation, is transformed into an enownment. The soil bears the imprint of my own idea. What before was merely an idea in my head is now projected out into the world and impressed on it so that the world, in this little spot, exhibits itself as my work. It is obvious that this picture of practice can be enlarged to embrace every kind of praxis.

If a number of medical practitioners spend a substantial amount of their time and labor in working together to build up an institute for the practice of their kind of medicine, bringing themselves together with other workers, buildings, equipment, social arrangements, legal arrangements, etc., then the meaning of this activity lies in the fact that they have projected out into the world and impressed on it a plan which they formulated in their heads in such a way that their work exhibits itself in this piece of world. They worked out the necessary alienation—the necessary differentiation of things, humans, institutional arrangements, etc., as being other than they should be—and subsequently the necessary enownment, the being as they ought to be, made own through appropriation to and by the joint plan.

Also, as we have seen, the meaning of thinking, as cognitive theoretical activity, lies in its specific character as a mode of enownment. Thinking, too, is a form of practice in which there is first a differentiation into alienation—a challenging of thought by problems which cannot as yet be accounted for in terms of principles hitherto obtaining—and an attempt thereupon to enown the alien data by developing concepts that will conform to them and bring them into conformation. In the process, thinking enowns thought to reality. This aim, to enown thought to reality, is the practice-aim of thinking as practice. In thinking, I practice on my thought-capacity, working to make it appropriate the unorganized data into a coherent scheme.

In both cases, that of normal practice and that of the special kind of practice which is called cognitive, or the practice of knowing, the aim is an enownment, while the explicit subject matter can be anything you please. A lumberjack works on trees, cutting them down. A sailor works on a ship, making it sail. A doctor works on a patient, making him well. A microbiologist works on bacilli and works on his mind at the same time, making the mind conform to the bacilli. A physicist works on subatomic particles and works on his mind at the same time, making the mind conform to the particles. A linguist works on comparative Indo-European grammar and works on his mind at the same time, making the mind conform to the grammar.

These are variations on the theme of enownment. But in none of these instances does the worker work on enownment, as such, as his subject matter. It is the latent subject matter, to be sure, but not the manifest one. All the way through, each one in his work is working at enownment. He is working on enownment without specifically bringing it to consciousness as such. He works at it in the particular vesture with which it is clothed in his special kind of work, so that he sees the clothing without bringing out thematically what it clothes. It clothes enownment. Enownment is the healing of the breach brought about in alienation. All work and labor is enowning the alienated. Everybody works—when and as he works—at healing. Working is healing.

All the time, the human mind keeps working at healing. Or, to put it more truly and fully, at breaching and healing and breaching and healing and so on. The name for this is freedom. When I speak of enownment, I mean to speak both of the breaching and the healing. There is no stage at which the human mind stops at an enowning and lets it be. Every stage of enowning becomes a fetter on freedom. Every stage exists to be broken through, departed from, left behind. But also, it is broken through so that an affirmative enowning can happen again. The liberation has two shapes, liberation from and liberation into.

The third form of life, beyond the normally cognitive and the normally practical, is the form of life whose subject matter is itself enownment, freedom, liberation, from and into. This is the form of life that shows itself first in community of human existence. From the outset of human existence, humans belonged together and were known to one another in organizations of kinship. Practicing kinship is not a normal kind of practice. It does not consist in making our kin our subject matter in the way in which the lumberjack, carpenter, sailor, doctor, or any other normal practitioner proceeds. We do not go at our kin with our own will, reifying them, treating them as clay in our hands, wood under the saw, patient on the table. That would be worse than despotism and tyranny; it would be the violent negation of kinship.

Practicing kinship is learning to live with and living with our kind as own with own, in mutual caring, concern, respect, and cooperation. Associated with this is thinking kinship. This kind of thinking is not like thinking lumber or thinking tooth-repair or thinking atomic particles. The difference lies precisely in the fact that the kinship which is the subject matter of this thinking is an explicit ownness. Kinship is ownness made explicit. It is above all in our kinship relations that we experience what it is to belong—in the nuclear family, the extended family, the lineage, clan, tribe, race. When we begin to look for our Being, we begin first and most obviously to find it where we belong. So even our names, which are supposed to say what and who we are, come to us from the kin.

Kinship is not the only form of community. Sociologists and philosophers make distinctions among kinds of community (*Gemeinschaft*) and society (*Gesellschaft*). Friendship, professional corporative association, membership in institutionalized organizations such as the military, the university, the government, are instances. In all of these communal/ social associations there is a specific kind of thinking by which the mutual belonging of members becomes articulated. You have to live in friendship, in the army or navy, the university or the town, to know what it is to think these matters in the specific form of thinking belonging. It is not the same as studying them from the outside like a sociologist or psychologist, not even like studying them from the inside like an anthropologist, although the latter already begins to participate. The dominant form of your life (*Lebensform*) has to be cast in the shape of the community in order for your thinking to be the specific thinking belonging. It is like the musical thinking of the instrumentalists in the Budapest Quartet when they are playing Beethoven's Opus 130.

An extremely important form of such communal existential thinking consists in the thinking that is involved in citizenship in the nation-state as it exists at present. The mind of each of us is permeated by categories, forms, principles, and values that owe their character to the nation-state of which we are members. We think matters of domestic and

foreign concern as participants and undergoers. Even the re-
sisters and revolutionaries are permeated. The scope of the
story of alienation and enownment is so vast when one turns
to this sphere, that it does not lend itself to a simple passing
description. I mention it only by name, despite the fact that
the basic issues of war and peace, humanity and inhumanity,
advance and decline, totalitarianism and libertarianism en-
gross all of mankind's thinking here in the most urgent way.

Beyond political thinking in its historically living form as
the enownment thought of participation and undergoing,
there are still other forms of thinking whose explicit subject
matter is enownment, freedom. These are the modes of
thought that belong to art, religion, and to the special kind
of theoretical meditative thinking that specifically makes enownment into its subject matter.

Art is concerned with making objects show enownment for
direct apprehension (intuition), whether in classical or ba-
roque modes as harmonious and reconciled, or in mannerist,
romantic, or dadaist modes as alienated. Different categories
are used to describe the effect at different times, so that we
speak of beauty and ugliness, harmony and discord, unity
and disunity, rightness and wrongness, working and failing.
Religion is concerned with overcoming the fundamental
alienation by which man's finite, mortal existence is bur-
dened: alienation in death, life, time, eternity. Religion is
man's desperate attempt to find an ultimate enownment in
and of the totality of his own existence.

Again, all that can be remarked now is that the scope of
these matters is enormous. They are only named here. The
point is just that, like all practice, the practice of art and
the practice of religion include a mode of thinking specific
to each, and this thinking makes explicit to itself the specific
enownments to which art and religion are dedicated. Art
thinking has its own language, the language of the studios,
creators, performers. Religious language equally has its own,

different language, that of prayer, church, community, which is spoken in the cultic practice; and here, too, the subject matter of thought and language is religious enownment, the union which is the object of prayer and the life of the spiritual community.

Thinking that is the most specifically "thinkingful" of all is thinking that belongs to the explicit practice of the life of enownment. Its language tries to say the things needed to be said in living in enownment. Ofttimes it is a language of silence, like the language of lovers together. It can try to speak in the outward shape of poetry. It can also try to speak in the language of prose, like the stumbling language of this essay. But, for the most part, it does not yet exist. The reason is that, for the most part, our race has not yet begun to live in enownment in the way necessary to constitute it our dominant life mode. How, then, could such a language have taken shape?

To know enownment as such, so as to be able to comprehend it as it shows itself explicitly in religion and art and communal existence, and less explicitly in other forms of existence—this is the indispensable precondition of a genuine knowledge of what heals. So much of the life around us and in us today is so breached that, to anyone who has some small glimpse of the practice and thinking of enownment, it brings the near hopelessness of despair.

Does one need to name names? Let us look about us—and not last at ourselves.

BIBLIOGRAPHICAL NOTE

The concept of *enownment* is adumbrated throughout Hegel's writings. Chapter 6, "Logic Further Defined and Divided," in *The Logic of Hegel,* 2d ed., in *Encyclopedia of the Philosophical Sciences,* trans. W. Wallace (London: Oxford, 1972), gives his clearest simple statement of the nature of a dialectical logic. All of the major works, beginning with the *Phenomenology of Mind* (New York: Harper Torchbook, 1967, with introduction by G. Lichtheim), are developments of the fundamental pattern of the process of alienation and enownment, the latter treated under such names as identification, self-recovery, self-consciousness, and reconciliation. From a psychological viewpoint, the *Phenomenology of Mind* and the *Philosophy of Mind* are most important. *Hegel's Philosophy of Mind,* in *Encyclopedia of the Philosophical Sciences,* pt. 3, trans. W. Wallace, translation of the *Zusätze* by A. V. Miller, foreword by J. N. Findlay (London: Oxford, 1971).

Writings of Martin Heidegger that would be closely related include: *Identity and Difference,* trans. with introduction by J. Stambaugh (New York: Harper, 1969); *On the Way to Language,* trans. P. D. Hertz (New York: Harper, 1971); *Poetry, Language, Thought,* trans. with introduction by A. Hofstadter (New York: Harper, 1971); and *On Time and Being,* trans. J. Stambaugh (New York: Harper, 1972).

Writings of the present author relating to the subject include *Truth and Art* (New York: Columbia University Press, 1965); and *Agony and Epitaph,* especially the chapters "The Vocation of Consciousness" and "Being: the Act of Belonging" (New York: Braziller, 1970). The article mentioned in the text, "Ownness and Identity: Rethinking Hegel," appears in the *Review of Metaphysics* (Summer, 1975); and there is an article entitled "Enownment" in *Boundary* 2, 4, no. 2 (1976), the issue entitled *Martin Heidegger and Literature,* edited by W. V. Spanos.

5

Analytic Philosophy, Phenomenology, and the Concept of Consciousness

Harold A. Durfee

At long last there are hints that contemporary philosophy is beginning to transcend the sharp separation between analytic philosophy and phenomenology, which has so deeply divided twentieth-century Western thought for fifty years. The same conflict pervades psychological theory as well as philosophy, and will, apparently, be overcome only with great difficulty. The hints of emerging dialogue are no more than hints, but in this volume of essays devoted to meeting points of psychoanalysis and philosophy—and more specifically concerned with philosophy of mind—it seems appropriate to focus further inquiry upon a controversy that seriously divides both disciplines.

Moreover, it would seem that diverse interpretations of the nature of consciousness lie at the heart of this controversy. Consequently, I shall try to locate the center of the controversy between these two powerful positions by establishing four main areas of divergence; and furthermore, I shall attempt to indicate how the diverse interpretations of consciousness are a central feature of the dividing line in each of these four areas.[1] If the few hints of conversation are to

1. A volume of essays reflecting upon the relationships of these two movements is presented in H. A. Durfee, *Analytic Philosophy and Phenomenology* (The Hague: M. Nijhoff, 1976). In addition, the most useful evidence of attempts to transcend the division are K.-O. Apel, *Analytic Philosophy of*

develop into genuine dialogue, careful attention to these features of the division in philosophy of mind and in psychological theory will be necessary to move either discipline beyond its current theoretical impasse. Let it be noted immediately that there are innumerable and important fundamental similarities, which ought not be neglected, and which I have not attempted to elaborate upon in what follows. Transcending the cultural division, however, in either field, may necessitate that one focus upon the differences, for only when these are located and diversities in the interpretation of consciousness in each are specified can one hope to narrow the schism in either discipline.

Although the channel separating the European continent from Great Britain is narrow, it has always been both physically and philosophically a stormy sea, and may have threatened philosophical shipwreck in our day. Perhaps the appropriate subtitle for these remarks should be, "Can A Philosopher Swim the English Channel?" No one will expect me, I trust, to swim from shore to shore—from English analysis to European phenomenology—in these few pages. I shall be content to have located deep undertow and to stay afloat on rough seas. Only separate attempts devoted to each issue would suffice for the fulfillment of the program, and I hope that someone may be enticed to try the water.

A most exciting history has yet to be written of the dialectical relationships that Western reason has elaborated among four, or perhaps five, components of the philosophical drama: history, transcendence (including self-transcendence),

---

Language and the Geisteswissenschaften (Dordrecht: D. Reidel, 1967); S. A. Erickson, Language and Being: An Analytic Phenomenology (New Haven, Conn.: Yale University Press, 1970); W. Mays and S. C. Brown, Linguistic Analysis and Phenomenology (London: Macmillan, 1972); A. Montefiore, Philosophy and Personal Relations (Montreal: McGill-Queens, 1973); A. Montefiore, Philosophie et rapports interpersonnels (Montreal: Les Presses Universitaires, 1973); E. Pivcevic, Phenomenology and Philosophical Understanding (London: Cambridge University Press, 1975).

subjectivity, consciousness, and perhaps language. The permutations and dramatic relationships of these features of our intellectual universe form the setting for the philosophical drama of the twentieth century. In regard to our current concern, the divergences between analytic philosophy and phenomenology revolve around attempts to maintain and creatively illuminate—or to minimize—crucial dialectical features. I have attempted to identify these, in turn, as: (1) Being and Clarity; (2) Ontological Powers and Consciousness; (3) Consciousness and Meaning; (4) Meaning and Intentionality.

Being and Clarity

One feature of the dialogue that seems to stare one in the face at first encounter—and is undoubtedly the occasion for many unkind remarks, if not downright laughter—is the dialectic of Being and Clarity. Although this feature is central on the philosophical landscape, it has, strangely enough, seldom been addressed directly. It may strike some as unduly metaphysical, and thereby prejudicial, to put the issue in terms of Being and Clarity, but I do not think that that is the case. It is not crucial that it be stated in this way, for the matter could be elaborated in terms of Language and Clarity, but to do so would seem to neglect important elements. If Austin was right in believing that language is only the first word and functions itself to get us to "the realities which we use the words to talk about," [2] some reference to more than language would seem appropriate.

In contemporary philosophy, the Cartesian desire for clear and distinct ideas has taken on renewed vigor among analysts in the uniquely linguistic form of clear and distinct language. We need hardly be reminded of the intimacy, at times almost approaching identity, that contemporary philosophers have

2. J. L. Austin, *Philosophical Papers* (London: Oxford University Press, 1961), p. 130.

elaborated between language and consciousness. Thus, differences in the concept of consciousness begin to appear already in differences about language. Such a Cartesian and linguistic model, however, remains in constant tension with a more Hegelian dialectical thesis concerning clarity, in which ambiguity seems built into the human and linguistic situation, at least until one arrives at some total gestalt. Analytic philosophy has promoted the model of clarity and "exact" philosophy. To vote against clarity is but one step removed from a negation of motherhood. Most philosophers, even if not for God, are at least for country and for clarity. Unfortunately, the model itself seems far from clear. Some may be concerned that clarity is not enough, but whether it is sufficient or insufficient, we would be helped tremendously by clarification of this normative feature of philosophical discourse. Clarity about clarity itself would illuminate immensely. It may well be that ordinary language is in good order, and that our task is not to change anything but to leave everything as it is and only describe. If that is the case, let us begin by describing the content of the norm itself.

Appearances to the contrary notwithstanding, the goal of clarity is not confined to one side of the channel. Although there may be disagreement about this, I am not convinced that many desire ambiguity for its own sake, but only as seems demanded by the philosophical considerations at hand. Obfuscation for its own sake is philosophical abdication. There is, nevertheless, a major European thesis within phenomenology that puts it in some dialectical tension with the analytic call for clarity. Put most directly, the thesis is "Being hides." I have in mind not only Heidegger, but such late work as Merleau-Ponty's *The Visible and the Invisible*. It might be argued that the theme is not essential to the phenomenological program. Even this seems highly debatable, but in any case it has become a major theme among central phenomenologists.

Heidegger reminds us of the Heraclitean Fragment 123, "Being inclines intrinsically to self concealment." [3] Being, in its revelation is inevitably a kind of concealment. This suggests that there are serious limitations to clarity, and that in regard to the revelation of the real, we neither have clarity nor are we to expect it. Being shows itself, but when it does, such revelation is only partial and thereby ambiguous. Any illumination will involve, at the same time, a concealment —one that is even so subtle as to conceal its concealment. This theme, with pre-Socratic origins, suggests that there are serious ontological limits to the ideal of clarity, and that these limits need exploration. Hence the theme Being and Clarity.

Phenomenologists do not urge that we cover up and obscure whatever illumination is available, but they are implicitly raising serious questions concerning the analytic model. Can we expect the reality of language, even ordinary language, to present itself without concealment, so that once discovered, at least the being of language will be clearly revealed, and thereby the knots will be untied? Has the concealment of the concealment been so successful in analytic circles that this very feature, at least insofar as language is concerned, has been quite lost, and have we been led to expect a revealing—a clarity—that, because of this loss, is in fact not available? If such clarity is, in principle, available, that would suggest a unity of philosophical insight and the structure of language, at least if not of reality, a unity of insight and structure which is, in principle, denied by the philosophical proposals associated with the Continent.

Thus, the differences between the more monistic and the more dialectical positions begin to make their appearance at the very foundational point of the analytic demand for clarity. To find ordinary language in good order, and thereby

3. M. Heidegger, *An Introduction to Metaphysics* (New Haven, Conn.: Yale University Press, 1959), p. 114. See also M. Merleau-Ponty, *The Visible and the Invisible* (Evanston, Ill.: Northwestern University Press, 1968).

therapeutic, is, to say the least, to minimize the dialectic of concealment and unconcealment. Do we have any reason to suspect that reality, simply the reality of language, neglecting all else for the moment, emerges unambiguously and without hiding in this aspect of itself any more than it seems to at any other locus of human existence? Furthermore, if language is designed to reveal reality, as Austin suggests, can we seriously expect reality to become clearly present by such linguistic unconcealment?

This matter of clarity is not neatly divided, however, by the English Channel. There is serious dialogue in Wittgenstein between the activity of saying and the phenomenon of showing, for there is that which cannot be said but must be shown. In addition, there are the too-neglected features of Wittgenstein's mysticism (although that may not be the most appropriate word). Showing occurs, evidently, when we have "thrown away the ladder," and yet have arrived at a peculiar understanding.

It is at just such boundary situations that analytic philosophy and phenomenology appear to meet. The phenomenologist is, perhaps, more prepared to attempt to speak about, or somehow illuminate, what others may consider the unspeakable. Frequently the relationship of phenomenology to analytic philosophy would seem to be that of supplementation and complementarity, although one will always need to decide if the complement or supplement is meaningful and illuminating. Analytic philosophers keep such elements of the difficult-to-speak-about at a minimum and at the very boundary of their philosophical position, on the edge of the *Sprachtwelt;* these elements include such features as the nature of forms of life, facts in logical space that are the world, the metaphysical subject as the limit of the world, the fact that the world is my world, the seeing of the world aright after discarding the ladder, the mere fact (is *mere* the right word?) that the world is.

To repeat, such features seem to form the logical boundaries for the analysis of our language games. Since these issues remain on the boundary, however, and philosophical concentration is upon the games themselves, the dialectic between these boundary features and the games people play is minimized, with the implication that—regarding these games, at least—clarity is possible and reality will not hide. This points again to the question of whether there are limits to clarity itself even within the world of language—a question that opens into an arena for serious philosophical discussion.

Ontological Powers and Consciousness

In this section of the essay, those with serious aversion to the metaphysical enterprise, and especially to recent phenomenological metaphysics, will be most unhappy. One of the unwritten assumptions of this paper, however, is that both analytic philosophers and phenomenologists are doing metaphysics, and thus the issue is not the appropriateness of the metaphysical venture, but rather the content of any particular metaphysical proposals.

Let us concentrate upon two major aspects of this theme: the activity of ontological powers, and a new philosophy of mind.

THE ACTIVITY OF ONTOLOGICAL POWERS

Ontological realities seem to be minimized in analytic philosophy, even though we have just noted their presence on the edge of the *Sprachtwelt*. In order to emphasize a distinction, one should note that these ontological entities are present within the philosophy primarily as known, as objects of knowledge, as features of philosophical or logical space, as objects of philosophical affirmation. Even analytic philosophy of action is primarily about human action.

Phenomenology, on the other hand, frequently places an emphasis upon the activity of the ontological powers themselves. The universal logos is active, and employs us in its endeavors. I have in mind not only *Dasein,* as the field of Being for Heidegger, to which I shall return, but Dufrenne's proposals as well—to the effect that language has man, that language speaks, that "language is then the Word in which Nature . . . fulfills itself in coming to consciousness." In referring to Schelling, Hegel, Heidegger, and Heraclitus, he writes, "the human being who speaks is not the one who initiates the language." [4] Being speaks, the world speaks, even if ambiguously. One might say that it is Being which plays language games. I realize that this is an accent with which analytic thinkers are not overly familiar, and that they may not appreciate, but the Greek ontological powers of Being are still alive and well and living in Paris, still at work in phenomenological ontology.

There seems no significant analogous feature of analytic ontology. For analysis, the powers of Being are silent, and the activity lies exclusively with the human subject to penetrate the deep silence of the real. The attention of the analytic philosopher is then turned to our own talk, with which we attempt the penetration, and to the confusions that such talk generates. The transcendental turn regarding the analysis of language is seldom made, or if made, is carried out in a radically different manner, so that the horizons within which language itself is set remain cloaked in silence. As analytic philosophy has developed, it would seem that not only is it the case that certain matters are not said, but one has even abandoned the attempt to show, at which point we have a fundamental difference in the ontology of language itself. Let us note again the more dialectical character of the phenomenological analysis as compared with the analytic.

4. M. Dufrenne, *Language and Philosophy* (Bloomington: Indiana University Press, 1963), p. 16.

A NEW PHILOSOPHY OF MIND

The suggestion above concerning ontological powers was made primarily as background for the matter to which we now turn. We frequently think of the philosophy of mind as a major development in recent Anglo-Saxon philosophy, and surely it is that. Less frequently, however, do we consider the development of the European philosophy of mind. Nevertheless, in the dialectic of ontological powers and consciousness, there is emerging a philosophy of mind or consciousness quite distinct from that currently proposed by analytic philosophy. Consciousness is viewed, not primarily as an observer of some objective presence—physical, sensory, or otherwise—but in dialogue with Being, as an instrument of reality, as the way Being works in the world for self-revelation. Consciousness is the field, the clearing of Being. Being uses consciousness as its clearing through which and by which realities appear in the world, and thereby Being reveals itself. Consciousness is the locus where Being decides what will be.

If this is too much German mysticism, it is also available in a French version. Consider our earlier quotation from Dufrenne, "language is then the Word in which Nature . . . fulfills itself in coming to consciousness." Dufrenne continues, "Man, who gives a name to things, is the agent of this fulfillment." "In speaking, the human being, by his words, accomplishes a purpose that quite surpasses him." He continues, "Language is nothing more than a mediation between man and the world." "In other words, man can speak of the world only if the world speaks to him." [5] Consider one final quotation:

> This is the essential point: the world speaks to us; it comes and lets itself be caught in the snare of words; the words that these grand images wrench from us are full

5. Ibid., p. 71.

of its presence. And here perhaps we are at the very source that we sought to regain, at that point where the world reveals itself to us, where what is spoken is itself speaking. This communication of consciousness with the world is precisely the thing which, according to Husserl, or at least according to certain of his interpreters, transcendental logic seeks to explore.[6]

Consciousness thereby plays a unique and dialectical role, as a mediator, as a revealer of Being (which is only possible because ontological powers are active), and as that which determines the way the real will be. One is reminded of mirror images. It was not accidental, but true to the very nature of consciousness as interpreted by phenomenologists, when recently it was suggested that "The mirror is, of course, the phenomenological instrument *par excellence*." [7] Consider how consciousness itself, in Sartre for example, is that by which particular "thises" arise within the *en-soi*. Throughout the phenomenological movement, the problem of freedom is situated in this dialectic of consciousness and ontological powers.

Thus, in phenomenology, the relationship between consciousness and ontological powers is significantly different from that in analytic philosophy. It offers thereby a basic difference in the ontology of language and its intimacy with the real. In analytic philosophy, the intimacy of language games and forms of life, or facts, or sense data, is somewhat monistic, so that one reflects the other, thereby providing language as the avenue to therapy, where one may be at peace with the world, and the fly would be out of the fly bottle. For phenomenology, however, the relationship of consciousness, including language, to Being is much more dialectical, inevitably mantaining a tension, for Being hides,

6. Ibid., p. 96.

7. A.-T. Tymieniecka, *The Phenomenological Realism of the Possible Worlds* (Dordrecht: D. Reidel, 1974), p. 327.

and consciousness provides the opportunity for man to be distinguished from his world while discovering its meaning and learning to live his world. As Dufrenne asserts, "Communication is not unity." [8]

Consciousness and Meaning

It was suggested earlier that two of the major factors in the dialogue that is modern philosophy are history and transcendence, and these are relevant to our next consideration. At one time the feature of meaning was analyzed in terms of propositions, or "sense," as Frege suggested, and these propositions are what a sentence means. I would call attention to, but shall not go further into, the compatability of this with the Husserlian analysis of meaning.[9] More recently, however, analytic philosophers have tended to eliminate such sense or meaning, and have turned to the realm of ordinary language, where meaning was to be discovered in its use. The use, of course, would be totally embedded in the way that ordinary language terms worked or behaved in the language to carry on the work of the world. Such a move eliminates the realm of sense—or meaning, or proposition—which stood somewhat independent of, or transcendental to, the sign itself, as that which the sign was about, not as its referent but as its sense. There is negated, thereby, the dialectic between the meaning or propositions and the linguistic structure itself, and meaning is reduced simply to the behavior of the linguistic formulations. We need consider nothing but the historical linguistic activity, and no feature of the phenomenon of language transcends this. Once again the monistic impetus is evident, and we are left with history by itself—in this instance, linguistic history.

8. Dufrenne, *Language and Philosophy*, p. 96.
9. See R. C. Solomon, "Sense and Essence: Frege and Husserl," *International Philosophical Quarterly* 11 (1970): 378–401; also reprinted in Durfee, *Analytic Philosophy*.

Language is not seen as ciphers, to use a Jaspersian term, symbolic of some horizon of discourse or reality; nor is it seen as relative to any ultimate horizon of Being or meaning beyond the cipher. The cipher in itself in the way it functions is self-sufficient for meaning and thought. Our philosophical problems will be dissolved if we but turn to the arena of historical linguistic activity and watch it behave, to see how its good order works to carry on daily life. Interestingly enough, however, this proposal itself is not one of ordinary language, and is not itself an elimination of or dissolution of a philosophical problem, but is, rather, a philosophical suggestion. How we are to discern its meaning while our philosophical problems are dissolved, simply by turning to the use of the ordinary, not philosophical language, is somewhat difficult to discern. It is not accidental, but should be of more than passing interest for the philosopher, that the analysis of philosophical propositions themselves furnishes a frequent source of difficulty—as it did for logical empiricism, as it seems to for ordinary language philosophy, and as it does for the attempt to analyze the relationship between scientific and empirical language and the language of the a priori or the analytic.[10] It is at least intriguing that philosophical language itself becomes one of the major perplexities for philosophical reflection. Perhaps we are our own most pressing problem.

The attempt of analytic philosophers to find in ordinary language the conditions or preconditions of science, or to search there for the a priori conditions of language itself,

10. See J. Compton, "Hare, Husserl, and Philosophic Discovery," *Dialogue* 3 (1964) : 42–51; R. Schmitt, "Phenomenology and Analysis," *Philosophy and Phenomenological Research* 23 (1962–63) : 101–10. See also P. Ricoeur, "Husserl and Wittgenstein on Language," in E. N. Lee and M. Mandelbaum, *Phenomenology and Existentialism* (Baltimore: Johns Hopkins University Press, 1967), to which I am especially indebted in this section of the essay. The Compton and Ricoeur essays are both reprinted in Durfee, *Analytic Philosophy* (n. 1).

creates some tension within the movement. At least in some analytic circles, language itself is the avenue to the rediscovery of the a priori. There are those who are convinced that by moving from the very nature of language itself, they can find a priori necessities that offer firm foundations for the rest of the philosophical enterprise. Western philosophy has moved from theological concerns to ontological; from ontological concerns to epistemological; and now from epistemological concerns to linguistic ones. Within each of these— God, Being, Reason, Sensation—it held out the hope of firm and indubitable foundations. It therefore comes as something of a surprise that the analysis of language now holds out the hope of success in accomplishing what theology, ontology, and epistemology could not accomplish. If this dream is fulfilled, the intriguing question will remain as to why we can do with the linguistic features of the universe what we could not do with any other aspect of reality. What is there about language, even deep grammar, that allows it, rather than anything else, to serve as the entrance to ultimacy and necessity?

The introduction of such foundations of language, however, grounding community, society, knowledge, and science, and the introduction of such theoretical considerations as concepts, structures, abstractions, or principles may hardly be reduced to ordinary language and the historical. Rather, the introduction of such theoretical structures would seem to be a breaking of the peace of ordinary life; while the return to the ordinary, supposedly, offered the hope of a peace that would rid us of such theoretical knots in the head. The simple return to the ordinary would eliminate any dialectical tension between the historical and the transcendent conditions of meaning, for our reabsorption in the prephilosophical, found in good order, its use now clarified, would leave the linguistic animal at home in his original linguistic universe. In such a philosophical eschatology, having identified philosophy, or at least meaning, with the historical, the occasion for raising questions about the meaning of the ordinary and the unambiguous would have been dissolved. The ordinary would not be transcended by any arena of significance which gave it status, foundation, and meaning. Otherwise, all of the conundrums requiring therapy would reappear, and once again we would need to get the fly out of the fly bottle.

Phenomenology, on the other hand, maintains a dialectic of the transcendent and the immanent, or historical, called forth by the phenomenological reduction. It is anxious to discover the structure of the ordinary, the *lebenswelt;* but it focuses upon the ordinary world, not simply ordinary language—a *lebenswelt* in which there is deeply and intimately embedded a *sprachtwelt.* It is not, however, prepared to reduce the philosophical dialectic to the historical. An arena of significance, meaning, intentionality, remains as never reducible to the realm of ordinary language and its use; for ordinary language analysis, as seen by the phenomenological orientation, is but a part of the natural attitude. Maintaining a dialectic of the ordinary with the dimension of meaning provides for the conceptual, the theoretical, and the significant, serving as the very ground of meaning, even of the *lebenswelt.*

The ploys and hopes of antiphilosophical reductionism, however tempting they may appear, cannot maintain the significance of the ordinary, or even the significance of the natural attitude, or the significance of philosophy itself. The monistic project, which would establish the identity of meaning and the historical and would eliminate all features of self-transcendence to the significant, is to eliminate the very dialectic that gives meaning to the philosophical endeavor itself. Phenomenology insists upon the retention of such a dialectic, for the realm of the ordinary as the abode of peace is nothing more than twentieth-century philosophical romanticism. This phenomenological proposal, however—that consciousness intends the significant, that language dialectically points to both an arena of meaning and to the world, and that the significant is not reducible to the behavior of the ordinary—is the entrance to our final fundamental theme of divergence between these two attitudes.

Meaning and Intentionality

Finally, let me suggest a difference between these two movements that may be the most difficult to overcome—one that centers upon the doctrine of intentionality. There is, as far as I can determine, a fundamental difference in the very concept of an experience. What it is to have an experience receives quite diverse analysis, and the very nature of consciousness is at stake in this divergence.

It should be emphasized that I am not referring to the factor of context, horizon, or gestalt, which has been a central feature of phenomenology as opposed to atomistic sensa and the doctrine of association of analytic philosophy, although this in itself may offer a serious difference. I refer, rather, to more specific features in the doctrine of intentionality.

As is well known, the doctrine of intentionality has been a central feature of phenomenology, and many would suggest that it is the fundamental pivot of the phenomenological program. It is less clear, however, to what extent the analytic philosopher intends to maintain a doctrine of the intentionality of consciousness, for, to a considerable degree, he seems to have avoided the question. If the analytic philosopher is prepared to maintain that consciousness is always consciousness of, there will be little debate, or at least the focus of the debate will change, but the analyst has spoken to this issue so seldom that his position regarding intentionality is, at best, ambiguous.[11]

11. It is clear that some analytic philosophers do maintain major features of the doctrine of intentionality. See S. Hampshire, *Thought and Action* (London: Chatto and Windus, 1959).

There are, however, a few specific analytic comments that clearly, explicitly, and vigorously oppose this doctrine, and it is those which form the controversy as I shall consider it. In a paper presented to the Aristotelian Society some years ago, Ryle was most explicit in his critique of intentionality.[12] Let us bear in mind that this came from a period in Ryle's reflection when he had devoted serious attention to phenomenology. In this paper he not only criticized Husserl's theory regarding intentionality but, happily, he indicated as well, albeit briefly, the nature of the appropriate position.

We are not concerned now with the history of Ryle's intellectual development in order to trace the extent to which he maintained and developed the position, but are concerned only to note the conflict, the alternative interpretation of consciousness and experience. The issue as posed stands in what one might call the tradition of the Husserl-Hume controversy, and the very heart of the concept of intentionality is at stake in this brief comment. We should also note the way in which, once again, the dialectical character of consciousness is minimized, if not eliminated, so that a more monistic theory of experience replaces the subject-object dichotomy. Strangely enough, while there has been a discussion of the Husserl-Ryle difference regarding the philosophy of mind, to the best of my knowledge the controversy as posed regarding intentionality has been largely neglected.[13]

After a considerable elaboration of Husserl's position, Ryle turns explicitly to the doctrine of intentionality and writes,

> He *should* hold (I believe) that what was miscalled 'The object or content of an act of consciousness' is really the

12. G. Ryle, "Phenomenology," in *Phenomenology, Goodness and Beauty,* Aristotelian Society Supplementary Volume 11 (London: Harrison, 1932). Also reprinted in Durfee, *Analytic Philosophy.*

13. It is especially strange that Mohanty does not deal directly with the controversy as posed and discussed by Ryle. See J. N. Mohanty, *The Concept of Intentionality* (St. Louis, Mo.: W. H. Green, 1972).

specific character or nature of that act, so that the intentionality of an act is not a relation between it and something else, but merely a property of it so specific as to be a *differentia* or in some cases an individualizing description of it. He does in fact, however, continue to speak as if every intentional act is related, though related by an internal relation, to a genuine subject of attributes.[14]

A similar position was captured some years later by Ayer, also before the Aristotelian Society. In a discussion of phenomenology with Charles Taylor, and speaking specifically of the doctrine of intentionality, he says, "It is a way of rejecting any analysis of cognition which invokes only the presence of mental contents, or actual or potential behavior. . . ." "His interpretation of the special or 'modern' thesis of intentionality is that the objects of consciousness, and specifically the objects of perception, have significance in the sense that they refer beyond themselves; in short they are not significata but signs. As applied to all the possible objects of consciousness this thesis seems exceedingly implausible." A bit later he writes, "My own preference is for a behavioral theory, which would eliminate intentionality." [15] It will just sidetrack our considerations if we enter the complex issues of behaviorism, and Ryle's statement is even more direct than Ayer's to the point that we have before us. Ayer offers only a bit of further confirming evidence regarding analytic reactions to intentionality.

As I interpret it, the proposal is that consciousness is not intentional and that it is not necessary or appropriate to deal with experience as consciousness of; or, if one does say that consciousness is of, one does not mean what phenomenology

14. Ryle, "Phenomenology," p. 79.
15. A. J. Ayer, "Phenomenology and Linguistic Analysis," in *Proceedings of the Aristotelian Society*, Supplementary Volume 33 (London: Harrison, 1959), pp. 111–15. Also reprinted in Durfee, *Analytic Philosophy*.

suggests. One does not have any subject-object dichotomy, a conscious subject aware of X as object. Any such dialectic of subject-object vanishes into a more monistic moment of experience, or perhaps one should say behavior. The different contents of consciousness are not as subjects relating to differing objects, but simply a differing "specific character or nature" of the act, "merely a property of it," which property thereby is specific enough to offer a "differentia" or to perform an individualizing of one act from another. Consequently, consciousness in its acts of intending is not the presence of "a relation between it and something else, but merely a property." Consciousness is not some empty form with its content filled in by the objective content-giving pole. Consciousness is apparently differentiated by its own nature, and this differentiation within the moment of consciousness offers all of the object or content present or needed.

Let us not concern ourselves with the implicit elimination of the subject, and with the subjective pole of consciousness hereby accomplished. This has been dissected ad nauseam, and is obviously Hamlet banishing the ghost. Such a concentration upon subjectivity, however, would offer another way to focus the controversy between these two positions, for the centrality of the ego and the radical Cartesianism of phenomenology are well known. Let us concentrate, rather, on the more neglected feature of the very elimination of intentionality in the moment of and content of consciousness. Consciousness of has now become a moment of behavior or a particular differentia of some moment of consciousness without relation.

It is just such a monistic status in the tradition of Humean epistemological entities that the doctrine of intentionality was designed to counteract. Unfortunately, to the best of my knowledge, phenomenologists have not dealt with this matter with sufficient precision. They have constantly emphasized the doctrine of intentionality, and there has been considerable elaboration of the intuitive content of the noema of consciousness, with endless debate as to the extent to which this involves a Platonism, and endless elaboration of how this noema is a move away from the natural attitude involving the bracketing of questions of existence. However, although the Rylean alternative analysis of consciousness has been available for some time, there has been little direct consideration of his suggestion, and we lack an analysis of why it is not satisfactory to make the Rylean move—that is, to replace intentionality simply with content reduced to the differentia of consciousness.

I am not suggesting that the Ryle or Ayer positions are adequate for our epistemological situation. In this paper I am merely trying to locate, with some precision, the locus of the controversy, and in regard to the doctrine of intentionality it seems to me that this is where the debate needs to focus. We need a phenomenological analysis of precisely how intentionality significantly differs from Ryle's analysis of "differentiae," which claims that such differentiae or properties will provide all that is necessary for the differences in the content of consciousness without an intentional referent. Equally important, we need clarification of why intentional analysis necessitates the very relation that Ryle denies is present, and which he replaces with the concept of property. The more monistic tendency in interpreting consciousness is clearly evident in the concept of property and the elimination of relation, and the phenomenological doctrine of intentionality is, in its most serious depths, the insistence upon the dialectic of the relations.

The hints of a more serious conversation between analytic philosophy and phenomenology are long overdue. There are already numerous similarities and supplementary relationships. Regarding differences, however, the aforementioned matters will need special attention. Deep and compelling forces have led some thinkers to expect clarity rather than ontological ambiguity, to understand that the initiative was with man to penetrate a vast silence which itself takes no initiative, to form consciousness in a reflection of objective forms of life, to reduce the meaningful to the objective behavior of words, and to replace the intentional relation with the properties of momentary states. Others have found themselves compelled to contemplate the ambiguity of the real, and the action of its powers as well, to find consciousness as the semiautonomous servant of such cosmic forces, to recognize the sign as pointing dialectically, not only to the world, but to its meaning, and to see consciousness as also pointing beyond itself by the relation of intentionality.

We have failed to raise what is perhaps the most serious question of all, and that concerns the impelling forces, or decisions, or claims of truth, that have led wise men in such diverse directions. What lies behind this monistic impetus on one side, and the insistence upon mystery and the dynamic of the more dialectical on the other? This issue itself ought to give one pause, so that one does not attempt to deal too quickly with the issues raised above and to offer too simple and facile responses to the concerns upon which I have focused. At the root of the division between reductionism and antireductionism lies a great divide, not only in contemporary philosophy but in the entire history of Western philosophy. The foundations—both psychological and philosophical—of that division still call for exposure. Furthermore, the surface manifestations of that division in contemporary philosophy reflect vast and profound cultural diversities. While I have attempted to expose central loci of the contemporary debate, the deeper cultural and philosophical orientations increasingly call for an intensive analysis of a philosophy of comparative culture, which might provide the foundation for such epistemological differences even in the philosophy of consciousness.

The Construction of the Real

6

On Reality: An Examination of Object Constancy, Ambiguity, Paradox, and Time

JOHN S. KAFKA

The ancient philosophical problem of the nature of reality tends in a psychiatric context to lose much of its abstract quality and to gain a personal poignancy, because estrangement—alienation from reality—may mean tragic personal isolation. There have, however, been recent developments in the history of science and in the history of thought that make the very expression "alienation from reality" sound rather obsolete. A reference to "estrangement from consensually validated reality" would correspond more closely to our current awareness of the relativity of realities. Modern physical science has made us acutely aware of the limitations of commonsense reality.

The psychologist Heinrich Klüver (1936), in studying the building blocks of psychological reality, has developed and experimentally applied the concept of "subjectively equivalent stimuli." I shall here attempt to relate some of his formulations to clinical data and to psychoanalytic concepts by showing their relevance to our understanding of object constancy (Kafka, 1964b) and, in turn, to the related issues of ambiguity, paradox, and time.

Hartmann (1939) deals with some aspects of the relativity

Some of the ideas in the section on Time (p. 148) were presented during a symposium on The Experience of Time at the midwinter meeting of the American Psychoanalytic Association, New York, December, 1971.

of reality, but for him this relativity is circumscribed, and he still finds a fairly solid foothold in an "average expectable environment." This stability, even though limited, becomes acutely problematic for such authors as Loewald, Wallerstein, Novey, and Lichtenstein. They differ in their emphases on developmental social or psychic structural issues and perhaps in the degree to which they see the social and psychic structural-reality problems as separate or related. The collapse of ideas about commonsense reality, the crisis in consensual validation, and the waning of agreement on the "average expectable environment" are, however, their shared concerns. Novey goes so far as to emphasize the fundamental similarity between ordered reality systems and delusional systems. Lichtenstein traces "the transformation of 'reality' since Freud" (p. 353) and illustrates with case material the "Changing Function of the Id" (p. 358) and of the superego that results from a radical alteration of reality perception. With reference to id, Lichtenstein says: "to use the sexual experience in the service of a desperate effort at affirmation of the reality of the self and the other . . . is a shift in the function of psychic structures" (p. 360). With reference to the superego, he describes a patient who was not schizophrenic but who, after some experimenting with psychedelic drugs,

> became aware that there are really no objects, that everything is force, energy that flows through what is living, as well as through inanimate objects, in unbroken waves or vibrations. She began to read articles on modern physics in *Scientific American*, which bore out her feeling that there was no objectivity, no mechanistic laws, and that the ordinary reality of everyday life represented only one limited dimension of what was real. . . . She is, however, unable to bridge the inner gap between a reality perception that absorbs her, as she calls it, into an inner space, and the competitive world around her.

She feels temporarily at peace when she can be in touch with nature, but she yearns for a shared life with others, emotional contact, and meaningful communication, and this, more and more, evades her. [p. 363]

In my own clinical work, I have been brought face to face with the problem of multiple realities (1964b), and as a result have become particularly preoccupied with paradoxical "reality" experiences, the need for tolerance of ambiguity, and the causes and consequences of the failure to achieve such tolerance. In the course of investigating these issues, I have also reconsidered the influential double-bind theory, which relates disturbed behavior to paradoxical communications from parent to child. As I shall indicate, I have had difficulty in reconciling clinical observations with this theory. The study of formal aspects of ambiguity and paradox is important in these theoretical and clinical contexts (Kafka, 1971) and is linked with the study of such basic components of psychological realities as object constancy and the temporal aspects of reality systems.

Object Constancy

I will begin by examining object constancy and its connection to subjective equivalence. In psychoanalysis, object constancy usually refers to the coalescence of partially conflicting images—for example, the bringing together of the images of the gratifying "good" mother and the frustrating "bad" mother into one internal representation of a mother figure. Anna Freud, in an address at the International Psycho-Analytic Congress in Vienna in 1971, spoke of the ability to maintain object constancy as the ability to still love the frustrating object. General and experimental psychology use the term "object constancy" to describe the maintenance of psychological, usually perceptual, continuity despite different retinal images—for example, a table is perceived as one and the same object when seen from different angles.

Klüver's "subjective equivalence" is related to object constancy—that is, to the identity of objects—in that it refers to different but related stimuli that elicit the same response. Klüver had made the observation that increasing refinement of experiments in comparative psychology—that is, study of the smallest difference between two stimuli to which the organism can respond—led to decreasing psychological significance of the findings. He therefore thought that it would be more meaningful to study how *great* the difference between stimuli could be before the animal would fail to recognize similarities. For example, if an animal has been trained to jump for food in response to a symbol (stimulus) contrasted with another on the basis of size, shape, and color, how much could one change the various combinations of attributes and still have the animal jump for the food? Since different species and different individuals have different response thresholds to different patterns of distinguishing characteristics, subjective equivalence differs from species to species and from individual to individual. The relative strength or dominance of competing equivalence patterns in the absence of the original stimulus can also be studied. Findings obtained by this sophisticated method are consonant with subtleties of individual and species differentiation. Greater complexity of equivalence patterns corresponds to higher placement in the evolutionary scale.

This concept of subjective equivalence, developed in experimental psychology, lends itself more readily to clinical issues. This can be seen in the case of Lichtenstein's patient; for her, there "were really no objects" since no one pattern of subjective equivalence was consistently dominant. She was *aware* of a kind of floating energy or force flowing in waves through both inanimate and animate objects and creating, in rapid succession, different patterns of subjective equivalence. Previously (Kafka, 1964b), I have presented clinical data and more fully developed the thesis that because of the subjective equivalence of some fragmentary self-representations with fragmentary mental representations of others, distinctions between subject and object, between self and nonself, may disappear or recede into the background. I have encountered these analogous issues in investigations of psychotic phenomena and psychedelic drug experiences (Kafka, 1964a, b). In Lichtenstein's patient it would appear that such blurring of borders made communication difficult with those around her, who perceived the world differently—that is, in terms of more stable, more lastingly differentiated objects.

Among the factors that influence the formation of a system of subjective equivalences must be counted motivational factors—the drive organization and its current state of activation. The organization of patterns of subjective equivalence is obviously related in some way to the nature of early object relations (mother). For the development of more or less stable patterns of object constancy in the psychoanalytic sense, relatively stable patterns of object constancy in the "perceptual" sense are also almost certainly necessary, and the two meanings of the term have overlapping elements, arising out of the same matrix.

Related to the concept of object constancy is the concept of synesthesia—the blending of sensory modalities, as in the mental linking of colors with music or other sounds. This, too, is a concept that is clinically useful—as in the experience of déjà vu, or in LSD reactions in which the usual sensory synesthesia (seeing, hearing, tactile sense, and so forth) is extended to include mood, emotion, space, and time (Kafka, 1964a). The theme here is the problems created by the overlapping of different patterns of organization of sensory data in judgments of reality; the overlapping produces a feeling of familiarity with a perceptual *pattern,* but because of the simultaneous *lack* of familiarity with the perception in any one compartmentalized sensory modality, it also produces an accompanying sense of uncanny ambiguity.

The following case excerpt will illustrate the clinical use of the concept of synesthesia.

The patient was an attractive woman in her early thirties, a wife and mother of superior intelligence and advanced academic education. The symptom leading to referral for psychoanalysis was a fugue state—the most marked of several—an episode lasting several hours, in which she was in a recreation room in her home with her children, apparently functioning appropriately, but of which she could not recall her actions. The period was filled with déjà vu sensations and was experienced as uncanny and frightening. During it she experienced fragmented dream images dealing with operations and giant surgeons. Her symptoms also included phobias regarding driving a car and answering telephones, and long-standing preoccupations with possibilities of disaster. The phobias had emerged gradually over the past several years but had become more definite during the last three years, since her husband's brief hospitalization for an unconfirmed coronary occlusion.

In the course of psychoanalysis lasting several years, the meaning of the dreamlike images of the fugue states became understandable. The patient had grown up in a small French Canadian town in which her father's family was prominent. Her mother had grown up in an orphanage and her background had been an extremely deprived one. The patient's father had some scientific training, but he operated a small appliance repair shop and never became financially and otherwise fully independent of his parental family. During the mother's pregnancy with the patient, a two-year-old brother of the patient died of a renal disease. The patient was thus the only child of a mother who was grieving and chronically depressed. The patient herself had recurrent episodes of pyelitis with high fevers during her childhood. The home atmosphere was often experienced as oppressive by the patient. Somewhat masklike smiles, parental—especially maternal—interest in what the patient called "peace of mind literature," and the mother's description of her own deprived childhood reinforced the patient's fear of disaster and loss, and also contributed to feelings of guilt. Premature demands were often made of her. For example, when she asked her mother what she should do about bullies who threw stones at her on the way to school, her mother answered blandly that she should search in her conscience and there would find the right thing to do. The patient had felt reproached when "things came easy"—when, for example, without much effort she was a good student. As the only surviving child, the patient could powerfully influence the mood of socially fairly isolated parents, and thus contributed to the development and maintenance of the patient's feelings of omnipotence. The father, who "could make any toy with his hands," was seen as omnipotent until the patient's early adolescence, and the patient's identification with her father was marked in many areas. Gradually, however, the patient had recognized the extent of her father's inadequacy and dependence on his own parents. On this basis she had formed some very derogatory opinions of men. When she left home at 18 to go to college—the same one that her father had attended—she was going to be "a better man than Father," and she experienced leaving home as liberation.

Soon after the patient left home to attend college, her father died suddenly. The patient had made light of her father's anxiety—expressed in his letters to her—concerning anticipated gall bladder surgery. He died on the operating table, heart disease having apparently been misdiagnosed as gall bladder disease. The patient's fear of her destructive powers, especially when her omnipotence operated in the service of competition, became marked, and she began to feel that it was dangerous to be liberated from oppressive feelings, dangerous to take matters lightly, and even more dangerous not to anticipate disaster. The dreamlike fragments of the fugue state related to her father's death, the patient identifying both with the destructive surgeons and the victim suffering retaliation for destructive wishes. The fugue episode had occurred when hostile and competitive feelings toward her husband and resentment about her feminine and maternal role were particularly marked.

As this patient's history unfolded, she was able to see connections between many previously dissociated and isolated areas. Experiencing a sense of continuity between dream material, dreamlike elements of the fugue states, and remembered events and feelings was surprising to her and offered relief.

Although the analysis, of course, involved transference distortions and their interpretation, I would like to focus now on one particular aspect of this case: advance in understanding occurred during what might be described as minor repetitions of the so-called fugue states during psychoanalytic hours. In these hours, characterized by a somewhat trancelike atmosphere, references to ongoing experiences of synesthesia were prominent. A shiny object in the office, for instance, would be experienced and described as a "shrill [sounding] object." At this point a déjà vu experience would be reported and frequently a comment made about the uncanniness or awesomeness of the moment. After several minutes of "heavy" silence, an early memory of the "atmosphere"—that is, a synesthetic blending of the sounds, sights, rhythms, tastes, smells, and so forth, of a certain place or time would emerge. (The atmosphere of the father's shop was experienced with particular vividness.) A fragmented image from a fugue episode could then be traced to either a fact or fantasy associated with the time or place characterized by the remembered "atmosphere."

To clarify the association of synesthetic and déjà vu phenomena in cases of this kind, I wish to draw a schematic analogy. Let us imagine that a certain wave pattern on an oscilloscope can represent visual, auditory, or tactile stimuli. A responding organism or electronic scanning machine may be asked if this is a familiar *visual* pattern, or it may be asked if this is a familiar *pattern*—visual, auditory, or tactile. Obviously, if the *response* is to the *pattern,* whatever the sensory modality involved, the likelihood that it will be familiar is much increased. In other words, if a certain pattern of stimulation, let us say a visual pattern, occurs at a time when the sensory compartments are particularly interwoven, particularly blended, the chances that this pattern will arouse a feeling of familiarity—that is, a déjà vu or related sensation—are multiplied.

Arlow has reviewed much of the literature on déjà vu phenomena and has made a major original contribution to our understanding of these experiences. Freud's early view, as summarized by Arlow, was that the déjà vu experience corresponded to an activation of an unconscious impression. Freud came to think, however, that the memory of an unconscious fantasy might be involved and not necessarily the unconscious impression of an actual event. Arlow has also summarized later extensions of the concept by Ferenczi and Oberndorf, among others, to the effect that not only unconscious fantasies but also repressed fragments of past dreams, and consciously experienced intentions that were subsequently repressed may play a part in déjà vu phenomena. Arlow stresses Oberndorf's emphasis on the reassuring quality of the déjà vu experience ("you've been through this before and will come out all right again this time"), and also Marcovitz's emphasis on the déjà vu reaction as an expression of the wish to have a second chance. Arlow's original contribution is his formulation, supported by detailed psychoanalytic observations, that the déjà vu reaction contains in its *formal* structure latent elements of defensive reactions and wish-fulfillment. He treats the déjà vu experience reported to him as he would the manifest content of a dream. The person having a déjà vu experience feels that the actual, the manifest, situation has occurred previously, whereas it may be that it is not the situation that is familiar, but the latent meaning behind the situation.

Arlow criticizes previous contributions by pointing out that they usually do not make any attempt to "account for the uncanny, disconcerting, unpleasant, anxiety-tinged affects which usually accompany this form of experience" (p. 614). He adds that "the lingering sense of uneasiness or the uncanny which characterizes déjà vu appears to be in proportion to the underlying anxiety and indicates that the ego has not fully succeeded, through the various mechanisms already mentioned, in mastering this anxiety" (p. 629).

Arlow seems to relate the particular uncanny affect to the ambiguity arising from a sense that a manifest situation has occurred previously, and at the same time a sense that only the latent meaning of the situation is familiar. The ambiguity here involves several levels of abstraction, since *manifest* and *latent* imply different levels of abstraction.

Ambiguity

The ambiguity and "uncanniness" of the déjà vu experience, often clinically upsetting, provide an example of the power of ambiguity—whether it arises from sensory blending, from manifest-latent conflict, or from some other source—to produce anxiety. Since systems of abstraction are in flux from one level to another, from moment to moment, "ambiguities" pertaining to human communication are usually ambiguities of types. (Ambiguity of types in the literature dealing with the formal logic of ambiguity refers to contradictory statements on different levels of abstraction.)

Ambiguity may be particularly strange and unacceptable to persons of whom well-compartmentalized ego-functioning was demanded prematurely—as with the patient described above. Normally, a child can indulge without danger in the richness of blending or other ambiguous experiences, secure in the knowledge that his parents are able either to resolve or to tolerate any conflicts produced by such ambiguities.

It is, of course, primarily Winnicott to whom we owe the formulation of the importance of ambiguous objects in normal development, and I postulate that sensory blending—synesthesia—is a special case or aspect of a broader issue: the importance for normal development of acceptance of ambiguous "transitional" states. Schachtel has developed the idea that childhood amnesia is related not so much to the content of the experience during this period as to the fact that the schemata of adult memory are so different from the schemata of childhood experiences. In his paper "Fausse Reconnaissance in Treatment," Freud says, "There is another kind of *fausse reconnaissance* which not infrequently makes its appearance at the close of a treatment. . . . the patient may say: *'Now I feel as though I had known it all the time.'* With this the work of the analysis has been completed" (p. 207; Freud's italics). In the analysis of my déjà vu patient, I believe that there was rapprochement in terms of the schemata of the knowledge of childhood and the schemata of the knowledge of the adult. In this particular case synesthetic aspects of the childhood schemata were reactivated. The uncanny quality, experiences related to depersonalization, I see as related to premature demands for unambiguous ego functioning; and I see analysis as containing a process of learning to be less uncomfortable with feelings of estrangement, a process leading to their tolerance or acceptance.

The link here to Winnicott's transitional-object concept was exemplified clinically for me by a patient of mine whose foremost symptom consisted of cutting herself and interfering with wound healing (Kafka, 1969). I developed the thesis that the patient's own body was treated by her as a transitional object. Uncanny affects in the transference-countertransference seemed related to the persistent ambiguity concerning the aliveness or deadness of the body into which she could slice with some gusto. This patient, too, had experienced premature demands that she avoid the ambiguous.

Just as uncanniness is an integral part of the déjà vu experience, it is also characteristic of ambiguous transitional states. Without reviewing Freud's paper "The 'Uncanny' " in any detail here, I would like to call attention to his point that the ambiguity of not knowing whether we are dealing with a living or dead person is a frequent characteristic of the uncanny.

Paradox

In the formal logical sense, ambiguity and paradox can be substituted for each other (Kafka, 1971), but psychologically the terms carry a somewhat different meaning, *paradox* implying a more defined confrontation with an unsolvable problem. The consideration of the quasi-physiologic ambiguity of synesthesia and the ambiguities of transitional objects of transitional states can lead one to further examination of double-bind theory, and to the problems of paradox in general. First, to return to Winnicott:

> There is the third part of the life of a human being, a part that we cannot ignore, an intermediate area of experience, to which inner reality and external life both contribute. It is an area which is *not challenged,* because no claim is made in its behalf except as it exists as a resting place for the individual engaged in the per-

petual *human* task of keeping inner and outer reality
separate yet inter-related. [p. 230]

In this statement Winnicott talks of the positive, constructive, healthy aspect of ambiguity, just as Freud has commented that children accept, without feelings of uncanniness,
ambiguity concerning the animate or inanimate nature of
dolls and the like. It is with respect to this issue that doubts
arise concerning double-bind theory. Double-bind theory, at
first glance, seems to underline the positive and healthy aspects of unambiguous communication and the pathogenic
features of certain contradictory communications. Bateson's
concept of the double-bind situation is as follows: it involves
(1) two or more persons, (2) repeated experience, (3) a primary negative injunction, (4) a secondary injunction conflicting with the first at the more abstract level, and, like the
first, enforced by punishments or signals that threaten survival, (5) a tertiary negative injunction prohibiting the victim
from escaping from the field. Even this brief statement makes
it quite clear that much more is involved than contradiction
at the more abstract level. Despite the apparent rigor of
double-bind theory, close examination reveals significant
flaws in it.

Double-bind theory is supposedly based on Russell's theory
of types as elaborated in Whitehead and Russell's monumental *Principia Mathematica*. But Whitehead and Russell propose that recognition of the hierarchy of types permits escape
from logical paradoxes after one has been trapped in certain
classical paradoxes. As examples of classical paradox and its
relation to ambiguity, I shall describe two photographs from
Watzlawick et al.'s book *Pragmatics of Human Communication*. One picture shows a stop sign onto which another sign
is nailed, saying "No stopping at any time." The other picture indicates an overpass onto which a sign has been attached reading, "Ignore this sign." Presumably the latter sign

has been placed on the overpass by a practical joker. One could choose either to stop or not to stop in response to the signs in the first picture, feeling ambivalent about either decision. But ambivalence does not describe one's response to the "Ignore this sign" sign. One's affective response to being trapped in this paradox—or ambiguity of types—bears a resemblance, I believe, to the affective component of some naturally occurring, "typically" ambiguous situations, such as déjà vu phenomena and certain other transitional ambiguous states.

For Whitehead and Russell, the "Ignore this sign" paradox would be solved by pointing out that the actual sign and the words "this sign" involve different levels of abstraction. Whitehead and Russell add, however, that reasoning would have to come to a standstill if attempts were made rigorously to avoid the possibility of paradox even in the most formal logical chain, to say nothing of the processes involved in less formal tasks. Specifically, they talk of the necessity of ambiguity of logical types in order to "make one chain of reasoning applicable to any of an infinite number of different cases, which would not be possible if we were to forego the use of typically ambiguous words and symbols."

Furthermore, Gödel proved formally that we must accept the possibility of internal contradiction in order to proceed even in the most rigorously defined areas of mathematical logic. Oversimplifying almost shamelessly the concepts involved, let us consider the classical syllogism, "All men are mortal. Socrates is a man. Therefore, Socrates is mortal." Not quite so, says Russell; we don't quite know that Socrates is mortal until he is dead. Alexander the Great, cutting the Gordian knot, symbolizes individuation—the escape, if you will, from a "double bind" by introducing a new category of solutions to a knotty problem.

Bateson and his coworkers have emphasized that the formal aspects, not the content, of double-bind communications are the significant pathogenic factors. This is hard to reconcile fully with the notion of the therapeutic double bind, which Bateson and his colleagues also introduce. Clinical observation indicates that it may be more accurate to say that communication by parent or analyst of tolerance of ambiguity facilitates individuation. Double-bind theorists talk of metacommunication—that is, communication about a communication. To be understood, however, this metacommunication must be appropriate to the developmental level of the recipient, be he a patient in psychoanalysis or psychotherapy, a spouse, or a child in his family setting. Winnicott speaks of the importance for normal development of not challenging certain ambiguities at certain developmental levels.

While no one disputes our need for structures and categories, ambiguity is a visible relative of the uncanny structureless void. Intuitively well-titrated tolerance of ambiguity is that aspect of good parenting that promotes just enough familiarity with estrangement to avoid alienation. Freud has characterized the Unconscious (1915) as knowing no contradiction. The problem with which Gödel deals can be stated in a grossly oversimplified way as follows: a self-consistent system of abstraction is too limited for interesting tasks. Therefore, one has to jump to ever more-inclusive levels of abstraction. To escape from this always incomplete series, Gödel tries to have a system speak about itself. For this self-description he uses a kind of mathematical or formal logical projection—something like descriptive geometry—which can be thought of as a geometric system describing itself in algebraic forms. In the end, however, what the system says about itself is that it must necessarily be incomplete.

What is perhaps only an esoteric problem on the frontiers of formal logic, with thus far very little, if any, practical impact on the physical sciences, is a central problem in psychiatry, in psychoanalysis, and perhaps in biological systems generally. In psychoanalysis we are constantly dealing with such an attempted projection: we want the primary process to say something about itself in secondary-process language; we want consciously to apprehend something about the unconscious system (Freud's *System Ucs.*).

Perhaps Gödel has given us a formal logical description of the unconscious by picturing an infinitely regressing series of ambiguities of type, which must perhaps continuously be tapped to promote individuation, creativity, and psychoanalytic work. It is here that I see the link to a psychoanalytic consideration of the problem of the experience of time.

Time

The psychoanalyst's major concern with the experience of time is perhaps based on his ongoing observation of the restructuring in the present of past experiences. He is in a position to observe the effects of such restructuring on the experience of time and on temporal perspective; but related to the more general problem of paradoxical experience is the issue of integration of the discontinuous moment and the flow of continuity. This issue, which is the ego's task, can be more accurately described as the problem of toleration of qualitatively different, irreconciled, paradoxical experiences.

Bonaparte (1940) refers to a communication sent to her by Freud in which he talked of our "later" transformation into continuity of "successive cathexes . . . quanta issuing from the ego." Since when we talk of the nature of the experience of time, the very word *later* begs the question, I believe that the problem of integration of the discontinuous moment and the flow of continuity was neither avoided nor solved by Freud. The term *quanta,* however, with its implications in terms of the irreconcilable nature—within one closed system—of wave and particle theory, may be of some interest. Freud wrote during the same period in which quantum mechanics was being formulated. Quantum mechanics was developed primarily between 1900 and 1926; Heisenberg's uncertainty principle was formulated in 1927; and it was in 1929 that Bridgman warned against "licentious . . . philosophizing and psychologizing" based on it.

I shall nevertheless attempt some psychologizing, since self-observation of psychic processes confronts us rather directly with the static-fluid connotations of the observer-observed situation and, I believe, with its paradoxical implications, since different levels of abstraction are involved. An analogy is suggested between the particle and the wave, on the one hand, and the experience of the discontinuous moment and the flow of continuity, on the other. Self-observation attempts to bring together the static grasping the changing grasping the static—opposites on different levels of abstraction; these opposites can be seen as paradoxes, an infinitely regressing series of ambiguities of type, perhaps again something akin to what I have somewhat daringly called Gödel's formal logical description of the unconscious.

Loewald, in a powerful and beautiful paper, after considering the *now* active presence of past and future, arrives at the concluding formulation that "psychic structures are temporal in nature" (1962, p. 268), that the very fiber of mind is time. I wonder if the temporally conceived form of the paradox of the static and the fluid is not an especially poignant, or perhaps the extreme formal, statement of the problem we meet at the limits of our study of "what we call psychical" (Loewald, p. 268). William Fry, who says, "Whenever man seeks to inspect the self, he will confront the self and discover that the self is the inspector," also states, "I have . . . discovered no technique of illustrating the instantaneous simultaneity created in paradox" (p. 172).

In a philosophical tour de force, which it amuses him to paradoxically entitle "A *New* Refutation of Time" (italics mine), Jorge Luis Borges also brings home to what extent we experience time as the core of the psyche. Not only does he point out how even the idealist philosophers could not follow

their own logic to the invalidation of time—which Borges
proceeds to do—but he also jars us with his unusual conceptual integration of an experience that seems to have at
least some of the features of the déjà vu experience. "That
pure representation of homogeneous objects . . . is not
merely identical to the one present on that corner so many
years ago; it is, *without resemblances or repetitions, the very
same*. . . . I felt dead . . . an abstract spectator . . . the
possessor of a reticent or absent sense of the inconceivable
word eternity. . . . Time . . . is a delusion" (p. 226; italics
mine). Similar experiences, usually less explicitly conceptualized, are not unknown to us in our psychoanalytic work,
and when they occur, they may represent nodal points of reorganization of life perspective.

Even if we restrict the term *object constancy* to a specific
psychoanalytic meaning of continuing investment in an object even though this object may be frustrating, we cannot
disconnect the concept from continuity in time. The paradox
that we encounter at the core of time experience—the flowing and the saccadic—is inherent in the problem of object
constancy. In considering this paradox and our continuing
concern with tolerance of paradoxical and *qualitatively* different experiences, we may perhaps turn with profit to the
ego's more obvious task of integrating *quantitatively* different
and variable experiences of duration. Here some experimental approaches can be interdigitated with psychoanalytic observations.

In temporal terms, experimental data are typically classified as relating to (1) the experience of a very short interval—
the present, (2) the experience of a longer interval—duration,
(3) the experience of the future or of a temporal perspective,
and (4) the experience of simultaneity. Despite the methodo-
logical strictures of experimental approaches, all of these
areas are of interest to the psychoanalyst, and he in turn has
contributions to make from his vantage point. The part of

the experimental work that may appeal most directly to the analyst's interest, however, is that which bears on the effects of new organization of data on the experience of past duration, and some explorations of the *process* of structuring time experience.

In a series of experiments, Ornstein, for example, demonstrated the retroactive effects of new information on judgment of past duration. His type of approach, stated schematically, was as follows. Subjects were asked to learn an apparently random series of numbers, and then were asked how much time it took them to learn the series. Other subjects, after having learned the same series, were given a code that transformed the apparently random series into an ordered one. If these subjects had known the code before learning the "random" series, learning would have been easier and the learning period shortened. Although the actual learning period was the same in both groups, the subjects who were given the code that permitted them to reorganize their experience, to recode it retrospectively, estimated the learning period as shorter than did the subjects who were not given that information.

In an experiment some years ago (Kafka, 1957), I studied how persons given different sets of instructions approached the task of judging the duration of a series of intervals during which they were in a darkened room with an autokinetic light. These periods were interspersed with rest intervals in the same room lighted normally, and the subjects were also asked to estimate retrospectively the duration of these intervals. Each subject selected a particular interval as a reference for comparison with the other interval experiences. In the process of arriving at estimates, they constantly made judgments of equivalence and difference, and there was a general tendency to overestimate. The choice of reference intervals seemed to be related to clinically discernible moods and affects, although confirmation would require a predictive study.

In any case, the patterns of time judgments obtained did suggest that overestimators who used "dark" reference intervals tended to make larger "corrections" in arriving at estimates of "light" intervals, seemingly using self-observation operating below awareness. The effort to reconcile contrasting and differentially *grained* experiences of duration—that is, experiences in which the size of "now" (the temporal distance between moments of self-awareness) varies—can be studied in such a setting and can also be studied in our clinical work.

Without attempting to make a list that is exhaustive and that excludes the obvious, I shall indicate some time-related aspects of the psychoanalytic situation.

1. The patient's analytic hour, his extended "time out" (from work, from usual activity, from usual style of behavior, and from usual style of communication), is the analyst's extended and relatively usual "time in."

2. The analyst, more than the patient, assumes that contiguity of communication (and of experience) has *possible* "meaning" implications transcending contiguity as such.

3. The analyst, more than the patient, assumes that temporal distance between communications (and experiences) does not eliminate the possibility of *meaningful* connections between them, and may even be a *defense* against such connections.

4. The analyst may thus be said to be both a "condenser" and "dilator" of time.

5. Sequence may be translated in the context of clarifications and interpretations as having specific meaning as such. Sequential dream "phrases," for instance, may be translated into prepositional clauses.

6. The analyst may thus be seen by the patient as dealing with time in a peculiar way.

7. The patient who finds that some of these peculiar dilating and contracting ways are productive of further insight, are "meaningful," may by identification, by other mecha-

nisms, or for other reasons, learn from and utilize them in looking at his own temporal experience.

8. The stage may thus be set for reorganization—or in the language of experimentalists, for recoding—of time experience.

In analogy with the distinction between Federn's "bodily ego feeling" and Schilder's "body image," the word *recoding* can be understood to include time feeling rather than, or in addition to, a subjective time image. The following brief clinical illustration deals with "time feeling" rather than with "time image."

A professional man who had been raised by adoptive parents alternated in living with his mistress and his wife during the course of his analysis. In one analytic session, when he had again lived for a prolonged period with his wife, he spoke of his feeling of progress in his analytic work, but also spoke at length of his difficulty in "seeing himself" during his most recent prolonged period with his mistress, a period that had terminated almost two years ago. I commented that he had seemed more different, from hour to hour, during that period than now, and in response he gradually described the different time texture between periods spent with his mistress and those spent with his wife and children. Although his description of people, situations, and feelings was complex, his focus was on the struggle to reexperience and reinterpret his "time out," his discontinuity of experience; he was attempting to "see" himself both in more constant times and in saccadic periods of rapid mood changes. He then talked about the eventual termination of the analysis, his anticipated joyful and nostalgic feelings. This was followed by talk of his plans to ask his adoptive parents about his biologic parents, who he believed were known to them. Previously unmentioned historical details about

his adoptive parents began to come out, and fantasies
about his biologic parents. He then expressed the
thought that there might be a connection between characteristics of his mistress and his fantasied parents. In
the next session, in the context of expressing fears about
what he might discover concerning his origins and how
he would react to the discoveries—and in the context of
talking about plans, wishes, and fears for his future—he
reported a dream of being in a corner room from which
one could see in two directions.

I think that the process of connecting events and feelings
differently—in a sense, bringing new information to bear on
episodes reexperienced during psychoanalysis—permits a reorganization and reinterpretation of time feeling. The reorganization may enhance the sense of continuity and facili-
tate the widening of temporal perspective and its extension
into the future.

In the give and take of ordinary conversations, the timing
of our speech and gestures is determined in part by our assessment of the characteristics of the listener and by a complex network of mutual expectations. The better I know my
friend, the more accurately can I assess his mood, his interest
in a topic, his appreciation of the levels to which I carry the
consideration of the topic, and the many other factors that
codetermine, not only what I communicate, but also the rate
and changes of rate of my communications. Feedback—verbal
and nonverbal—constantly influences this rate. Certain patterns of unpredictableness can have disorienting effects
(Kafka, unpublished), and so, to repeat the obvious, can
the analyst's silence.

When the termination phase approaches, however, one
hopes not only that the analysand is in touch with his own
range of available temporal graining, but also that analyst
and analysand have a subtle mutual understanding of such

graining, the temporal perspective in which it is placed, and
how temporal perspective can be reexperienced in a tele-
scoped form in an individual hour.

Conclusion

In examining the paradoxical aspects of temporal structure, we can see that imbedded in the temporal framework—
the temporal mesh—are subjective equivalence patterns. In
terms of both the psychoanalytic and general psychological
meaning of object constancy—the idea of an *enduring* object—we can see the object emerging and disappearing as
the time span and the time patterns change, varying its guise
ambiguously as it moves between paradoxical roles, recur-
rently producing "subjectively equivalent stimuli," the building block of our momentary and more lasting realities. Conversely, our needs and drives largely determine on which
characteristics of the stimulus field we focus in order to form
our subjective equivalences. The time span necessary to locate characteristics—in changing stimulus fields—that lend
themselves to "perceptions" congruent with the current active drive state, must itself continually expand and contract.
Our drive states thus determine the subjectively equivalent
time spans that anchor our temporal world.

We have indications from tachistoscopic studies of perception that perceptual acts recapitulate the history of our
perceptual development. The adult's perception of tachisto-
scopically exposed Rorschach cards resembles the child's perception of normally exposed cards (Stein). Our "realities"
depend on the time grid of perception, but I visualize not
only different sizes of the holes in the grid, but also different
shapes and different textures of the mesh. Different meshes,
to carry the analogy further, permit the passage, so to speak,
of different ego states from earlier and later developmental
phases, various ego states in which object representations
have different qualities—as was the case for my patient with

the fugue states and the déjà vu experiences. The nature of
temporal graining—that is, the patterns and textures of the
available grids—contributes to the organization of the flow
of experience into object constancies. Elsewhere I have developed in more detail the notion that "Psychological reality
for a person at any one time is a pattern of organization of
stimuli and can be described in terms of a pattern of subjective equivalences" (Kafka, 1964b, pp. 576–77).

To the extent that the analyst is responsive to his patient's
own multiple ways of graining experiences of time, he is responsive to his patient's multiple—and perhaps paradoxical—
realities. As the analysand awakens—or reawakens—to the
possibilities of shared rhythms of organizing experiences, he
is better able to explore and develop his own individual
variations of those rhythms and those realities.

As we hesitantly reach for the limits of understanding, we
must return to Loewald's statement of the basic relationship
expounded here: "Psychic structures are temporal in nature"
(1962, p. 268)—in other words, mind is time.

REFERENCES

Arlow, J. "The Structure of the Déjà Vu Experience." *Journal of
the American Psychoanalytic Association* 7 (1959) : 611–31.
Bateson, G., et al. "Toward a Theory of Schizophrenia." *Be-
havioral Science* 1 (1956) : 251–64.
Bonaparte, M. "Time and the Unconscious." *International
Journal of Psycho-Analysis* 21 (1940) : 427–68.
Borges, J. L. "A New Refutation of Time." In *Labyrinths,* edited
by D. A. Yates and J. E. Irby. New York: New Directions,
1964.
Federn, P. *Ego Psychology and the Psychoses.* New York: Basic
Books, 1952.
Freud, S. "Fausse Reconnaissance ('Déjà Raconté') in Psycho-
analytic Treatment (1914)." "The Unconscious (1915),"

chap. 5. "The 'Uncanny' (1913)." In *Standard Edition of the Complete Psychological Works,* vols. 13, 14, 17. London: Hogarth, 1955, 1957.

Fry, W. F., Jr. *"Sweet Madness: A Study of Humor.* Palo Alto, Calif.: Pacific Books, 1968.

Gödel, J. "Über formal unentscheidbare Sätze der Principia Mathematica und verwandter Systeme I." *Monatshefte für Mathematik und Physik* 38 (1931) : 173–98.

Hartmann, H. *Ego Psychology and the Problems of Adaptation* (1939). New York: International Universities Press, 1958.

Kafka, J. S. "A Method for Studying the Organization of Time Experience." *American Journal of Psychiatry* 114 (1957) : 546–53.

———. "Some Effects of the Therapist's LSD Experience on his Therapeutic Work." *American Journal of Psychotherapy* 18 (1964a) : 236–43.

———. "Technical Applications of a Concept of Multiple Reality." *International Journal of Psycho-Analysis* 45 (1964b) : 575–78.

———. "The Body as Transitional Object: A Psychoanalytic Study of a Self-mutilating Patient.' *British Journal of Medical Psychology* 42 (1969) : 207–12.

———. "Ambiguity for Individuation: A Critique and Reformulation of Double-Bind Theory." *Archives of General Psychiatry* 25 (1971) : 232–39.

———. "On the Experience of Duration in Psychotherapy." Unpublished.

Klüver, H. "The Study of Personality and the Method of Equivalent and Non-equivalent Stimuli." *Character and Personality* 5 (1936) : 91–112.

Lichtenstein, H. "The Effect of Reality Perception on Psychic Structure: A Psychoanalytic Contribution to the Problem of the 'Generation Gap.' " *The Annual of Psychoanalysis,* vol. 2. New York: International Universities Press, 1974.

Loewald, H. W. "The Superego and the Ego Ideal. II. Superego and Time." *International Journal of Psycho-Analysis* 43 (1962) : 264–68.

Novey, S. "Some Philosophical Speculations About the Concept of the Genital Character." *International Journal of Psycho-Analysis* 36 (1955) : 38–94.

Ornstein, R. E. *On the Experience of Time.* Baltimore: Penguin Books, 1969.

Schachtel, E. G. "On Memory and Childhood Amnesia." *Psychiatry* 10 (1947) : 1–26.

Schilder, P. *The Image and Appearance of the Human Body* (1935). New York: International Universities Press, 1950.

Stein, M. I. "Personality Factors Involved in Temporal Development of Rorschach Responses." *Rorschach Research Exchange and Journal of Projective Techniques* 13 (1949) : 355–414.

Wallerstein, R. S. "Psychoanalytic Perspectives on the Problem of Reality." *Journal of the American Psychoanalytic Association* 21 (1973) : 5–33.

Watzlawick, P., et al. *Pragmatics of Human Communication.* New York: W. W. Norton, 1967.

Whitehead, A. N., and Russell, B. *Principia Mathematica.* Cambridge: Cambridge University Press, 1910.

Winnicott, D. W. "Transitional Objects and Transitional Phenomena." In *Collected Papers.* New York: Basic Books, 1958.

7

Cognitive Aspects of the Paranoid Process—Prospectus

W. W. Meissner

There is hardly a single subject to which contemporary psychoanalysis addresses itself that is more far-reaching in its theoretical implications and in its impact on the understanding of the way in which man's mind works than the problem of the internal versus the external in human experience. The differentiation between what we experience as somehow internal from what we experience as external raises important and perplexing questions having to do with how, to begin with, such a sense of the internal arises and comes to oppose itself to a sense of the external. It also raises significant problems for our attempts to articulate our concepts of the inner life of man within a framework of his experience of reality.

The problem of interiority versus externality has plagued psychoanalysis from its very beginnings, and leaves the tenuous ambiguity of its mark on psychoanalytic thinking and theorizing even to this day. Freud was confronted with the tension between fantasy and reality from the beginning of his work with hysterics. The question hovers in the background and only comes into sharper focus at more or less critical points. He was confronted in a powerful way with this very dilemma when he began to realize that the hypothesis by which he linked the development of neurosis to the effects of actual seduction could not be maintained. Freud leaned heavily in the direction of explaining neurotic symptoms by an appeal to real experiences, but he increasingly came to realize—not only through his growing clinical experience, but by virtue of his deepening self-analysis—that the role of reality was questionable in many cases and that, in fact, he was dealing with the patients' fantasies, which were generated from and motivated by an unconscious wish.

This theoretical intuition proved to be a vital turning-point in the history of psychoanalysis, since it redirected Freud's attention to the unconscious dynamics lying behind mental fantasy productions. Following this theoretical turn-about, Freud's investment was directed toward the exploration of the realm of internal experience and particularly the instinctually derived, unconscious realm of fantasy. It was only some years later, when Freud had begun to think in terms of the separation of ego functions and their role vis-à-vis drive derivatives, that the role of reality in psychoanalytic theory came back into more specific focus.

The problem of the tension between reality and fantasy, however, created a constant latent ambiguity that he never seemed to be able to resolve satisfactorily. It is interesting, for example, that in his treatment of the Wolf Man (1918) he advances the hypothesis of primal scene exposure to explain the patient's intense sadomasochism. However, the evidence for such real exposure was not direct or specific. Freud found himself unable to argue directly from a real primal scene experience and was forced to reconstruct the possibility of such an experience from other suggested data. Nonetheless, when the argument was boiled down to its essentials, Freud still had to admit the possibility that the primal scene content might have been a product of the Wolf Man's own childhood fantasy.

In any case, the problem of the interplay between reality and fantasy lives on to plague us still. In the study of development, for example, we can never be sure whether the critical variables that determine personality development have to do with the child's real experience with objects, or whether it is more the internal economy of how those developmental experiences are processed that carries the explanatory weight. Analysts have been repeatedly impressed with the disparity between identifiable real behaviors and the dimensions of the fantasy account that the patient presents.

To compound the difficulties, it is not always clear what the significance of internal as opposed to external might be. Our attempts to disentangle this problem are carried on in the shadow of the famous Cartesian split, which radicalized the separation between the realms of the subjective and the objective. The methodology of the objective (positive) sciences more or less insists on this split, and on the correlative application of the criteria of objective verifiability to scientific knowledge. This seems to imply somehow that scientific knowledge leads to an understanding of objects "out there" in reality, somehow existing independently of the observer's experience. Thus the Cartesian split has emphasized the separation between internal and external, and this separation has been consolidated by the Kantian *Critique*—"das Ding in sich ist das Ding unbekannt." The Kantian critical approach to knowledge places the thing in its objective existence beyond the reach of man's knowledge. We are left only with a grasp of phenomena, out of which we can only construct the world of our experience.

It is this ambiguity that Hampshire (1959) engages when he addresses himself to the complex interplay between thought and intention and action: "But these vaguely expressed ideas do go together to form the commonplace notion of action, which is ordinarily contrasted with the 'inner' processes of thought and feeling, which are preliminary to action. . . . The contrast between 'inner' and 'external' processes is closely connected with the contrast between that which is a source of action, or the effect of action, and that which is the bringing about of a change in the world" (pp. 154–55). The Cartesian agent ends in a disembodied state, connected to real events and external actions only by divinely inspired accident.

But the capacity for movement and action in a world of constant objects as referents of such action requires that the agent be acting and moving as an object among other objects, as a body persisting among others. The capacity to move my own body at will and to manipulate external objects is basic. Hampshire comments:

> I not only perceive my body. I also control it; I not only perceive external objects. I also manipulate them. To doubt the existence of my own body would necessarily be to doubt my ability to move. My own body is in action felt to be continuous with other resisting bodies, some of which can be made to move at will as my body moves. . . . I find my power of movement limited by the resistances of objects around me. This felt resistance to my will defines for me, in conjunction with my perceptions, my own situation as an object among other objects. Both perceptions and bodily sensations contribute to this elementary discovery; even taken together, they do not constitute the whole of it. I know directly, that I tried, or set myself, to move, or that I did not try, but was rather moved by something else. No knowledge is more direct and underived than this knowledge of the fact of my own intention to move or bring about a change. It is therefore wrong to represent experience of the external world as some synthesis of impressions of each of the five senses. A physical object is recognized as a potential obstruction, or as something to be manipulated, occupying some definite position in relation to me at the moment of perception. The use of any of my senses, or any combination of them, gives me the means of recognising the obstruction, the thing to

be manipulated, as of a certain kind and as liable to resist my intended actions in a certain way. [pp. 47–48]

If we were to be trapped within our own experience, how could we ever find our way out of such an enclosure? What would it mean for us to know something outside of our own experience, to know objects that are somehow distinct and separate from our knowing and that constitute the reality within which we live and experience? What is there within the mass of our human experience that allows us to differentiate between that which we describe as internal to that experience and that which we describe as external to it?

The dilemmas of internalization versus externalization have recently prompted Roy Schafer (1972) to resort to an attempt to regard internalization simply in terms of fantasy and to categorize the language of internal process in terms of spatial metaphor. He says:

> The gist of my argument is that internalization is a spatial—actually, pseudospatial—metaphor that is so grossly incomplete and unworkable that we would do best to avoid it in psychoanalytic conceptualization. Incorporation (and the incorporated object or person) is the only term that has a real reference, namely archaic fantasies of taking objects into the body. Logically, internalization cannot mean anything more than that: it refers to a fantasy, not to a process. [p. 434]

Thus Schafer recommends that we abandon the ambiguous territory of internal versus external, along with the metaphorical language that describes psychic processes and their consequences in terms of the internal and the external, and resort to a psychological language that deals without such complexities.

Hartmann (1939) had originally formulated the notion of internalization as an aspect of the phylogenetic progression toward an increased capacity for internal regulation. In these terms, the increasing capacity for delay and the relative independence of stimulus conditions serve to support the argument that such capacities were related to the development of internal apparatuses within the organism. Schafer notes that this evolutionary concept of internalization involves an illogical inference from increased organismic complexity and environmental independence to a localizing of thought and experience. Schafer concludes that the psychological observer has no warrant to locate mental activity anywhere, particularly within the organism. To locate thought, experience, or affect "inside the self" or "inside the mind" is to resort to a spatializing metaphor, which tries to make a place out of an abstraction. The mind has no other boundaries than the boundaries of a concept; it does not have the boundaries of place. If we dispense with the spatializing notion of inside as opposed to outside, we can then say that if an individual keeps ideas or feelings to himself, that is not the same as keeping them within himself. The private world is not necessarily equivalent to an internal world (Schafer, 1972). Schafer's argument is important insofar as it points to the critical difficulties concerning the concepts of internal and external. His argument forces us to face this critical dilemma.[1]

It is worth noting in connection with these problems that the vantage point of psychoanalysis, in terms of its methodology, is relatively unique among empirical disciplines. The psychoanalyst stands, as it were, with one foot in external reality and the other foot in the world of internal subjective experience.[2] The analyst's methodology imposes on him the

1. It is not my intention to put Schafer's argument to the test here. I have tried to make a critical evaluation of it elsewhere (Meissner, 1976) and would only wish to note at this juncture that the problem to which Schafer addresses himself is not irrelevant to the main theme of this paper.

2. This formulation will later have to be modified in terms of the analyst's additional vantage point in the realm of transitional experience. Nonetheless, the analyst's emergence into the realm of transitional experience with the patient does not invalidate his assessment of both objective and subjective reality.

task of discriminating and gathering as much objective data as possible to illuminate the real nature of the objective context of the patient's experience, both in development and in the patient's current world experience. At the same time, the analyst must be in touch with and responsive to the inner world of the patient's subjective experience. The availability of that subjective realm cannot be direct or observational, but can be made available only through more indirect avenues of the patient's own introspective report, to which the analyst can add his own internally grasped subjective experience as he engages with the patient in the analytic process.

In terms of the necessity of not losing sight of either of these poles of experience, it is essential to the working of the analytic process that the analyst be able to keep both the subjective and objective dimensions in contact with each other, and in the appropriate perspective. Thus, an essential part of the analytic work is the gradual discrimination in the patient's own experience between that which is real and that which is a product of fantasy, both in terms of his current experience and in terms of his past experience, as derivatives of infantile determinants. The psychoanalytic methodology is placed in the difficult and peculiar position of being able to retreat from neither the external objective parameters of the patient's involvement in the world nor the internal subjective realm of the patient's experience. The analytic process must find its way through these complex thickets to enable the patient, together with the analyst, increasingly to discriminate between these aspects so that in some ultimate and integrative sense they can be brought into harmonious resolution (Schimek, 1975).

One can say, then, that the immersion of the psychoanalytic perspective in both the internal and the external is one of its greatest strengths, but the source of its greatest vulnerability as well. Analysis can neither retreat to the ordered and objectivized assurance of extrinsic behavioral observation and measurement, nor fall back to the posture of internally derived and subjective expressions of meaning and fantasy. It must keep itself within the tensionful field of the interplay and opposition—ambiguous and often contradictory—of the internal and the external. Thus it is no surprise that the dilemmas posed by this oppositional polarization are an integral part of the heritage of psychoanalysis. My attempt in the present reflection is to articulate the dimensions of the problems and particularly to focus the issues raised by this inherent tension of analytic experience for the understanding of cognitive aspects of man's involvement in, as well as separation from, his environment.

Aspects of the Paranoid Process

My approach to these problems has taken shape in the context of work with the paranoid process. I would like to set the present reflection in the context of the paranoid process, in the hope of gaining some further purchase on these difficulties and articulating a frame of reference and an orientation toward their delineation and understanding within the psychoanalytic perspective.

In using the term "paranoid process," I refer to a process that has both developmental and defensive components, but which most critically operates in the realm of gradually delineating the individual's inner psychic world and his experience of an emerging sense of self. Correlatively, the paranoid process operates to shape the individual's experience of the significant objects in his surrounding experiential world. Consequently, the paranoid process contributes in important ways to the progressive individuation of a sense of inner cohesiveness and self-awareness, while at the same time it shapes and directs the progressive and continuing interaction with significant objects (Meissner, 1977).

While the paranoid process arises descriptively from an examination of paranoid forms of psychopathology, it is not limited to such pathological expressions; rather, it plays itself out in a general way, not only influencing nonparanoid forms of pathology, but also functioning equally and significantly in the shaping of normal personality development and in the construction of a consistent and coherent and well-integrated sense of mature identity. The three core dimensions of the paranoid process that I would like to discuss are introjection, projection, and the paranoid construction. The notions of introjection and projection are familiar to psychoanalysts, but in view of the variety of usages, it may be well to point out that in the present context the concepts have a somewhat broader significance.

Without doubt, the concept of introjection is the central dimension of the paranoid process, in that projection is a correlative secondary derivative from the organization of the introjects, and the paranoid construction serves to bolster, reinforce, and articulate the projective system. The notion of introjection relates to Freud's original formulation of narcissistic identification, which arose originally in his analysis of melancholy and was later applied as the essential mechanism of internalization in the formation of the superego. The mechanism of introjection implied abandonment of an object relationship and the preservation of the object intrapsychically by its internalization through introjection.

Reflection on the process of introjection in terms of the paranoid process has considerably broadened the meaning of introjection from the relatively narrow focus of Freud's original formulations. Introjection comes to refer to that process of internalization by which aspects of objects or object relationships are taken in to form part of the subject's inner world. There is difficulty in illuminating how this process takes place. Jacobson (1964) sees the process in terms of the merging of object-images with self-images and regards them as more or less psychotic phenomena. I think the process is more complex. While there is little question that the process of introjection plays upon and influences the organization of self-representation, this seems to be a secondary phenomenon. To envision the organization of the self simply in representational terms bypasses the obvious structural referents of the self along with the structuralizing aspects of introjection (Meissner, 1971, 1972). Rather, in terms of the paranoid process, introjection gives rise to the inner organization of the core experiences around which the sense of self shapes itself. The process of introjection and the forming of the introjective configuration plays itself out in the developmental process and is expressed in an increasingly individuated and integrated sense of self.

The process is, of course, subject to all the vicissitudes of development itself. I shall return to this subject shortly, but the point to be emphasized here is that there is a progressive differentiation in the organization of the introjects and their economy. At the earliest development levels, the introjective configuration is relatively primitive, undifferentiated, and global. At progressive stages of development, it becomes more delineated, more specifically differentiated, and increasingly structuralized.

While the developmental aspects of introjection are of major significance, it should not be lost sight of that the mechanism functions basically in defensive terms—that is, broadly speaking, the mechanism of introjection is thrown into operation by the defensive need to salvage and preserve the residues of narcissism that are jeopardized by the developmental progression. The intimate involvement of introjection and the introjective organization with issues of narcissism and defense gives a characteristic stamp to the introjective organization. The introjects thus become the vehicle for the organization of drive derivatives and defensive configurations within the intrapsychic organization (Meissner, 1977).

The critical notion here is that intrapsychic development involves a progressive modification of infantile narcissism at sequential stages of the developmental process. At each stage, further modification of the original narcissism takes place so as to protect and preserve the emerging sense of self. Only gradually is the early infantile omnipotence and grandiosity modified and integrated. Kohut (1971) has described a first stage of this introjective organization in terms of the grandiose self. The preservation of such narcissistic remnants gives the introjective process, by which emergent self-components are formed, a defensive character. Later, the evolution of introjection leads in the direction of minimizing separation anxiety (loss of significant objects) or of defending against intolerable ambivalence.

The psychoanalytic literature has carved out certain introjective configurations and described them in terms of the aggressor-introject (Anna Freud's [1936] "identification with the aggressor"), the victim-introject (Meissner, 1977), or even the grandiose self (Kohut, 1971). Developmentally later and more structuralized introjective configurations have been traditionally described in terms of the ego-ideal or the superego. Clearly, the limited focus of the classic description of introjective processes has not exhausted the understanding of this component of the paranoid process.

In any case, the introjective organization must be regarded as organizing and expressing a specific configuration of drive derivatives and as serving specific defensive functions. By implication, the drive-and-defense organization of the introjects leaves them relatively susceptible to the regressive pulls of drive influences, and also allows them to serve as the point of origin for further defensive operations, specifically that of projection. Consequently, in a clinical frame of reference, it is the inherent relationship of the introjective organization to drive derivatives—whether libidinal, aggressive, or narcissistic—its susceptibility to regressive pulls, and its propensity to projection that allow us to delineate and identify it (Meissner, 1971).

The question inevitably arises as to where this internalized,

introjective organization is situated. Is it inside or is it outside? Is it internal or is it external? Is it in the mind? In the
self? In the ego? The answers do not come easily, nor can the
questions themselves be unambiguously posed. If we can
agree that such introjected, internalized objects are properly
internal psychic formations (as opposed to external), we are
unavoidably confronted with a number of difficult metapsychological questions. The questions are not to be resolved
here, and I will hope at least to suggest a direction of the
metapsychological reflection in a later section of this study.

The critical questions have to do with the relationships between such introjective formations and the structure of the
self, and consequently the relationship of the self to the traditional structural components of the tripartite psychic apparatus—id, ego, and superego. In regard to the interiority
versus exteriority of the introjective organization, the answer
must be neither yes nor no, but more or less. The notion of
"degrees of internalization" was introduced by Loewald
(1962). Referring to superego introjects, he described them
as being "on the periphery of the ego system" (p. 483)—that
is, the introjective formations have a more peripheral character as opposed to the more central character of components
of the ego system. Schafer's (1968b) clarification in terms of
activity and passivity bears on the same issue. In these terms
the introjects are conceived as imaginary, "felt" presences—
Schafer elsewhere calls them "primary process presences"
(1968a)—by which the patient feels himself assaulted or grati-
fied and in relation to which he feels himself to be relatively
passive. The passivity is a matter of degree and stands in contrast to degrees of activity, particularly the more purely self-
originative and active quality of ego activities. Schafer describes the peripheral quality of the existence of introjects in
the following terms:

> An introjection is an inner presence with which one
> feels in a continuous or intermittent dynamic relation-

ship. The subject conceives of this presence as a person, a physical or psychological part of a person (e.g., a breast, a voice, a look, an affect), or a person-like thing or creature. He experiences it as existing within the confines of his body or mind or both, but not as an aspect or expression of his subjective self. [1968a, p. 72]

Both Loewald and Schafer are careful to exclude the introjective formation from any connection with the ego, and there are good metapsychological reasons for doing so. Attempts to dissociate the introjective organization and isolate introjects within the psychic realm do not meet with as much success, nor do such attempts find good theoretical support. The tension between the subjective and objective is reflected in Schafer's further description of the introject:

The internal object seems to be located within the subjective self. And yet it is not part of that self, just as food may be experienced as being inside the mouth and stomach and yet not part of either. In subjective experience, the person aware of his engagement with internal objects or introjects feels himself to be engaged with something other than himself; yet he will acknowledge that the object is within him and thus within his subjective self. This observation seems not to fit the usual conception of the self as all that is not object and vice versa. [1968a, p. 80]

In the light of these difficulties—namely, in conceptualizing degrees of internalization and in formulating the relationship between introjective formations as self-modifications and as influencing correlative ego structures, it seems to me to make greater sense to regard introjective organizations as part of the self-system. The degrees of internalization within the self-system, then, would reflect the extent to which a particular introjective configuration has been successfully integrated and harmonized with other components of the self-system. The "primary process presences," to which Schafer gives such discriminated and quasi-externalized status, reflect the separation of such introjective material from the rest of the self-content, against which it stands in relative opposition. Such primary process presences would have to be regarded as occupying a position on the periphery of the self-system.

At the same time, it has been my clinical experience that such primary process presences often evolve only as a result of extensive therapeutic clarification and delineation. Patients, more often than not, begin the therapeutic process in a condition in which the introjective formations are more or less undifferentiated from the main mass of the subjective sense of self. It is, in fact, only to the degree to which such patients are able to begin to put some distance between particular introjective formations and the rest of the subjective sense of self that therapeutic progress is made and the ground is laid for eliminating or revising such introjective configurations (Meissner, 1976, 1977). As already noted, these formulations call for the further exploration and elaboration of complex metapyschological issues.

The mechanism of projection is both correlative to and derived from the introjective organization. In terms of the representational economy, following Jacobson's formula, projection can be described in terms of a transferral of elements from the self-representation to object-representations. Consequently, the externalization involved in projection is an intrapsychic process—external objects are not changed or modified by the projection itself.[3] The role of projection in

3. External objects may be modified secondary to the projection from the subject's inner world, but the modification is not a direct causal effect of the projection process. The modification of the object may take place by a response to the subject's expectations or by corresponding internalizations

modifying object-representations gives it a critical function in relation to object relationships. The correlative interaction of projection and introjection plays itself out throughout the whole of the developmental course, as we shall see later. Thus projection is a central dimension of the process by which the differentiation of objects is established and in terms of which the quality of object relationships is continually being shaped and reworked.

Insofar as the projections serve to externalize elements of the introjective configuration, they bear the characteristic stamp of introjective components. Thus the projective derivatives are reflective of the organization of drives and defenses inherent in the introjects. Projection deals in the commerce between self- and object-images and is characterized by the quality of differentiation and complex organization that is inherent in such representational organizations. Consequently, projection does not exhaust the limits of externalization. Externalization in its turn may also function in terms of relatively dissociated and depersonalized elements of the intrapsychic frame of reference. Thus, in certain forms of phobia, aggressive components may be externalized and experienced as external threats without the particular configuration of more personalized and organized qualities characteristic of projections as such. More often than not, however, when such externalizations take place they carry with them the stamp of

(Meissner, 1977). Brodey (1965), in fact, describes externalization in the following terms: "1. Projection is combined with the manipulation of reality selected for the purpose of verifying the projection. 2. The reality that cannot be used to verify the projection is not perceived. 3. When this mechanism is prominent in a stable group where people are learning from each other (as in a family), information known by the externalizing person but beyond the *Umwelt* of the others is not transmitted to these others except as it is useful to train or manipulate them into validating what will then become the realization of the projection. Reality testing is subverted in this process. Interlocking systems of externalization shared in a family potentiate disturbed ego development" (pp. 167–68).

introjective organization. Thus, the analysis of phobic contents can be made through the externalized elements to their introjective derivatives and, in the therapeutic work, can be traced back to the generative and pathogenic object relationships. The classic paradigm for this process was established by Freud in his case studies of Little Hans (1909) and the Wolf Man (1918).

In consequence, the effects of projection are experienced particularly in terms of object relationships. This is the primary focus and area of expression of the projective function. However, the projective operation may play itself out in other nonhuman contexts. The mechanism may operate in any context in which human qualities can be attributed to external realities. This may take place in primitive animistic or magically superstitious interactions with the environment, but it also takes place in more mundane contexts of interaction with pets or other forms of animal interaction, or even in determining the quality of interaction between the individual and his social environment—social organizations, institutions, business organizations, government, and so forth.

It should be noted that the operation of the paranoid mechanism of projection may be accompanied by denial or it may not. If the projection is motivated by a defensive need to dissociate oneself from an intolerable or somehow noxious self-element, the projection will usually be accompanied by a denial. Thus, in the classical form of the persecutory paranoid projection, hostile and destructive intent is attributed to the object and at the same time denied to the subject. Rather, the introjective components of helplessness and vulnerability serve to defend against the more destructive and threatening aggressive components. Where such defensive need does not operate, however, projection may take place without denial. This most usually is the case in the projection of more benign and tolerable or acceptable attributes. A similar set of circumstances would seem to operate in the context in which the combined functioning of introjection and projection subserves certain forms of empathic responsiveness.

It can be seen that projection is a highly complex phenomenon with many gradations and variations. Moreover, it can be readily seen that the functioning of projection plays a critical part in the working-through of the gradual elaboration of forms of introjection. The modification of object-representations by projective components sets the stage for subsequent reinternalizations, which serve to modify the introjective organization. Thus the interplay of introjection and projection provides a form of feedback process that allows for the progressive modification and differentiation of introjective organizations and their correlative projections.

The progressive interlocking of introjective and projective mechanisms and their correlative and mutual influence provides the central mechanism for intrapsychic development, as we shall see in a moment, as well as the medium through which various forms of psychopathology are expressed. It is when these processes are somehow cut off from the main forces of synthetic integration operating within the psyche and become contaminated by regressive drive influences or external reality-based distortions that pathological influences are effected. The point to be stressed here in terms of the cognitive aspects of the paranoid process is that both introjection and projection are mutually and interactionally involved in the continual processing of cognitive experience, in reference both to the experience of the subjective realm of the self and to the objective experience of the external environment. Their role in the building-up and shaping of object-representations is critical in the latter regard.

It must be simply stated that the projective system, whatever the degree of its elaboration and complexity, does not stand on its own. The projective components, as we have indicated, derive from the subject's inner world and are reinforced by the motivational components—the drive and defensive configurations—that characterize that realm of inner experience. But the projective elaboration cannot be sustained simply by means of drive-derivative exigencies. This is particularly true in the case of more or less pathological projective distortions, which unavoidably run afoul of other dimensions of the subject's experience of reality. Without some secondary considerations, one would have to anticipate that such projective distortions would be equivalently self-limiting and self-correcting.

But clinically we know that such is not the case, particularly in the cases of the most severe projective distortion found in the forms of paranoid psychopathology. Here the projective system acquires a delusional fixity and a conviction that make it all the more impermeable to therapeutic intervention and correction. In fact, the projective system is reinforced and maintained by what I have chosen to call the "paranoid construction" (Meissner, 1977). The paranoid construction is equivalently a cognitive reorganization of one's experience of reality in such a fashion as to include and integrate the elements of the projective system. The function of this cognitive organization is seen most dramatically in paranoid states where an elaborate system of beliefs, attitudes, convictions, and formulations serves to justify and sustain the projective components. These organizations may take the form of elaborate and extensive belief systems, or may take the often more concrete form of what Cameron has called the "paranoid pseudo-community" (1959).

The paranoid construction thus plays a critical role in the operation of the paranoid process. Its immediate function is to sustain and reinforce the projective elements. However, these projective elements in turn are derived from and reflect specific aspects of the introjective organization. The function of the projections themselves is related to the inner necessity for sustaining, to whatever degree possible, a sense of cohesiveness and integration within the experienced sense of self. Insofar as the introjective organization forms the core elements around which the sense of self organizes itself, the maintaining and the reinforcing of the introjective organization becomes a vital issue in this economy of self-organization and integration. Thus the entire apparatus—paranoid construction, projections, and introjective formations—serves the overriding purpose of preserving and sustaining a coherent and organized and integrated sense of self. This is the inner driving force and motivation behind the paranoid process. Moreover, this motivation not only operates in pathological aspects of the paranoid process, as in the case of severely depressive or paranoid pathologies, but also plays itself out in the relatively normal and adaptive development of human personality and its maintaining of a mature and integrated sense of identity.

The paranoid construction can therefore be envisioned as providing a context within which the organization of the self finds a sense of belonging, participation, sharing, meaningful involvement, and relevance. We do not have far to go in our own experience to understand the importance of this dynamic in human life and experience. If the paranoid process operates in certain ways to separate and divide us from a sense of communion and belonging with our fellow men, that same process creates pressures that drive us in the direction of establishing another context, another matrix, within which these needs can be adequately satisfied.

This inherent dynamic lies behind the shaping of social groupings and provides the inner dynamism for social processes. At its most pathological extreme, these same dynamisms find their distorted expression in the creation of a paranoid pseudocommunity. Even without such a persecutory confabulation on a larger scale, the persecutory bond, which is established between the paranoid individual and his persecutors or the terrifying forces that threaten him, serves as a form of paranoid construction that reinforces his projective delusions; these in turn serve to stabilize and consolidate the pathogenic sense of self that has formed itself around the core introjective configurations having to do with victimhood and vulnerability. Thus the victim-introject is a constant feature of these pathological expressions, yet it forms the core around which the individual's fragile sense of self is able to achieve some sense of perdurance and cohesiveness.

Developmental Aspects

I have noted in passing the role of the paranoid process in development, but since that role is of considerable significance it will merit further discussion.[4] In terms of my present focus, the critical influences of the paranoid process come to bear on the differentiation and articulation of both self- and object-representations. Through the operation and interplay of the mechanisms of introjection and projection, the intrapsychic components around which the emerging sense of self takes place are gradually established. The commerce of these processes, in other words, contributes both to the organization of object-representations and to the gradual internalization of object-representational elements to compose the core elements of an intrapsychic substructural organization.

These inner structural modifications and the organization of object-representations are in the beginning primitive, undifferentiated, and global. Only gradually does the process build up the residues, both internally and objectively, and increase the degree of differentiation between these elements so that the critical developmental step of the differentiation between self and object can begin to take place. Thus it is the operation of these processes in the earliest stages of psychic development that lays the ground for the emerging distinction between what is internal and what is external.

We can translate this process into the more familiar terms

4. An amplified discussion may be found in Meissner, 1977.

established by Margaret Mahler's (1975) research into the separation-individuation process. In Mahler's terms, the infant begins life in a state of autistic immersion within the mother-child unit. Within this normal autistic unity there is no differentiation, but rather a state of absolute merging, a condition of primitive hallucinatory disorientation in which need satisfaction belongs to the child's own global sense of omnipotent and primary narcissism. In this phase, there is no distinction in the child's experience between internal and external stimuli.

Within this omnipotent autistic orbit, the infant's waking experience centers around the continuing efforts to achieve physiological homeostasis. The mother's ministrations are not distinguishable from the infant's own tension-reducing processes—including urination, defecation, coughing, spitting, and so forth. Little by little, however, the infant begins to differentiate between the pleasurable and the less pleasurable or painful qualities of his experience. Differentiation is achieved only in terms of levels of tension. Gradually a dim awareness of the mother as a need-satisfying object begins to take shape in the child's experience, but the child still functions as though he and the mother form an omnipotent system, within which the duality is contained within a common boundary. Distancing emerges without separation. Gratification is sought from an emerging and distancing configuration ("nipple") that is not yet perceived as an object. This marks the transition to a more symbiotic phase of the child's development of which the essential feature is a delusional omnipotent fusion with the representation of the mother, as well as the delusional maintenance of a sense of common boundary between these two physically separate individuals.

It is in terms of these primitive physiological affect states, governed by the experiences of pleasure and unpleasure, that the first differentiations begin to emerge. The cathectic attachment to the mother and the response to her ministrations is governed by the pressure of physiological needs. In the symbiotic phase, primary narcissism still prevails but in a less absolute form than it had in the first few weeks of life. The perception dawns ever so dimly that need satisfaction derives from a need-satisfying object—even though that object is still retained within the orbit of the omnipotent symbiotic unity. Only to the extent that separation begins to take place does the infant experience receiving milk that is not his own narcissistic (omnipotent) creation.

As these developments take place there is a critical shift of cathexis from a predominantly proprioceptive-enteroceptive focus toward the sensory perceptive and peripheral aspects of the infant's body. This is a major shift of cathexis and is essential for the development of a body-ego. At this juncture, the operation of projective mechanisms comes into play, not merely to contribute to the construction of a more or less separate need-satisfying object, but to begin to serve the specific defensive functions of deflecting more destructive and unneutralized aggressive impulses beyond the gradually emerging body-self boundaries.

As this developmental process works itself out, the organization of object-representations not only is contributed to by external inputs, derived from external reality and, particularly and most significantly, from the primary objects of the infant's experience, but also is modified in some degree by the interplay between such inputs and projective elements. The organization of object-representations becomes increasingly differentiated as the child's cognitive capacities become more developed and articulated. Thus the capacity for the development of sensory and perceptual images, the gradual emergence of more complex forms of memory organization—shifting from more immediate and stimulus-bound forms of memory processing to the gradual emergence of more sophisticated and persistent forms of recognitional and finally evocative memory—the emergence of object constancies, and a variety of important influences from various forms of developmental learning, all contribute in meaningful and important ways to the gradual building-up, differentiation, and organization of object-representations (Meissner, 1974).

As the object-representation is increasingly elaborated, elements of the object-representation are correlatively internalized and introjected as parts of the infant's globally emerging and relatively undifferentiated sense of self. Even in the earliest phases of the symbiotic matrix, these internalizations are taking place so that critical elements of the inchoate core of the infant's self are being shaped. At this point, we can only guess at the significance of the balance of pleasurable versus unpleasurable components and the significance of the contribution of maternal attitudes to these nascent stirrings within the child. Winnicott (1965) has stressed the importance of "good-enough mothering" and a "holding" environment in the laying down of these primitive, yet crucial, early internalizations.

As these processes continue their interplay, the organization of elements of the self become more decisive and is more clearly and definitively separated from representations of the object. This process has been described by Mahler and her coworkers (1975) in terms of separation and individuation. In the view I am proposing here, projection and introjection are the inner mechanisms which subserve the overriding process of separation-individuation. At each step of the separation-individuation process, there is a critical reworking of internalized elements that gradually allows the child to establish a more autonomous sense of self and to separate himself from the dependency on the parental object. In this sense, the individuation would seem to be related to the building-up of an articulated sense of self through progressively differentiated introjections, while the gradual separation from the matrix of parental dependence is accomplished through the progressive projective modification and delineation of object-representations.

The process is even more complex. The building-up and integration of introjective components sets into operation critical identificatory processes that extend the processes of internalization and structuralization at a metapsychologically distinct level. These identifications have to do with the structural integration of the ego and with the transformation of superego (introjective) elements in terms of their integration with ego structures (Meissner, 1972). Reflexively, this further order of structural integration sustains and consolidates the organization and experience of the self. The degree to which such structuralizing identifications are brought into play is a function of the degree to which introjective formations are conflict-free, unambivalent, and not caught up in the pressures of drive and defense.

The threat to the separation-individuation process is particularly that of separation anxiety. Mahler has described the various forms in which separation anxiety expresses itself, and the distortion that can work in the normal progression of separation and individuation. Separation as an inherent threat to development not only arises from the natural developmental impulse in the child and his burgeoning wishes and autonomous self-determination and expression, but also can be reinforced and intensified by the reactions of the maternal figure. If the mother reacts to the child's bids for autonomy by excessive rejection and precipitant pushing of the child away from the comforting support of his dependence on her, the child is forced into a premature posture of self-sufficiency. On the other hand, if the mother is excessively threatened by the loss of the child as a dependent appendage, her efforts will be directed toward stalling his bids for relative autonomy and a prolongation of symbiotic dependence.

These varieties of maladaptive emergence from the state of maternal dependence can play upon the interaction of projection and introjection in a variety of ways. These distortions create defensive pressures, which make it necessary for the child's development to rely excessively on the utilization of these mechanisms in ways that are specifically and excessively caught up in defensive patterns. Thus, an excess of separation anxiety can lead the child to resort to an excessively regressive and global introjection of the parental image as a defensive means for preserving the contact with the need-satisfying dependency-gratifying object and as a means of preserving narcissistic integrity. The basic threat, after all, of separation anxiety at this level is the loss of the object. That object, in turn, is essential to the preservation of the infant's sense of narcissistic integrity and omnipotence. If the infant is allowed to make the separation from the maternal orbit without excessive stirring of separation anxiety, introjection will in fact take place, but not under the intense pressures of narcissistic need and defensive exigency.

As the developmental process advances, there is a progressive modification of infantile narcissism and an increasing differentiation of the sense of self, which gradually modifies the quality and nature of the introjections involved at each phase and correspondingly changes the quality of defensive organization. At each phase of the separation-individuation process, there is an increasing capacity for autonomous existence and a diminishing intensity of the child's dependence on need-satisfying objects. As the respective differentiation of object- and self-representations and their inherent stability is gradually increased, there emerges an enlarging capacity for toleration of the separateness of objects.

The capacity to tolerate the separateness of objects is perhaps one of the primary goals of the development in object relationships. It implies that the object-representation has been sufficiently developed so that the realistic qualities of the object are recognized and acknowledged, with a minimal complement of projective distortion. Thus the discrimination between one's self and the object is clearly established and maintained. In fact, the capacity to relate to the object in relatively realistic terms and to tolerate the separateness and autonomous independence of such objects is intimately related to the stability and cohesiveness of the self. The capacity for realistic object relationships depends upon the organization of a sense of self that has at its core the internalization of a good and loving parent, which serves as the focal point for the integration of successively positive introjective elements. Modell (1968) has expressed this relationship succinctly in the following terms:

> The cohesive sense of identity in the adult is a sign that there has been a 'good enough' object relationship in the earliest period of life. Something has been taken in from the environment that has led to the core of the earliest sense of identity, a core which permits further ego maturation. . . . it is a fact that these individuals who have the capacity to accept the separateness of objects are those who have a distinct, at least in part, beloved sense of self. If one can be a loving parent to oneself, one can more readily accept the separateness of objects. This is a momentous step in psychic development. [p. 59]

At the same time, correlative to the emergence and integration of increasing self-cohesion and identity, there is a process of integration and consolidation taking place in the organization of object-representations that leads in the direction of object constancy (McDevitt, 1975; Meissner, 1974). This process evolves not only the perceptual object constancy, which allows for the consistency and persistence of perceptual experience under the constant variation of stimulus conditions, but also the more complex forms of libidinal object constancy that contribute to and form the basis of stable and relatively consistent and mature object relationships. Thus, the differentiation and consolidation of object-representations play their parts, along with the development of self-cohesiveness, in the articulation of important capacities to know and respond to external reality.

We are left, then, with a momentous conclusion—namely, that the capacity to know, recognize, and accept reality is a critical developmental achievement, and not a given or presumable quality of human cognition. Moreover, the attainment of that capacity depends upon the critical working-through of developmental issues and the gradual consolidation of a cohesive sense of self, along with a differentiated and objectively articulated capacity for object-representations. To the extent that object-representations are contaminated by defensive needs, which motivate the coloring and modification of object-representations by projective determinants, the capacity to know and understand reality is in that degree impaired.

In the discussion from this point on, we can only satisfy ourselves with a superficial sketching of the broad realms of human cognition and hope to link them with the aspects of the paranoid process that we have been discussing. In the ensuing sections, I will be examining the three broad areas of human cognitive functioning—the subjective, the transitional, and the area of realistic cognition—in an attempt to indicate their complex relationships with the paranoid process. Unfortunately, I can be little more than programmatic in these areas, since they represent relatively unexplored areas in terms of psychoanalytic implications. In this sense, we stand only at the beginning of an immense theoretical task.

The Realm of Subjective Experience

The realm of subjective experience is the area of specific psychoanalytic investigation. The psychoanalytic vantage point is taken within the context of subjective experience and views all other data resources, whether they concern themselves with historical factual detail or with current ongoing experience, from that special vantage point. Kohut (1959) has made the point that the phenomena that we designate as mental, psychic, or psychological include by implication the idea that the mode of observation of such phenomena involves introspection and empathy as essential constituents. He writes:

> The inner world cannot be observed with the aid of our sensory organs. Our thoughts, wishes, feelings and fantasies cannot be seen, smelled, heard, or touched. They have no existence in physical space, and yet they are real, and we can observe them as they occur in time: through introspection in ourselves, and through empathy (i.e., vicarious introspection) in others. [p. 459]

Moreover, introspection and empathy are the modalities of psychoanalytic cognition par excellence. The analytic patient is required to give free rein to his powers of introspection in his attempts to free associate. Consequently, the resistances to free association are at the same time impediments to the exercise of introspection. Similarly, it is the capacity for empathic experience—that is to say, the sensitivity of the analyst's own capacity to experience his inner states as resonating with the patient's inner experience—that provides him with important clues and avenues of access to the understanding of the patient's inner world.

The complexity of subjective experience and the variety and shading of its inherent qualities provide us with the basis for a distinction—even though the elements of the distinction are difficult to disentangle experientially and may in fact be combined in varying degrees. Introspection is, in effect, a form of self-observation. The activity of self-observation requires some degree of experienced distance between the introspecting self and the introspected self. Those elements

of the self that are thus cognized are to that degree objectified, even though they do not become objective. The introspected aspects of the self remain part of the self, retained
within the sphere of the subjective experience of the self—
yet somehow distanced, somehow objectified, capable of
inspection, representation, and examination. Yet at the same
time, in the process of such objectifying introspection, the
experiencing self does not lose contact with the originating
source of the introspective activity. While there is an experienced split within the self-cognition, it remains a split within
the self, and not a differentiation between or separation
between self and object. It is this introspective split between
the experiencing and self-observant capacity of the patient
that is basic to the therapeutic alliance and the establishing of
the therapeutic situation.

The point I am making here is that introspection is a
heterogeneous experience, which is related to the organization of introjects. The introjects serve as structural elements
in the organization of the self and enjoy a greater or lesser
degree of internalization (Meissner, 1971). Some of the introjective content, therefore, is maintained more or less at the
periphery of the experienced self—in other words, in the
process of internalization, derived from the experience of
objects through the integration of object-representations,
that which is internalized in a greater or lesser degree retains
the stamp of its origins, namely, the quality of object deriva-
tion and object relatedness. Thus the introjective content
holds a greater or lesser degree of internalization within the
organization of the self and is more or less objectified as a
potential object of introspective experience.

Specific introjective formations may be integrated more or
less at the periphery of subjective experience in the sense of
Schafer's (1968a) "primary process presences," and thus attain a relatively more objectified, somewhat distanced, often
dissociated or quasi-autonomous status within the organiza-

tion of the self. Sandler (1960) has noted that such introjective formations, which in part contribute to the building up of the superego, often have a quasi-autonomous quality in the organization of the self that enables them to serve as the internalized source of gratification or aggression—replacements for the external parental objects. Or introjective formations may be more closely integrated with the internal aspects of the self and thus carry with them a closer association with the experience of activity, intention, purposefulness, and so forth. Schafer (1968b) has described these dimensions of relative activity and passivity of internalized contents.

This consideration raises an important metapsychological issue—namely, the relationship between the experienceable organization of the self and the tripartite entities. As Kohut (1971) has noted, the organization of the self and the organization of the structural entities of the tripartite intrapsychic organization cannot be simply identified. The self-organization is much closer to experience and operates at a different level of psychic organization than the structural entities. Moreover, the organization of the self is more explicitly related to the vicissitudes of narcissism than are the ego and superego.

In addition, the structural entities in the strict theoretical sense are understood to be organizations of specific functions. This concept applies not only to the ego as such but also to the superego. Even though the theory at various points attributes more or less personalized, anthropomorphized metaphors to the operation of these structures, they nonetheless can be given an adequate account within the theory simply by a cataloguing of specific functions belonging to either structure.

A defect in the structural theory from this point of view is that it has difficulty in integrating and accounting for complex experiential states. One of the major difficulties in the structural concept is that it leaves no room for the experience of one's own self as an integrated and relatively autonomous self-originating focus of action. The lack of a personal ego in the systematic psychoanalytic ego psychology has been a recurrent point of theoretical criticism—a point that has been belabored particularly by Guntrip (1973). If the realm of subjective experience can be specifically related to the cognition of and organization of the self, then there is room for a subjective experience of self as an active and organizing principle within the intrapsychic apparatus. Our understanding of the ego as the experiencing source of intrapsychic cognition and activity would seem to imply, as a requisite for maintaining the unity of the human personality, the ultimate identity of the functional ego with the subjective experiencing self.

There has been some ambiguity in the understanding of self-observation in psychoanalytic metapsychology. It was originally envisoned as a function of the superego, undoubtedly related to the superego's function of self-evaluation and criticism. But the function of observation and judgment involved seem much more properly attributed to the ego. Thus, in this perspective, the ego is the ultimate agency of introspection. Or at least, ego functions must be involved in the introspective activity. Along the same lines, the self is introspectable insofar as it is representable—that is, insofar as self-representations are the cognitive media of self-cognition and introspection. In this sense, only those aspects of the self that stand at some remove from the subjective polarity of the self can be articulated in self-representations and therefore can become the objects of introspection. The introspective subject—that is, the self-ego as the originating source of inner experience—is not, therefore, representable. It can only be grasped in the subjective experience of the self as a knowing source of cognition or action—not as a represented component of the self.[5]

The critical point here was addressed in a note added by Gill to Rapaport's (1967) discussion of the relation of the superego to the self. He observes:

> The self in subjective experience is something which can observe itself. The ego is free of this: the ego is something which functions, it does not observe itself. That is why the topographic systems had to be discarded in favor of the structural systems—because the most important things about the ego are not at all conscious. The self will have to be so defined in the psychological apparatus that it is observable by an ego function which is at the same time defined as a subsidiary organization within the self. [p. 689]

Further, it is in terms of the complex relationships of ego and superego, and their relationship to the self-organization, that some of the complex problems of the vicissitudes of narcissism must be worked out. Complex problems of subjective experience, affects, consciousness, and altered states of both subjective and objective awareness impinge upon these central theoretical concerns.

A specific question that has to do with the realm of subjective experience concerns the issue of self-cohesion. Such cohesion is, as I have suggested, a developmental achievement related to the progressive differentiation and resolution of

5. It should be noted that it is this heterogeneity of the organization of self-components that forced Schafer (1968a) to distinguish between the self-as-agent, the self-as-object, and the self-as-place. Schafer's inner objects, which he identified with introjects—the "primary process presences"—remain objectified, that is, as part of the self-as-object ("me"). The self-as-place has more or less explicit bodily reference, closely related to the body-ego. It is not clear that Schafer's self-as-agent is identical with the experiencing subject described here. Rather, he specifically locates the internal objects in the self-as-place, and not in the subjective self-as-agent and self-as-object.

infantile narcissism. The working-through of the crises of separation and individuation and the resolution and refinement of narcissistic vicissitudes lead in the direction of the establishing and maintaining of a cohesive sense-of-self. In terms of our present discussion, such cohesiveness is reflected in the integration of introjective formations that constitute the organization of the self to a greater or lesser degree. If such introjective formations are mutually compatible and can be integrated not only with each other but with the subjective experiencing ego-self, then the basis is laid for a mature, adaptive, autonomous, and functional sense of identity. To the extent that specific introjective formations remain contaminated by drive derivatives and fixations, those components resist integration and serve as the nidus for psychopathology.

An important point to be emphasized here is that introjective components are continually being reprocessed during the course of development by identifications (Meissner, 1972). Their function is similar to that described by Kohut (1971) in terms of "transmuting internalizations." Thus, relatively nonambivalent introjective organizations, or narcissistically integrated introjective configurations, serve as the object of further internalization processes that are metapsychologically distinct and provide the basis on which further structuralizing internalizations takes place so that introjective components can be transformed into ego and superego structures. As this further internalization takes place, introjective components are drawn farther away from the relatively passive and objectivized aspect of self-organization and are drawn into closer proximity to the subjective integration of the experiencing self.

Within the realm of subjective experience the organization of components of the self follows topographical principles, so that elements of the self are either descriptively unconscious, preconscious, or conscious. By inference, then, the self and the experience of self are not coextensive with consciousness. Thus, introjective contents may be subject to varying degrees of repression and, just as we have noted in reference to the paranoid process, may be removed from the areas of conscious experience by mechanisms of denial and projection. By projection, then, elements of the self can be removed from the experience of the self and located in the realm of objects. Within this context, the objective of the analytic process is to reactivate such introjective elements and bring them into contact with conscious experience. By hypothesis, when such introjective formations are sufficiently objectified and separated from the other aspects of the experience of self, they can be effectively abandoned and mourned.

It should be noted that the economy and organization of the introjects, together with their introspection and subjective experience, are intimately related to and expressive of affects. The experience of affects takes place uniquely within the realm of subjective experience. In this sense affects are an integral part of the organization and structure of the introjects. Thus, the internalization process that gives rise to internal objects serves to organize and integrate affective elements derived from specific drive determinants and vicissitudes, as shaped by the ongoing commerce with objects and as reflecting the parameters of those object relationships. The view taken here is that the close link between the affects and their integration with introjective formations means that it is particularly the affects that serve as the vehicle for the subjective experience of introjective organizations. Correspondingly, the affects tied up in repressed introjective formations also remain unconscious. The critical question here is the role of affects in the organization and experience of the self. Needless to say, the theoretical integration of affects with their correlative introjective organizations and their relevance to the structuring and experience of the self remain important metapsychological tasks for the future.

Transitional Experience

The concept of transitional objects or transitional phenomena stems from the work of Donald Winnicott (1971). Winnicott describes transitional objects as a developmental experience—that is, the infant's first attachment to an object as a substitute for the mothering figure. The transitional object is therefore the child's first original "not-me" possession. The onset of such transitional phenomena comes in roughly the second half of the first year of life, when the issues of separation from the mother begin to assert themselves. In Winnicott's view, the organization of transitional phenomena sets the conditions for a realm of illusory experience somehow intermediate between the experience of one's inner psychic reality and the experience of an external objective world. He comments:

> I am here staking a claim for an intermediate state between a baby's inability and his growing ability to recognize and accept reality. I am therefore studying the substance of *illusion,* that which is allowed to the infant, and which in adult life is inherent in art and religion, and which becomes the hallmark of madness when an adult puts too powerful a claim on the credulity of others, forcing them to acknowledge a sharing of illusion that is not their own. We can share a respect for *illusory experience,* and if we wish we may collect together and form a group on the basis of the similarity of our illusory experiences. This is a natural root of grouping among human beings. [p. 3]

The transitional object, therefore, is neither part of the realm of subjective inner experience nor part of the external shared experience of reality. Yet it is the possession of this transitional object in its intermediate realm of experience that allows the child eventually to separate from the infantile dependence on the mother, thus cushioning and by gradual increments increasing his capacity to tolerate her separateness. Accordingly, the transitional object embraces within its own organization elements of both the extrinsic reality and the child's inner world. Further, the emergence of transitional phenomena is paralleled by the beginnings of meaningful introjections correlated with the distancing and incremental separation of child and mother within the symbiotic orbit. My position here is that the transitional object and its correlative transitional phenomena are organized through the interplay of projection and introjection.

Intrapsychically, what is being formed is a transitional object-representation, compounded of elements derived from the real objects together with projective elements derived from the subjective inner world. The attachment to the external transitional object itself is thus paralleled by intrapsychic developments that take place as a form of intermediate object modification that is ultimately in the service of critical internalizations. The transitional object is created by the infant in order to bring this developmental gap, and to serve as a vehicle through which he not only buffers the threats of separation but begins to relate more meaningfully to reality. As Winnicott notes, when the mother's adaptation to the infant's inner needs is "good-enough," this allows the infant to create the illusion that there is an external reality that is somehow congruent to the infant's creative capacity.

The existence of such transitional phenomena remains an operative part of the child's growing experience. This area of intermediate illusory experience never entirely disappears, but rather is transformed and integrated into the individual's experience as an area of privileged creativity or play—in which there is no need for a decision as to whether what it contains is altogether real or altogether subjective. Winnicott (1971) observes:

in health the transitional object does not 'go inside' nor does the feeling about it necessarily undergo repression. It is not forgotten and it is not mourned. It loses meaning, and this is because the transitional phenomena have become diffused, have become spread out over the whole intermediate territory between 'inner psychic reality' and 'the external world as perceived by two persons in common,' that is to say, over the whole cultural field. [p. 5]

It is worth reflecting for a moment on the implications of such a transitional realm of experience. My view here is that the transitional realm is compounded out of elements of object experience, related to the formation of object-representations, and projective components derived from the realm of subjective inner experience. Certainly, as Winnicott suggests, this enables us to envision the manner in which the whole realm of creativity and the forms of self-expression operate. The illusory quality of artistic productions and their symbolic value, expressive of aspects of the artist's inner world, fit this model quite aptly.

The model, however, of such a realm of illusory experience demands further exploration and understanding. While the illusory quality of a painting or a piece of poetry is more immediate and obvious, the quality of illusion as an expression of creativity becomes less obvious in other areas of human creativity, such as, for instance, the scientific. The way in which, for example, the complex mathematical and symbolic manipulations of theoretical physics serve as a vehicle for the creative illusion within the scientist's experience—a realm of experience that is neither wholly subjective nor objective—challenges our usual view of such knowing activities. The sense in which the scientific community, at a farther remove, operates in terms of areas of shared illusion in going about its cooperative business requires even further illumination. To bring it even closer to home, the sense in which psychoanalytic understanding itself may serve as an area of such shared creative illusion challenges our more traditional paradigms of psychological understanding.

Closer to our own psychoanalytic understanding, however, we can suggest that important aspects of the psychoanalytic process partake of the illusory quality of the realm of transitional experience. Most particularly, I would focus on the transference and the transference neurosis as the area where such illusory qualities enter the psychoanalytic process with particular pertinence. I would suggest that the transference experience can be envisioned as a shared creative experience on the part of both the analyst and the analysand, in which the activation of introjective configurations within the patient gives rise to projective derivatives that somehow mingle with the forming object-representation of the analyst to provide a composite phenomenon, a transitional object operating within a realm of illusory experience that re-creates in a dramatic, intensely affectively toned way, derivatives of infantile experience. This experience, however, does not arise solely within the patient, but is entered into and shared by the analyst in a specific and therapeutically useful form of creative collaboration. It is by reason of participation in this illusory realm that the analyst is capable both of meaningful empathic responsiveness as a vehicle for understanding the patient's experience, and of countertransference reactions that reflect his own projective involvement in the creative illusory experience of the transference.

In this sense, as the patient and analyst emerge into this shared experience, they participate in a form of transitional object relationship. In the usual context of analytic therapy, however, the capacity of the patient for object relationship is not limited to this transitional modality. He is also able to form a more realistic object relationship with the analyst, which ultimately serves as the basis for the therapeutic alliance. As Modell (1968) has indicated, however, some forms of psychopathology reflect the incapacity of the patient to transcend the transitional mode of object relatedness, or at least an inability to sustain realistic object relations in any meaningful way. In the transitional object relationship, the object is envisioned within the illusory realm of experience and cannot be clearly conceptualized in an objective mode. This relates to Brodey's (1965) distinction of object-mode and image-mode in object relationships. The image-mode reflects the inability to separate self and object in narcissistically impaired individuals. Narcissistic impairments prevent the articulation and discrimination of the object as a separate real object and its investment with object-libido.

Thus, the transitional object spans the distance between the realm of that which is created from the subject's inner world and that which exists in the environment. The individual does not simply create the transitional object, as if it were a hallucination, but rather appropriates an object that is something in the environment. It remains outside of the self, but its separated status outside of the self is only partially acknowledged. It is a form of creative environment insofar as its properties reflect elements of the subject's inner world. Within the analytic setting, the analyst's real personality, his separateness as an individual person with his own interests, investments, and commitments independent of the patient, cannot be wholly tolerated. In this modality of object relationship, the image of the analyst is created to be congruent with the patient's need. The analyst then exists for the patient alone, and the relationship is tense, exclusive, and narcissistically gratifying.

Modell (1968) has succinctly summarized the quality of such transitional object relationships:

the transitional object is a substitute for the actual environment—a substitute that creates the illusion of encapsulating the subject from the dangers of the environment. The transitional object is not a hallucination—it is an object that does exist 'in the environment,' separate from the self, but only partially so. It is given form and structure, that is, it is created by the needs of the self. The relationship of the subject to the object is fundamentally ambivalent; the qualities of the object are magical and hence there is an illusion of connectedness between the self and the object. The relation of the subject to the object is primarily exploitive, the subject feels no concern for the needs of the object and cannot acknowledge that the object possesses his own separateness and individuality. The transitional object relationship is dyadic—it admits no others. [p. 40]

As Modell suggests, the transitional modality of object relationship is found in certain forms of psychotic psychopathology and in the borderline syndrome as well. These, however, form the pathological extremes. Intermingled projective elements, which constitute the basis of the transitional object relationship, nonetheless operate in a variety of other pathological expressions and in a wide range of functional and adaptive human activities. It would seem likely that Kohut's (1971) description of self-object relationships represents another form of the transitional mode of object relatedness. Similarly, following Winnicott's lead, I can suggest that the transitional mode of relationship has significant implications for the formation of groups and for the genesis of shared symbolic experience, which are critical elements in human cultural involvement.

The Experience of Reality

In the historical beginning of the psychoanalytic experience, the nature of reality was more or less taken for granted.

In other words, there was a fairly self-evident and mutually validated consensus about the existence and nature of an external reality. The development of psychoanalysis in its early phases could take place within that more or less stable context. I have already commented on the role of reality in Freud's early thinking, its fading into the background subsequent to the *retorquendo* of the seduction hypothesis, and finally its reemergence in a position of renewed significance in his later thinking.

Critical focal points in Freud's attempts to deal with reality had to do with the reality principle, with the function of reality testing, and with the vantage point of the ego in the structural theory as mediating among the demands of id, superego, and reality. The impulse to turn in the direction of reality received a significant boost from the addition of the adaptive hypothesis that Hartmann added to the metapsychological perspectives. In these terms, the apparatuses of primary autonomy were somehow preadapted and ordered to the realm of real experience so that their coordination to reality was more or less maturationally determined. The emphasis here, however, was still on the development of psychic reality as an intrapsychic phenomenon that took place in the context of the assumed stability of the reality field. Thus Hartmann could appeal to the need for adaptation to a presumably unvarying "average expectable environment." As Wallerstein (1973) has pointed out in his brilliant reassessment of the role of reality in analytic thinking, this presumption is no longer operative. He points out that "what's new in emphasis or perspective in this is the explicit view that—in order to achieve maximal explanatory leverage —the outer must be seen in as intricately patterned and discriminated and *variable* a manner as we have developed in order to look at the inner" (p. 15).

We can usefully remind ourselves that the task we have before us here is limited to merely surveying a vast complex area. We are not at the point of building the edifice—not even of putting up the initial scaffolding. We are more or less at the stage of staking out potential vantage points for future construction. We are dealing with disparate areas of dynamic flux which follow their own respective principles of organization and process. The ultimate question must deal with those factors that contribute to and allow degrees of congruence between the inner subjective world of experience and the objective world of what is experienced. That congruence can be tested in a variety of ways—reaching from the endless variety of private and pragmatic testings that constitute the fabric of daily experience (Dr. Johnson's rock), through a variety of forms of predictive verification, to more or less complex techniques of consensual validation. The question, then, is not the strictly epistemological one of whether and what external reality exists independent of mental operations, but rather the psychological concern over the conditions that contribute to or impede the potential congruence between knowledge and reality.

Hartmann's (1956) view of reality is a composite one—on the one hand there is a given, preexisting reality existing externally, and on the other there is a reality that is the creative construction of man's cognitive capacity. Thus, the world of personal reality stands in contrast to the experience of objective reality, and the two exist in irreducible polarization. It is the opposition of the reality of science (objective) to the reality of personal experience based on meanings, values, personal significance, and affective experiences.

Our discussion of the developmental aspects of the paranoid process drew us to the conclusion that the sense of reality is a developmental achievement that reflects the vicissitudes of object relations, and particularly the emerging capacity for separation and the tolerance of the separateness of objects. Thus the inner resources of the ego, including both the emergence of the cognitive capacities of the ego and the differentiation and stabilization of self, march hand in hand with the articulation and differentiation of a sense of reality. In Loewald's (1951) terms, "the primitive ego detaches an external world from itself" (p. 14). But the dichotomy between the objective knowledge of reality and the personal knowledge of reality cannot be so discretely maintained. Even our most objective systems of knowing—the physical sciences —cannot escape from their immersion in human experience. In this connection, Polanyi (1959) observes "that no meaningful knowledge (not even, that is, in the so-called hard sciences, the physical sciences) can be acquired, except by an act of comprehension which consists in merging our awareness of a set of particulars into our focal awareness of their joint significance" (p. 44).

The upshot of these considerations is that the nature of reality is by no means clear or unequivocal. In terms of the cognitive dimensions of the paranoid process, my conclusion is that there is no realm of human experience that is not potentially (if not actually) influenced by the interplay of introjective and projective mechanisms. Thus the knowledge of reality and our experience of our objective environment, whether physical or social, is caught up in a continual commerce, interchange, interaction, and reciprocal influencing between the inner world of man's experience and the external reality. This does not mean, however, that man's experience of his world is delusional; it may, and often does, become so. But the point is rather that, even in the most objectified and realistic dimensions of man's knowing experience, that experience continues to be a basically human one that cannot extrapolate itself from the rich complex of his inner life.

To pose the question in slightly different terms, the problem can be cast in terms of the difficulty of finding that discrimination point at which the transitional realm of illusory experience passes over into the realm of objective experience.

In terms of intrapsychic formations, this requires the differentiation between transitional object-representations and, more strictly speaking, object-representations as such. However, this is not merely a matter of cognitive reorganization in the framework of the subject's representational world (Sandler and Rosenblatt, 1962). It is also a question of the degree to which structural components of the organization of the self come to bear by way of projection on representational organizations.

Turning more explicitly to the levels of cognitive organization in objective experience, we are confronted with a vast, extremely complex, richly interwoven, and far-reaching series of cognitional phenomena. It must be stated at the very outset that human cognitive experience is an integrated experience. While we are able to make introspective delineations and conceptual distinctions between aspects of man's cognitive functioning, in the concrete order it is difficult to separate aspects of cognition from the other interrelated dimensions of cognitive functioning operating within the same experimental context. Thus, if we can separate levels of cognitive organization and functioning—as, for example, the areas of sensation and sensory experience, perception and perceptual experience, conceptualization and, finally, at the most developed and elaborated level of cognitive functioning, various forms of belief systems—we cannot at the same time treat them as relatively autonomous and independent forms of knowing. Rather, they are combined in complex forms of interaction. The knowledge of external reality existing independent of the subject requires some form of sensory input, but that input is not simply a given: in some degree and in some manner it is an interactional product of other levels of cognitive processing.

At the lowest level of cognitive organization, the order of sensation and sensory processing, we are dealing with cognitive elements that are in the closest relationship to the organization and functioning of the sensory receptors and the neurologically based central nervous system organizations that process and integrate such sensory input information into cognitive patterns. Thus an examination of sensory processes would have to look at the nature of sensory input information in relation to specific sensory modalities. This would concern the way in which the visual system, for example, picks up fragments of sensory input information and gradually modifies and integrates it into more complex components. This processing begins to take place at the earliest interface between the patterning of visual illumination and stimulation of the retina. The retina is in fact a sensory extension of the central nervous system, so that input stimulation is immediately translated into patterns of neuronal firing, which are then transferred to higher levels of the visual system, and at each level reprocessed and reorganized into an integrated visual experience. The work of neurophysiologists in recent years has only begun to suggest the ways in which central nervous system information processing takes place and the complex neural networks required to produce them.

At this level the ultimate product of the sensory processing is the formation of an image that reflects the dimensions and qualities of the external object. The extent to which the imaging process is congruent with the structure of the external reality remains a nagging question, but from a biological (as well as psychological) point of view, the sensory apparatuses have evolved adaptively in order to be able to recognize, discriminate, and respond to patterns of external stimulation. This adaptive dimension is not only in terms of the overall biological adaptability of human experience and environmental interaction and control, but also in terms of the more or less normal functioning of individual men in the ongoing commerce with the environment—serves to reinforce and support the sense of reality and the capacity for reality testing. The fact that there is a certain variability in the capacity for processing sensory input information, or that the processing can be disturbed in various pathological states or states of variation of consciousness, does not undercut the basic hypothesis.

Our personal experience of the external world seems immediate and direct. The organized immediacy of that experience, however, is mediated by a complex series of sensory processes—whether in the present moment or as residues of past experience. The activation of sensory receptors and encoding systems that relay signals to various levels of brain integration serves to mediate a mental construct by which input signals are organized and represented. This was the point of Brunswik's (1952) well-known lens analogy—relatively diffuse sensory input is focused by central nervous system information processing to form representational images with a higher degree of congruence to the external world than at the receptor level.

It is rather remarkable, in fact, that this process works at all. The capacity for the human nervous system to handle input information is quite circumscribed. Miller's (1956) famous estimate of seven bits of information as the limit of sensory capacity is somewhat stunning in view of the known complexity and capacity of these processes. The upshot is that the reliance on strategies of selection and organization of such data plays a maximal role in cognition. The data derived from sensory channels are in fact constructed as a method for maximal utilization of sensory input. The patterning of such constructions depends on circumstances, motives, goals, and a host of other psychological variables.

It should not be forgotten, however, that the taking in of sensory information and its processing are not given or automatic. Rather, they are subject to a variety of influences that reflect a complex interaction between inner dimensions of the neurological and psychological processing of information and the activity of the sensorireceptors. The very operation of these receptors in all sensory systems is not only variable but selective—that is to say, the very reception of sensory information is continually being modified and influenced by feedback mechanisms from higher levels of central nervous system organization that introduce a factor of selectivity and variability in the very acquisition of sensory inputs. These selective feedback processes may in turn be in the service of higher-order needs and motivations.

Whatever can be said about this early level of cognitive organization, our theoretical understanding of the operation of these processes must leave room for the imposition of higher-order patterns of organization not only on the patterning of sensory information—for example, in terms of image formation—but also on the receptivity and selectivity of sensory input data at the very threshold of information acquisition. These phenomena are well known clinically. Hysterical blindness, hallucinations, denial of real events, selective attention, and other pathological distortions of the sensory processes suggest that the veridical perception of reality depends not only on specific integrative capacities within the sensory system, but also on the coordination of those systems with higher-level information processing resources.

My own preference is to keep the level of sensory organization discrete from and differentiated from the level of perceptual organization. The perceptual function involves a more complex and higher level of cognitive functioning, and correspondingly is much more reflective of and influenced by inner psychic components. The perceptual level is the first level of cognitive organization that can be said to be specifically psychological. We move beyond the level of sensory processing and its intimate involvement in neuropsychological systems to a more complex level, in which we must begin to confront the issues of higher-level cognitive functions as well as forms of organization.

At this level the question of imagination arises, and also

the various forms of memory and memory organization, dream cognition, perceptual defense, forms of social perception, and so forth. Beres (1960a), for example, has defined imagination as "the capacity to form a *mental representation* of an *absent* object, an affect, a body function, or an instinctual drive" (p. 327). But the same capacity must also operate in the perception of a present reality. Thus the cognitive function of imagination is in part the adaptation to reality—whatever else its uses in the service of fantasy and imaginative creativity (Beres, 1960a, b). The imaginative process involves complex levels of cognitive organization that reflect the integration of a number of ego-functions, each of which is susceptible to the vicissitudes of regression and conflict. The operation of imagination, therefore, in the perceptual process may reflect varying degrees of primary- versus secondary-process organization.

The perceptual process itself cannot be regarded as simply an acknowledgment of or acceptance of the products of sensory processing. Rather, the perceptual product is a complex result of the interaction of a variety of intrapsychic influences. Perceptual process involves a complex reorganization and interpretation of sensory images in terms of which the perceptual product is increasingly determined by the inner constellation of needs and drives and defenses. An examination of the phenomenon of perceptual defense, for example, indicates the degree to which perceptual organization reflects such inner dynamic processes. The process of perception, then, becomes overlaid with emotional needs, drive derivatives, personal significances, meanings, values, and so forth.

Perception thus becomes the realm of personal knowledge and is highly susceptible to the potential influence of projective influences. We have already observed that projective influences play particularly on the experience of object relationships, so that the area of social perception is one in which such influences play a particularly important role. It is here, too, that important interpretive dimensions of the perceptual process frequently play themselves out. In this regard, addressing the problem from a different theoretical orientation, Money-Kyrle (1961) has commented:

> There is a contant interchange between the outer world of perception, and conscious thought, and this inner world. . . . The very perception of a situation involves the projection into it of a meaning derived, in part from conscious or pre-conscious memories of similar situations, in part from primary, or near primary, symbols which belong to our innate endowment. The situation, with its symbolic meaning from which it derives most of its emotional importance, is also 'taken in,' internalised, and usually modified inside in accordance with the mechanisms operating there. If this internal and largely unconscious manipulation is comparatively free from paranoid-schizoid and manic elements, it will provide the unconscious basis for rational thought about the situation. But so far as there is violent splitting, projection or denial, in the inner world—mechanisms which are products of the destructive impulse and which, by preventing its fusion with more positive impulses, operate to maintain its strength—the result, when reprojected, will falsify the picture of the external world as well. Moreover, the pattern of the projective-introjective cycle elicited by a current situation tends to repeat that of the response to the last similar situation, and so back to infancy when these patterns were laid down. So far, therefore, as the paranoid-schizoid or manic defences of infancy were not overcome at the time, they will be likely to continue to operate in the inner world, and to distort the perception of the outer. [pp. 83–84]

In these terms, however, it is not simply the projective aspects of the paranoid process that are being expressed; other components of the paranoid process are at work. The modification of the perception of complex stimulus situations may also be modified by the overriding organization of the paranoid construction. In complex social interactions, for example, the paranoid construction may require that certain perceptual elements be minimized, overlooked, forgotten, repressed, ignored, or even denied. Such cognitive operations are not immediately reflective of the projective dimension itself, but rather operate in more broadly conceived fashion to provide a cognitive matrix within which such projections can be systematically integrated and sustained. This may also express itself in terms of cognitive styles; but the complex relationships between cognitive styles, forms of perceptual defense, and interaction with other cognitive elements remain to be explored and understood.

We are concerned here with the construction of a perceptual-and-conceptual integration of cognitive experience of the real that takes place within each individual consciousness. Each individual organizes and constructs his own phenomenological 'world' or 'world-model' (Money-Kyrle, 1961) by which he represents the external world and in terms of which he articulates his responsiveness to his external environment. Through this model he responds to and engages in the matrix of stimulation—selectively, adaptively, defensively, and with a variety of degrees and qualities of motivation. The individual cannot be divorced from his representational world—the organization and cathectic investment in this cognitive organization reflects and expresses the core of each personality.

The level of conceptualization shifts the focus of cognitive organization away from the level of concrete perceptual organization, which is more or less linked to specific sensory inputs and the realm of concrete cognitive experience, to a more general and possibly abstract level of cognitive organization. It is at this level that we have to deal not only with elements of concept formation but with elements of intellectual judgment as well. It is at the level of the formation of judgments that the truth value of cognitive formation becomes a relevant issue. Such judgments include not only judgments of fact as related to reality-testing and the sense of reality, but also evaluative judgments. We enter here the complex realm of categorical versus existential judgments, or objective versus organic meaning (Weisman, 1965).

Thus, the sense of the real and the evaluation of meanings and significances are not simply the byproducts of inner dynamics and the capacity for objectification. Rather, they are caught up in processes of social influence and the sharing of such meanings and significances, which dictate the terms of the consensual validation by which parameters of our experience are accepted and integrated in our view of the real world (Lichtenstein, 1974). Where such conceptual and consensual validation breaks down, we refer to the pathology of delusions. It is often difficult, however, to draw a line between pathological delusion formation and complex systems of shared illusions that may characterize large and significant cultural groupings. Once again we seem to be drawn back to that realm of transitional experience, the area of illusion that forms the matrix of cultural expression and experience. Thus, the shared beliefs of many may become the matrix within which reality is defined and experienced. The meaning of reality in such contexts becomes relative, and the conceptual integration involved in the sense of reality is correspondingly adaptively integrated.

At this level of conceptualization, we are dealing with the most complex and far-reaching systems of cognitive organization, which I have chosen to call "belief systems." Such belief systems may operate in a wide variety of socially and culturally determined contexts, whether they be religious, social, political, moral, or whatever. Such systems are complex constructions, elaborated forms of the paranoid construction, which serve to integrate and validate culturally devised attitudes and values. The most obvious examples that come to mind are religious belief systems; but other belief systems are often of equal importance in human affairs. Certainly, political ideologies play an overwhelmingly important role in the working out of the vicissitudes of human life. Thus, the Communist belief system is an elaborate ideology that serves to sustain certain attitudes, convictions, sets of values, and contexts of meaning, within which a certain patterning of life and behavior is played out. The ideology in this sense represents a paranoid construction that allows for and sustains other elements of the paranoid process. The extent to which such complex systems are pathological depends on the degree to which projective distortions and conceptualizations deviate from consensual validation. Certain forms of fanatical political belief may seem pathological to those who do not share such beliefs, but in the cultural matrix within which such a belief system functions, that ideology may be purposeful and adaptive. The fact that it serves to sustain pathological distortions and projections does not alter its cultural validity or significance.

In general, religious and political belief systems tend to offer the richest ground for pathological distortion, but they do not have an exclusive claim on pathology. Even those conceptual systems that we generally see in terms of maximal objectivity can also be seen in terms of the perspective of the paranoid process as operative belief systems of the same kind. Thus, objective natural science stands for a set of beliefs, attitudes, and values that dictate a particular orientation toward the world and an understanding of it. Not only does the scientific set of mind embrace a certain weltanschauung and an implicit ethical code, but the organization of scientific thinking itself tends to take place in terms of certain overriding paradigms (Kuhn, 1962). The paradigm is a shared set of convictions and attitudes that are embraced and adhered to by the scientific community. As Kuhn comments,

"A paradigm is what the members of a scientific community share, and, conversely, a scientific community consists of men who share a paradigm" (p. 176).

One of the pervasive paradigms of scientific theory is the objective paradigm, which postulates an objective world beyond the limits of experience—a world that scientific experimentation and theorizing progressively approximate. This is part of the scientific ideology or belief system that justifies and sustains the efforts and intentions of scientific work.[6] It goes without saying, in addition, that more specific forms of scientific paradigm, in terms of specific theories or constructs, may provide more or less private belief systems for individuals or groups of individuals. The history of science is filled with the gradual development of new paradigms, their confrontation with old paradigms, and a gradual conquest of the old by the new. Adherence to such belief systems, even though scientific, may become more than a matter of evaluation of objective evidences and theoretical understanding. Such systems may become vehicles for inner needs and motivations, which then shift the staunch adherence to them from the level of scientific conviction to that of delusion. The rigidity of such adherence may then take on a frankly paranoid quality.

Epilogue

At all of these levels of cognitive organization, then, we are confronted persistently with the same basic issues. The answers to the questions of what is inside and what is outside, of what is subjective and what is objective, do not avail themselves of easy resolutions. In an earlier and simpler day,

6. Only recently have we begun to question the ideological commitments embedded in scientific formulations, or even in scientific methods. Science is not an isolated noesis, but arises within a social process and is carried on within a matrix of active and determining social influences. The implicit role of various forms of ideology in scientific methods, particularly in the use of reductionistic paradigms, has been traced by Rose and Rose (1973) with reference to certain aspects of neurobiology.

psychoanalysis may have been able to allow itself the luxury of passing over these concerns and permitting certain basic if simplified assumptions about the nature of reality and our knowledge of it to stand unchallenged and unexamined. We no longer have that luxury, as I think the preceding assessment suggests.

But in making that admission, we open ourselves to even more complex and difficult problems than we have ever attempted to face before. The conclusion presented here is that the operation of the paranoid process plays itself out at every level of human cognitive experience and affects the organization of that experience in extremely complex ways. The conclusion brings us little solace, however, since it places a demand on us to explore further what has become a major theoretical concern.

The nature of reality, its impact on psychological functioning, its relationship to and influence on the processes of internalization and structuralization, which are so critically important developmentally and functionally, and lastly the role of reality and its implications for psychoanalytic treatment, are all areas that clamor for clarification and understanding.

The task is at least twofold. First, the advancement of understanding requires that we return in a more systematic fashion to an examination and evaluation of the data of modern psychology dealing with cognitive processes. The need for this effort in psychoanalysis was felt acutely by David Rapaport (1967) and his followers, and the exigency has hardly diminished since his pioneering efforts. The problem remains, and it has not simplified but has become more pressing and more difficult. Psychoanalysis requires a theoretical reassessment and integration of the understanding of cognitive processes, specifically in psychoanalytic terms, which would allow the understanding of such cognitive elements to be integrated meaningfully and productively with the rest of psychoanalytic theory.

The second part of the task before us lies closer to the traditional realm of psychoanalytic endeavor. We need to become more sensitive and responsive to the issues of real experience and the effects of real influences on the functioning of our patients. This applies not only in a developmental sense but also in the broader sense of the influence of social and cultural factors on the capacity for adaptation and maturity of functioning. If we keep these issues in the perspective of the paranoid process, we need not lose sight of the continuing interaction and mutual definition between reality and psychic structure. As the construction and perception of reality changes, new questions and theoretical challenges will be raised for psychoanalysis. The problem of the implications of changing perceptions of what is real for our understanding of id, ego, and superego functioning has already been raised (Lichtenstein, 1974). Thus the paranoid process continues to play itself out not only in individual histories but in human history as well.

REFERENCES

Beres, D. "Perception, Imagination, and Reality." *International Journal of Psycho-Analysis* 41 (1960a) : 327–34.
———. "The Psychoanalytic Psychology of Imagination." *Journal of the American Psychoanalytic Association* 8 (1960b) : 252–69.
Brodey, W. M. "On the Dynamics of Narcissism. I. Externalization and Early Ego Development." *Psychoanalytic Study of the Child* 20 (1965) : 165–93.
Brunswik, E. "The Conceptual Framework of Psychology." *International Encyclopedia of Unified Science,* vol. 1, no. 10. Chicago: University of Chicago Press, 1952.
Cameron, N. "Paranoid Conditions and Paranoia." In S. Arieti, ed., *American Handbook of Psychiatry,* vol. 1. New York: Basic Books, 1959.
Freud, A. *The Ego and the Mechanisms of Defense* (1936). New York: International Universities Press, 1966.

Freud, S. "Analysis of a Phobia in a Five-Year-Old Boy (1909)"; "From the History of an Infantile Neurosis (1918)." *Standard Edition of the Complete Psychological Works,* vols. 10, 17. London: Hogarth, 1955.

Guntrip, H. *Psychoanalytic Theory, Therapy, and the Self.* New York: Basic Books, 1973.

Hampshire, S. *Thought and Action* (1959). London: Chatto and Windus, 1965.

Hartmann, H. *Ego Psychology and the Problem of Adaptation* (1939). New York: International Universities Press, 1958.

————. "Notes on the Reality Principle (1956)." In H. Hartmann, *Essays on Ego Psychology.* New York: International Universities Press, 1964.

Jacobson, E. *The Self and the Object World.* New York: International Universities Press, 1964.

Kohut, H. "Introspection, Empathy, and Psychoanalysis." *Journal of the American Psychoanalytic Association* 7 (1959): 459–83.

————. *The Analysis of the Self.* New York: International Universities Press, 1971.

Kuhn, T. S. *The Structure of Scientific Revolutions.* 2d ed. Chicago: University of Chicago Press, 1970.

Lichtenstein, H. "The Effect of Reality Perception on Psychic Structure: A Psychoanalytic Contribution to the Problem of the 'Generation Gap.'" *Annual of Psychoanalysis* 2 (1974): 349–67.

Loewald, H. "Ego and Reality." *International Journal of Psycho-Analysis* 32 (1951): 10–18.

————. "Internalization, Separation, Mourning and the Superego." *Psychoanalytic Quarterly* 31 (1962): 483–504.

McDevitt, J. B. "Separation-Individuation and Object Constancy." *Journal of the American Psychoanalytic Association* 23 (1975): 713–42.

Mahler, M. S.; Pine, F.; and Bergmann, A. *The Psychological Birth of the Human Infant.* New York: Basic Books, 1975.

Meissner, W. W. "Notes on Identification. II. Clarification of Related Concepts." *Psychoanalytic Quarterly* 40 (1971): 277–302.

———. "Notes on Identification. III. The Concept of Identification." *Psychoanalytic Quarterly* 41 (1972) : 224–60.

———. "Differentiation and Integration of Learning and Identification in the Developmental Process." *Annual of Psychoanalysis* 2 (1974) : 181–96.

———. "A Note on Internalization as Process." *Psychoanalytic Quarterly* 45 (1976) : 374–93.

———. *The Paranoid Process.* New York: Aronson, 1977.

Miller, G. A. "The Magical Number Seven, Plus or Minus Two: Some Limits on Our Capacity for Processing Information (1956)." In *The Psychology of Communication,* edited by D. K. Stewart. Baltimore: Penguin Books, 1969.

Modell, A. H. *Object Love and Reality.* New York: International Universities Press, 1968.

Money-Kyrle, R. E. *Man's Picture of His World: A Psychoanalytic Study.* London: Duckworth, 1961.

Polanyi, M. *The Study of Man.* Chicago: University of Chicago Press, 1959.

Rapaport, D. *The Collected Papers of David Rapaport.* Edited by M. M. Gill. New York: Basic Books, 1967.

Rose, S. P., and Rose, H. " 'Do Not Adjust Your Mind, There Is a Fault in Reality'—Ideology in Neurobiology." *Cognition* 2 (1973) : 479–502.

Sandler, J. "On the Concept of Superego." *Psychoanalytic Study of the Child* 15 (1960) : 128–62.

Sandler, J., and Rosenblatt, B. "The Concept of the Representational World." *Psychoanalytic Study of the Child* 17 (1962) : 128–45.

Schafer, R. *Aspects of Internalization.* New York: International Universities Press, 1968a.

———. "On the Theoretical and Technical Conceptualization of Activity and Passivity." *Psychoanalytic Quarterly* 37 (1968b) : 173–98.

———. "Internalization: Process or Fantasy?" *Psychoanalytic Study of the Child* 27 (1972) : 411–36.

Schimek, J. G. "The Interpretations of the Past: Childhood Trauma, Psychical Reality, and Historical Truth." *Journal of the American Psychoanalytic Association* 23 (1975) : 845–65.

Wallerstein, R. S. "Psychoanalytic Perspectives on the Problem of Reality." *Journal of the American Psychoanalytic Association* 21 (1973) : 5–33.

Weisman, A. D. *The Existential Core of Psychoanalysis.* Boston: Little, Brown, 1965.

Winnicott, D. W. *The Maturational Processes and the Facilitating Environment.* New York: International Universities Press, 1965.

———. *Playing and Reality.* New York: Basic Books, 1971.

8

Some Comments on the Subject of Psychoanalysis and Truth

If, as psychoanalysts, we try to think about the material we are dealing with—the various forms of suffering and the host of complaints we are confronted with in our daily encounters with all kinds of people—we will agree that we consider what is communicated to us, verbally or nonverbally, with the intention of discovering "hidden unconscious motives" or "secret motives" (Freud, 1895, p. 293) beneath the surface. We know the compelling force of these motives. We also know that if such motives are "successfully" experienced *and* recognized, they will subside, and the patient will be given a chance to continue his life into the future with less suffering and discontent. Our belief in this process is based on an assumption that in itself already reflects a whole philosophy: that man "would be a perfect being, if he were perfectly self-determining, active, and free," and that he has a chance to attain such a state—or more correctly, he simply *is* in such a state, to the extent that "he truly knows"—that is, when "active thinking and knowledge" assert themselves "against the passive association of ideas in imagination" (Hampshire, 1971, pp. 193, 190, 191–92).

Oedipus Complex: Explanatory Pattern

I believe we also agree that by adopting a special attitude of noninterference and of benevolent patience, an attitude of carefully avoiding any action prompted by passionate love or hate (that is, by avoiding unsublimated, drive-dependent tendencies) we discover hidden, dynamically unconscious meaning, largely by relying on the *Oedipus Complex,* the *Nuclear Complex* of the neuroses (Freud, 1908, 1905) as a guiding and explanatory pattern. Understood as the necessity to exist in at least a three-person relationship (Balint, 1957), the Oedipal situation is in itself a structure, a setting representing the "limiting conditions" (the "antecedent conditions") for that which is going to happen if those who live in the "space" of this structure are possessed by certain forces. By introducing the concept of forces in connection with the three-person relationship of the Oedipus complex, I refer, of course, to the drives. And if we as analysts speak of drives, we should be constantly aware that in our clinical experience we understand above all as their outstanding feature, as their essential manifestation, the special, experiential, sensual pleasure—*"a capacity for a primary, distinctively poignant, pleasure experience,"* the "invariant—the shared factor of infantile and adult sexuality" (G. S. Klein, 1969, p. 140; Klein's italics).

In speaking of a drive, we usually refer to its representations—that is, the affects and the ideas that stand for it. But, and this is crucial, an additional essential part of this realm of the "representational world" (Sandler and Rosenblatt, 1962) is the *object.* Freud's introduction of the object as a "defining characteristic of the instinctual drive" was considered by David Rapaport to be "the outstanding conceptual invention in Freud's theory of the instinctual drive" (Rapaport, 1960, p. 202). In Freud's "Instincts and Their Vicissitudes," where he introduced the concept *drive object,* it is not clear whether he meant animate or inanimate objects. To me, however, it seems obvious that Freud always meant that initially animate objects are linked with the drives, though in a second step the original drive object may become equated with or replaced by an inanimate thing—for example, a fetish—which acquires its particular significance only from a drive-triggered experience.

I think that this view is supported by what Freud said in his paper "The Unconscious" about the "thing-presentation" that is synonymous with object-presentation (see James Strachey's footnotes in Freud, 1915b, pp. 213, 201; also Loch, 1971): "the latter," we read, "consists in the cathexis, if not of the direct memory-images of the thing, at least of remoter memory-traces derived from these" (Freud, 1915b, p. 201). And if we also take into consideration the fact that in "Mourning and Melancholia" (1917), and earlier in "Psycho-analytic Notes on an Autobiographical Account of a Case of Paranoia" (1911), the withdrawal of libido from an object was presented as one important explanation for these disorders, it becomes perfectly clear that, at least at first, the instinctual object always refers to an animate object, to the person, the significant other "in regard to which or through which the instinct is able to achieve its aim" (Freud, 1915a, p. 122).

The Search for Historical Truth and the Search for "Sense"

Still another preliminary point is the view that the psychic structure that gets built up within the triadic relationship has a period of formation; it comes into existence during infancy and early childhood out of the events and vicissitudes of a dyadic relationship. By speaking of a dyadic relationship as the area for psychoanalytic research—and let us make it clear right from the start that it is research we are striving to accomplish—and by stressing that the roots of the sought-after unconscious meaning belong to an early period, I have expressed two decisive things: (1) We work as historians who search for earlier events in order to grasp, to explain, and to make transparent the situation as it presents itself to the contemporary observer. In this connection, we must, of course,

inevitably ask whether that which we find out about the past
is true or just "fancy." (2) When we study the vicissitudes of
the drive—that is, its derivatives in the form of affects, ideas,
and, in particular, object-relationships, we must remember
that object-relationships are the very matrix and really the
source of the manifestations of affects and ideas. This amounts
to acknowledging that objects—the subject is in this sense an
object too—are indeed the responsible agents generating the
psychic reality of the inner world we are concerned with.[1]
Thus we are forced to study how the psychic world—the mental representations as, so to speak, "the third element" [2]—
is engendered within this field: how affects and ideas (both
understood in their widest possible sense) happen to come
into existence as emergent phenomena.

Scientific Truth and Existential Truth

In this task I believe we are confronted with the question
of the birth of reflective self-awareness. The constitution of
thoughts and consciousness is not to be apprehended in terms
of a notion of truth understood as *adaequatio intellectus et
rei,* nor in the sense of "exact or correct" information or the
solution to a mathematical problem (Bollnow, 1975). What
really counts in this context is whether the "third element"
(the psychic world) emerging from the field of investigation,
which is naturally at the same time the very field of experience, is of such a kind that it makes "sense" to both the participants in the experience, in the discourse that *is* the treatment ("in psychological medicine it is essential that the
therapy should make sense both to the patient and the doctor," Balint and Balint, 1961, p. 206).

Thus, we are confronted with two notions of truth: truth

1. For a description of the overriding importance of objects and the field
in which they come to play their role, see Loewald, 1971.
2. There is always a third element: the child, the word to be born (compare below).

understood as the correct statement, the historical fact—only
in need of discovery to be brought to the surface; and truth
as the emergent, the construction of something that makes
sense and that therefore permits one to rely on it and to continue living. The latter "truth" deserves therefore to be
called truth not so much in the Greek sense but in the sense
of the Hebrew tradition, as a "rock" that is reliable, strong
enough to be a foothold, a foundation for us to stand upon
in the sense of "Existenztragender Wahrheit" (existence-
carrying truth) (see Loch, 1974, pp. 220–21; Kamlah and
Lorenzen, 1967, p. 144). Truth understood as "sense" is, to
quote Heidegger, something that is antecedent to scientific
truth because "Sense signifies the where-upon [das Worauf-
hin] of the primary projection [Entwurfs], from where something may become comprehensible in its possibility as that
which it is" (Heidegger, 1927, p. 324).[3]

Sense, then, really is a fundamental attribute of *Dasein*.
When Merleau-Ponty says that we are condemned to find
sense, he makes exactly the same point. However, Merleau-
Ponty stresses that this sense is not to be understood on a
purely solipsistic basis but as an emergence born out of a
dual bond between the subject and the world, the "pre-
objectal presence" of a totality, or if we restrict ourselves to
animate subjects, as an interpersonal happening (Merleau-
Ponty, 1945, pp. 487, 492).

Oedipus Myth: Event of Truth

To repeat, in reference to the question of truth, psycho-
analysis has two tasks: (1) the search for the historical truth,
and (2) the development of sense out of a dyadic relationship.
Before discussing the relationship of these two psychoanalytic

3. "Sinn bedeutet das Woraufhin des primären Entwurfs, aus dem her
etwas als das, was es ist, in seiner Möglichkeit begriffen werden kann."
Translated by Macquarrie and Robinson as: "'Meaning' signifies the 'upon-
which' of a primary projection, in terms of which something can be conceived in its possibility as that which it is" (p. 371).

tasks to the problem of truth, I must make a further preliminary remark, and this concerns the connection between the
triangular Oedipal structure and the search for truth. It has
been stressed repeatedly by various scholars that the drama of
King Oedipus has several dimensions apart from the one that
psychoanalysis usually brings to the fore. It is important for
analysts to realize, as Bion emphatically underlines, that the
single facts of the myth are all linked with one another, forming a "train of causation," and, in particular, that the myth
"sheds light on the nature of" and "illuminates" the phenomena he calls "plus and minus knowledge," meaning constructive and destructive knowledge or insight (Bion, 1963,
p. 45).

In "pictorial" language, Bion refers here to the conflict between "Tiresias and Oedipus," not that between "Oedipus
and Laius" (p. 51), and in so doing, he draws our attention
to the fact that King Oedipus is also the "Tragedy of Truth"
(Ricoeur, 1965, p. 496), "The Event of the Truth" (Schadewaldt, 1960, p. 92).[4] Thus, truth also has a demoniacal nature
when the search for knowledge is undertaken without concern for the price to be paid. This is an issue of special interest to the present generation, which finds itself confronted
with the problem of whether or not the striving for knowledge, the driving power of curiosity, should be limited by
overriding moral values.

Truth: Aim of the Psychoanalytic Investigation

If we comprehend the Oedipus myth or the Oedipus complex as a structure that defines and illuminates the vicissitudes of the drives and also leads to the discovery of truth—
that is, if we realize the close interrelations between drive-
emotional and cognitive development (Freud, 1939; Abelin,
1975; Loch and Jappe, 1974)—then we easily understand that

4. On Oedipus and the search for truth, see Flügel, 1965; Loch, 1969,
pp. 88 ff.

the two analytical tasks (the search for historical truth and the development of "sense") are as intimately connected with the solution of the Oedipus complex as are the destinies of the drives. The drives come to an at least preliminarily stable structure through the formation of the superego, which, as Freud remarked, reaches the stage of "being normally developed" when it has become "sufficiently *impersonal*" (Freud, 1926, p. 223; my italics).

In considering this search for truth as being a dimension of the Oedipus myth or the Oedipus complex, it becomes understandable why Freud repeatedly assured us that psychoanalysis is bound to truth. Let me cite but two quotations: "I have told you that psycho-analysis began as a method of treatment; but I did not want to commend it . . . as a method of treatment but on account of the truths it contains" (Freud, 1932, p. 156). Then: "And finally we must not forget that the analytic relationship is based on a love of truth—that is, on a recognition of reality—and that it precludes any kind of sham or deceit" (Freud, 1937b, p. 248).

Similarly, other authors stress truth as the aim of psychoanalysis: "By definition and by the tradition of scientific discipline, the psychoanalytic movement is committed to the truth as the central aim" (Bion, 1970, p. 99); "analytic activity . . . a search for truth" (Meltzer, 1967, p. xii); and "the core of the whole psychoanalytic process is lived truth" (Yankelovich and Barrett, 1971, p. 425).

The Psychoanalytic Subject Matters: Description and Discovery Versus Construction of Sense

We may now proceed to ask how we attempt to discover the truth, by which methods we find it. Above all, the method of *free association* serves as a guide. I need not emphasize, I am sure, that the use of this method obliges the patient to behave in a genuine manner, requires him to be "truthful," for quite simply and plainly, he is obliged not to lie, though, of course, a tendency to lie may be one of his symptoms. But we must be aware that though not lying is certainly a prerequisite to the attainment of our aim—"truth"—it certainly is not in itself a sufficient basis for its realization. We may come nearer to this aim if we look at some of the possible preliminary results of free association. Free association may, for instance, lead to "screen memories," or to the "primary traumatic event," or "primal phantasies." With regard to "screen memories," Freud concluded,

> It may indeed be questioned whether we have any memories at all *from* our childhood: memories *relating* to our childhood may be all that we possess. Our childhood memories show us our earliest years not as they were but as they appeared at the later periods when the memories were aroused. In these periods of arousal, the childhood memories did not, as people are accustomed to say, *emerge;* they were *formed* at that time. And a number of motives, with no concern for historical accuracy, had a part in forming them, as well as in the selection of the memories themselves. [Freud, 1899, p. 322; Freud's italics]

If the quotation demonstrates, and to my mind it does so very convincingly indeed, that there is no evidence for the historical truth of the content of the screen memories, the situation as to the veridical nature of the primary traumas is more or less the same. I want to remind you only of Freud's famous exclamation or confession to his friend Wilhelm Fliess in his letter of September 21, 1887: "I will confide in you at once the great secret that has been dawning on me in the last few months. I no longer believe in my *neurotica"* (Freud, 1897, p. 259). And as he continued, a most important and far-reaching insight was born: "there are no indications of reality in the unconscious, so that one cannot distinguish between the truth and fiction that is cathected with affect" (p. 260).

As these passages indicate, Freud came to realize that there is a reality different from that which corresponds to the common, so-called "objective reality," or "external reality," and this he henceforth called the "psychical reality" (Freud, 1900, p. 620). We meet it in the fantasies, which ultimately converge in the "primal phantasies" (Freud, 1915c, p. 269). Today we believe that these are concerned with "the recognition of the breast as a supremely good object, the recognition of the parents' intercourse as a supremely creative act, and the recognition of the inevitability of time and death" (Money-Kyrle, 1971, p. 103).

Freud differentiated the following primal fantasies: observations of sexual intercourse between the parents, seduction, castration, and some that he left undefined. In speaking of them in his detailed discussion in the Introductory Lectures, he said, "If"—and he was here referring to the questionable authenticity of the events they relate—"If they have occurred in reality, so much to the good; but if they have been withheld by reality, they are put together from hints and supplemented by phantasy. The outcome is the same." He goes on to express his conviction that they should be looked at as "a phylogenetic endowment" (Freud, 1916/1917, pp. 370, 371). He stated his views on the inherited schemata with particular force at the end of the Wolf Man paper, schemata that "are concerned with the business of 'placing' the impressions derived from actual experience," thus often "triumphing over the experience of the individual," who is surmised to possess "*instinctive* knowledge" in analogy to animals. And Freud added what seems to be of utmost importance in the theory of trauma—that the traumas of early childhood have to be understood as events "contributing material to this unconscious [the instinctive knowledge] which would save it from being worn away by the subsequent course of development" (Freud, 1918, pp. 119, 120; Freud's italics).

With the acknowledgment of a psychic reality that assimilates the inherited, instinctual schema, which in itself exerts

an organizing activity upon individual life experiences, we
might feel that this amounts to asserting that here we reach
a truth of nature, of our biological nature, that has existed
previous to all personal experience. That truth, therefore, is
revealed in the material of the fantasies, which in themselves
take their content from everyday life as the dream does in
respect to the dream wish. At any rate, fantasies are not a
deliberate result of our own construction, of our invention.
The organizing schemata of nature, the laws of nature, form
a reality that we perhaps describe—and describe even in
somewhat different language in the course of time—but that
nevertheless is in itself independent, particularly independent in its origins and effects, of the ways we describe it.

But is this really the case with these fantasies, the primal
fantasies, and is it not as with the screen memories and the
reports about the traumas of childhood? It was Freud himself
who wrote, in the case of the rat man, that a patient, that
any individual, "in his phantasies about his infancy . . . as
he grows up *endeavours to efface the recollection of his auto-
erotic activities;* and this he does by exalting their memory-
traces to the level of object love"; and then he added the
plainly decisive thought, "just as a real historian will view
the past in the light of the present" (Freud, 1909, p. 206 n.;
Freud's italics). Freud's further insight, as expressed, for instance, in "Remembering, Repeating and Working-Through,"
was that in the "group of psychical processes—phantasies, processes of reference, emotional impulses, thought-connections.
. . . it particularly often happens that something is 'remembered' which could never have been 'forgotten' because it was
never at any time noticed—was never conscious" (Freud,
1914, pp. 148–49).

These ideas of Freud's are to me strong evidence that he
was very much aware of the extent to which all of the patient's recollections are affected by the actuality of his present
situation. And when we admit this, we also have to admit

that, although we understand ourselves only here and now, we project ourselves simultaneously into the future, insofar as we answer to the interminable task of sustaining a psychic life, an inner world. Thus fantasies, like recollections, are not brought into light like excavations—although Freud did use this comparison (Freud, 1937a, p. 259). Fantasies or recollections do not represent discovered truths of a historical character but are attempts to create a sense, a significance, in order to go on existing.

I believe, and this is a further step to be taken, that interpretations in the form of reconstructions have, in essence, the very same character and task. This is already implied by Freud's obvious predilection, as can be seen from his paper "Constructions in Analysis," for the term *construction* as against the term *reconstruction*. I find rather strong proof of his preference for understanding the analytical work in this way—that is, as a new creation—in his description of "the way in which a conjecture of ours [as to the reality of the patient's past] is transformed into the patient's *conviction. . . .* It does not always lead so far" as "to end in the patient's recollection," but "Instead of that, if the analysis is carried out correctly, we produce in him an assured conviction of the truth of the construction which achieves the same therapeutic result as a recaptured memory" (Freud, 1937a, pp. 265, 266; my italics). The word *conviction,* and also the phrase "produce in him an assured conviction," and the view that there is no difference as far as the therapeutic result is concerned, do they not clearly indicate that the "truth" of such convictions is not that of *adaequatio rei et intellectus?* This is particularly evident with the so-called borderlines, about whom I will say more later. With that group, it is fairly clear to most therapists who endeavor to treat them that the analysis "constructs a meaning which has never been created before the analytic relationship began" (Green, 1975, p. 12; see also Viderman, 1970).

But let us look further at psychoanalytical concepts, and let us ask if any of them demonstrate that in psychoanalysis we encounter truth in the sense of "correspondence theory." There is, for instance, the concept of "transference neurosis." Here again, if we want to be precise—and precise we simply must be when endeavoring to reach truth—we discover with Freud: "we can draw no direct conclusion from the distribution of the libido during and resulting from the treatment as to how it was distributed during the illness." For example, should we succeed "in bringing a case to a favourable conclusion by setting up and then resolving a strong father-transference. . . . it would not be correct to conclude that the patient had suffered previously from a similar unconscious attachment of his libido to his father" (Freud, 1916/1917, pp. 455–56).

Faced with such insights, which, of course, must be extended to transference in general, we see that it is indeed correct, as Ross states succinctly, that "Transference, therefore, has no inherent truth function" (Ross, 1973, p. 337) as far as past events are concerned (cf. Blos, 1972, pp. 109–10).

Thus, we may say that truth in its scientific sense cannot be what analysts are really concerned with. And this opinion is not invalidated if we concede with Freud that there are "fragments of historical truth" (Freud, 1937a, p. 268; 1939, pp. 129, 130) in all the productions of the patient and also in the analyst's constructions. Also, we see that it is not scientific truth that we are referring to when we think of "interpretation" as "something that one does to some single element of the material, such as an association or a parapraxis" (Freud, 1937a, p. 261). In therapy, we interpret with the explicit intention of securing "the best possible psychological conditions for the functions of the ego" (Freud, 1937b, p. 250). Since these ego-functions are above all concerned with mediating between the superego, the id, and external reality, then if, for example, we interpret a defense mechanism, we are only able to do so if we realize that the patient defends himself against something that he *erroneously* believes would, should it be brought into the open, prevent him from continuing to exist. I use this formulation to make clear that the real reason for the patient's defense is that his superego precludes the integration of the defended-against content, and it is exactly his attachment to its command that makes him act as he does. It is decisive that the patient supposes that if he did not submit to his superego, he would lose its protection, the guarantee for his very existence.

Now the interpreted defense, undoubtedly something real and tangible, is, in terms of content, a construction of the analyst's. He explains something, he gives a hypothesis. But this hypothesis functions not merely to give a reason for observed behavior. By demonstrating to the patient that a false notion has been governing his behavior, a notion we commonly "explain" from his past, the hypothesis also functions to anticipate, to conjecture, to give a push to the imagination [5] in a way that might, if pursued, prove useful to the patient.[6] It is the latter aspect that allows the analyst to escape from the direct impact of the patient's subconscious demands, and fosters the sublimative restructuring of those subconscious demands and the quest for new objects that will eventually balance the loss that initiated his discontent and his pathological adaption (Winnicott, 1956).

"Genetic History": Acquisition of Reflective Self-Awareness by Intersubjectivity and Language

The conclusion that we do not arrive at a veridical picture of past events has been supported by numerous psychological investigations, mostly instigated by Bartlett's (1932)

5. On "explaining" and "anticipating hypotheses," see Bollnow, pp. 154 ff.
6. As Freud said, "the unconscious acts which we have inferred" enable us "to construct a successful procedure by which we can exert an effective influence upon the course of conscious processes" (1915b, p. 167).

attack on the "trace theory" of remembering.[7] In psycho-
analysis, the impossibility of getting a factual, accurate recall
of the past is nowadays expressed by conceding that the
"genetic history" (Kris, 1956) that we arrive at in the course
of the treatment is not equivalent to the "true developmental
history." [8] This phrasing, "genetic history" in contradistinc-
tion to "developmental history," paves the way, I believe, for
a fresh and deeper understanding of what we do when we
attempt to make conscious the hitherto unconscious. In helping the patient to accomplish this transformation, we delineate to him the steps that were blocked or that he has to
undertake. This has a lot to do with the present and much
less with the past, because it is the genesis, the emergence, of
a new reflective self-awareness or insight.

If, for instance, I say to a patient, "It seems to me you
prefer to appear weak because if you displayed your power
you might be afraid of being attacked by XY, and perhaps
also by me, your analyst," this achieves at least two things
simultaneously: it recognizes that there is a hidden power in
the patient, and it attributes to the patient a reason for an
actual piece of behavior. If—and only if—this proffered reason is acceptable to him and has the strength to *convince* him
that it is "true," it will possibly set him free to behave differently from then on—for example, in respect to strikingly
submissive behavior. What I should like to stress is this introduction of reasons that make sense and are thus true—all
of which takes places in the *symbolic order of language*—and
appeal to the patient's wish to lead a life of his own, to be
self-reliant and to actualize potentialities he is only dimly
aware of, powers that if handled effectively would enlarge
his life.

7. A survey of these investigations is furnished by J. H. Paul (1967).
8. Anna Freud quite recently used this phrasing in the Pre-Congress on
Training, July 11–12, 1975, prior to the 29th International Psycho-Analytical
Congress in London.

But again, this is clearly all in the service of the present and therefore of the future also; it is in the service of the executive powers of his ego, an ego that as "subject," as "reason" (*ratio*), is "the convocation of the conditions for the possibilities, a priori, for nature and freedom" and "is that convocation only as the delivery of sufficient reason" [9] (Heidegger, 1957, p. 127). And these reasons that we are talking about to the patients explain *and* anticipate; they have this double character of referring to anxiety or guilt, phenomena I consider to be causal agents, and of including the dimension that Freud called "what for" and "whither" (Freud, 1916/1917, p. 284; see also Racker, 1958, p. 56) and that has the immensely important function of relating to the future as stressed. The personal history enters here, but in the sense of possibly making plausible the links between acts and thought that previously seemed to have no reasonable connections. Maybe it is here that the "fragments of historical truth" have their legitimate place.

But what seems to be of even more decisive importance is the individual's need to assure the continuity of his inner life; this makes it imperative for him to meld present conditions with patterns already in use, in order to create coherence in understanding. If we accept this concern for *coherence* as a guiding principle, then we realize that the truths a person is about to gain are its derivatives; expressed the other way round, the *coherence* that the person cannot escape looking for builds meaning and sense—that is, creates *truth*.[10] And we should not hesitate to admit not only that this coherence is a "logical consequence" of the reasons already at the disposal of the patient, but also that these rea-

9. In German: "Dieses Subjekt, d.h. die Vernunft, die ratio, d.h. die Versammlung der Bedingungen der Möglichkeit a priori für Natur und Freiheit, ist diese Versammlung nur als die Zustellung des zureichenden Grundes."

10. See Rapaport, who wrote, "The concept of meaning . . . a correlate of the concept of continuity" (1944–48, p. 188).

sons are to not a small extent acceptable to him because they exert a "peculiar charm" (Wittgenstein, 1938, p. 50), an effect which in itself is also a function of the "Zeitgeist," of the spirit of the age (ibid.). This close link between acceptable reasons and explanations and, let me say, fashion should not irritate us in the least, since even in science the interpretation of phenomena is based, as Copernicus admitted, on figures of thought that are "sufficiently absolute and pleasant to the mind" (quoted from Toulmin, 1961, p. 98).

Coherence as a criterion produces a concept of truth that runs into a number of difficulties, since it uses neither "facts" nor purely "logical" connections. Instead, its contents "involve" one another in the service of providing a person with a stable self-feeling [11] with continuity of the ego (both may be equated for our purpose). The main difficulty is the circularity of the definition of coherence and truth (see Körner, 1970, p. 131). We may, perhaps, avoid this circularity by considering the existing relations between truth and utility, between *truth* and its *maintenance- and growth-value* (Nietzsche, 1884, pp. 93, 116). A pragmatic notion of truth is also taken as the binding criterion (measuring rod) in the famous lines by Goethe: "Was fruchtbar ist, allein ist wahr" (Only what is fruitful is true) (1829, p. 130). I personally believe that an understanding of truth as something that is sustaining me, that permits me to go on living, is completely legitimate. As I mentioned earlier, this is a definition in the Hebrew tradition.

The objection may be raised that such a concept of truth opens the way for unbridled arbitrariness. But this is easily disproved if we take into consideration a further point of the utmost, absolutely decisive, importance: I mean the plain fact that truth—I think the following is valid for every definition of truth, and it is in a very special, central way linked to

11. See Noy's important contributions regarding the ego's task of preserving "self-continuity and identity" (1969, pp. 161 ff.).

psychoanalytic work—is never a solipsistic event but is by necessity always arrived at by consensus. "One man is always in the wrong: but with two, truth has its beginning. One man is unable to prove himself: but you cannot contradict two" ("Einer hat immer Unrecht: aber mit Zweien beginnt die Wahrheit. Einer kann sich nicht beweisen: aber Zweie kann man bereits nicht widerlegen."—Nietzsche, quoted by Bollnow, 1975, p. 203).

The defining of truth by consensus is of special interest in psychoanalytic work because, whatever we do in the psychoanalytic dialogue, we are predominantly striving to find in the patient's verbal and nonverbal communications—no matter whether they refer to a hidden, secret motive, or to unknown belief of delusional character, or a wish that has never been frankly admitted—something that can give him a fresh, reasonable order for his mental life and functioning, something that makes sense to him. But because it takes at least two persons to tie this "something" to a consensual world, and this in turn always and unavoidably requires that there be a link with sense impressions, the mirroring function is so very important. It is the appropriate method for arriving at mutual validation of sense impressions, validation of the one for the other, of the analyst for the patient. It is a mirroring function that also comprises the reflecting back of affects and emotions,[12] a reflection achieved in a great variety of ways, by words, by inflections, by gestures, etc.

But the construction of *sense,* of course, is only completed —and this only in a preliminary manner—when the something so established (with the help of the mirror validation) is transformed or, more correctly, is *created* into a *word,* a

12. Even "the sense of self" on which Winnicott commented so extensively, coming "on the basis of an unintegrated state" at first "not observed" nor "remembered by the individual," needs to to be "mirrored back by someone who is trusted . . . and who justifies the dependence" (Winnicott, 1971, p. 61).

statement. Here we are now inescapably confronted with the
problem of language, which is the common property of every
human community and which, as Wittgenstein has proved so
convincingly, at least to my mind, cannot exist as "Privatsprache." I do not believe, to approach a very central problem of our work, that emotions and affects are capable of
being recognized without having been pinned down by criteria. I remind you in this connection of Wittgenstein's famous example of the beetle in the box,[13] where he tries to
make it evident that any particular beetle, even its objective
existence, is of no importance whatsoever for the "language-
game"—that is, for the meaning of the word *beetle*—because
only the use we make of the language, its grammar, enables
us to understand one another (Wittgenstein, 1936–49, p. 403).

I believe Wittgenstein is right, although I know there are
scholars who would have it that there is a "Privatsprache,"
since "the transcendental subject," equivalent to "the interpreting subject," always has priority vis-à-vis "the interpretation itself" (Birnbacher, 1974, pp. 120, 121). But although it
may be necessary, a priori, to speak of a transcendental subject—despite the fact that we can do so only when we have
learned to speak (!)—we are simply forced to rely on criteria,
and these can only be defined, fixated, by mutual consensus:

13. A translation of the example appears in L. Wittgenstein, *Philosophical
Investigations,* 3d ed., trans. G. E. M. Anscombe (New York: Macmillan, n.d.
[1970]): "Suppose everyone had a box with something in it: we call it a
'beetle'. No one can look into anyone else's box, and everyone says he knows
what a beetle is only by looking at *his* beetle.—Here it would be quite possible for everyone to have something different in his box. One might even imagine such a thing constantly changing.—But suppose the word 'beetle' had
a use in these people's language?—If so it would not be used as the name of
a thing. The thing in the box has no place in the language-game at all; not
even as a *something:* for the box might be empty.—No, one can 'divide
through' by the thing in the box; it cancels out, whatever it is.

"That is to say: if we construe the grammar of the expression of sensation
on the model of 'object and designation' the object drops out of consideration as irrelevant" (p. 100).

a consensus, of course, rooted in a common way of life (Wittgenstein, 1936–49, p. 389).

Keeping these relations in mind and relating them to the psychoanalytic task, we may now grasp that "truth" can be seen as "a category of understanding" that is "essentially concerned with a critical understanding"—namely, an understanding of a "speech act which understands itself as an identity of understanding." This is achieved by the acknowledgment of a criterion,[14] which—and this again is extremely important—"requires a fundamental unity of intention" (Marten, 1972, pp. 295, 291, 312). The "unity of intention" is the "common way of life"; in our case, the wish to know oneself is an essential part of the "common way of life." The patient and the analyst must be intimately united in the intention to pursue the psychoanalytic method in order to gain the knowledge and the insight necessary for the achievement of their particular goal.

New Beginning: New Metaphors or Symbols

Here we encounter a further problem. To the extent that these motives refer to former ways of life that were and still are in more or less close correspondence with the present ones, we may say that what we arrive at with our interpretations belongs to "the grammar" of the given language and the rules for dealing with one another that it forces upon us, and has here its roots *and* its *truth*. This is a "criterional truth," which means that we agree upon a grammar of understanding in which phenomena are characterized by "tokens" (words). The accepted criterion is a reason and a principle of justification because it represents a measuring rod and method of measurement at the same time (Wittgenstein, 1936–49, p. 316; Birnbacher, 1974, p. 8). Eventually we come to the limits of a way of life as the new one begins, however

14. Marten (1972, p. 295) characterizes this criterion as an "ontological predication."

dimly, to come into existence; it may happen when we reach
the "New beginning" that Balint (1934) spoke about, or if we
succeed in letting the previously hidden "true self" develop
(Winnicott, 1959; 1965, pp. 133 ff.; 1955, pp. 212 ff.).

At that point, together with the patient, we may transcend
the limits of our existing language and our traditional thinking. Something new is called for. Here psychoanalysis comes
to resemble poetry or other arts, for the newly formed verbal
(or nonverbal) metaphor (picture), the symbol,[15] insofar as
it is recognized by at least one other individual—for example,
the therapist—gives to the creator a new foundation to stand
on, and a new truth to live with. This new truth may be a
temporary one, because there are multiple "action schemata
of critical understanding" (Marten, 1972, pp. 321 ff.). But in
order for the patient to gain access to his unknown—the "O"
as Bion expresses it (Bion, 1970, pp. 26 ff.)—it must become
knowable in the "language of achievement" (Bion, 1970,
p. 125).

This requires the fulfillment of special conditions, which
I think may best be described by Winnicott's term "facilitating environment." The establishment of this environment
enables the patient to feel the state of "quiet well being" that
Balint (1937) depicts as the counterpart of "primary love."
To my mind (Loch, 1971, pp. 182 ff.), this state is precursor—
to use well-known psychoanalytic technical language—to the
coming into existence of the reality ego, the latter always
being an organization of defensive character (Apfelbaum,
1966).

The Psychoanalytic Dialogue and the
Anticipation of a "True Way of Life"

In exploring the possibility of the actualization of the re-
gion of *Noch-Nicht-Sein* (not-yet-being) (Bloch, 1961), the

15. Green reminds us that a symbol is "an object cut in two, constituting a
sign of recognition when those which carry it can assemble the two pieces"
(1975, p. 12).

dialogue between patient and therapist must, in order to make sensible the actions of the patient to himself and to the analyst by leading to a consensus, be "herrschaftsfrei" ("free of domination") (Habermas, 1971, p. 138). For although the psychoanalytic situation is, in a sense, asymmetrical, it never indoctrinates the patient by brute force or seduces him by making use of the passions—that is, primitive drive tendencies—into adopting a faith to please us, to gratify our own passions.

The passionate search for reasons and sense requires, in certain phases, the toleration of complete "nonsense" produced by the patient. To do otherwise would be utterly detrimental to the aim of finding and building the "true self" (Winnicott, 1971, p. 56); [16] "the personal realities" require the capacity to acknowledge and to live with ambiguities and double binds (J. S. Kafka, 1971). If we reject permanently the patient's "irrational" products, we may risk the danger of nipping his creative potential in the bud, and may instead influence the *third element* emerging from the dialogue—the word, the sense—so that it has not a "commensal" but a "parasitic relationship" toward the two partners, "a relationship . . . which is destructive of all three" (the partners as well as itself) (Bion, 1970, p. 95). Here a lie, a "non-sense" would be produced, confusing the partners and preventing psychic growth, killing instead of promoting life.

But above all, the psychoanalytic dialogue, in order to proceed properly, presupposes in both its partners the anticipation of the realization of "the ideal speech situation"; although this is a fictitious assumption, we cannot dispense with it, just as we cannot treat our patients effectively without presupposing the existence of "a fictitious normal ego" (cf. Freud, 1937b, p. 235, where he speaks of the "ideal fic-

16. See also Balint, "tolerating it [the material of the patient] so that it may remain incoherent, nonsensical, unorganized, till the patient—after returning to the oedipal level of conventional language—will be able to give the analyst the key to understanding it" (1968, p. 177).

tion" of the "normal ego"). This anticipation, according to
Habermas, is in itself the anticipation of "a true way of life"
("Lebensform") (1971, pp. 141, 139; [17] 1973, p. 259).

A Brief Recapitulation

To review briefly, before proceeding further, the Oedipus
myth provides us with the pattern of our psychoanalytic interpretations, which in themselves, like King Oepidus, aim
at "discovering the truth." This is an aim that we men and
women of the West apparently believe is our sublime task,
to gain "absolute self-responsibility," in the sense of "a most
extremely radicalized relation to truth," which includes *"an
unconditional request* for justification," as Tugendhat
phrased it, following Husserl ("Absolute Selbstverantwort-
ung. . . . *auf's äusserste radikalisierten Wahrheitsbezuges.
. . . der unbedingten Forderung nach Ausweisung"* (Tugendhat, 1967, p. 190; my italics). Psychoanalytic procedure
is based on sincerity,[18] but psychoanalysis does not discover
truth understood as a correspondence between facts of the
past and propositions in the form of interpretations concerning this past. Rather, it *constructs truth* in the service of self-
coherence for the present and for the future, on the basis of
mutual agreement. This is the case for screen memories,
primal fantasies, or past traumatic events, transference-
neurosis situations or the interpretations of the ego's defense-
operations.

All these different kinds of constructions and interpretations may contain some "kernel of truth" (Freud, 1937a,
p. 268), and I do not underestimate the extreme importance

17. "Die kontrafaktischen Bedingungen der idealen Sprechsituation
erweisen sich als Bedingungen einer idealen Lebensform."

18. This candor embraces the acknowledgment of "the truth of the drives,"
of erotic as well as of destructive, murderous wishes directed against the self,
the next of kin, and against the analyst in particular; such candor goes hand
in hand with the destruction of "hypocrisy," a destruction that is the sine
qua non for any therapeutic result (see Bird's excellent paper, 1972).

of this "objective external truth"; the acknowledgment of these truths by the analyst is imperative in some cases to restore the patient's confidence in his own perceptions. We must also keep in mind that there would never be an "internal world" without the existence of an external one. On the whole, however, analytical material does not give a veridical picture of the past and therefore does not contain "scientific truth-values."

The Truth-Value of Transference

The one main "actual" truth that our interpretations deal with concerns the transference, inasmuch as it represents the dimension of the "what for"—that is, the libidinal object that is the focus of the patient's behavior (Freud, 1916/1917, p. 284)—behavior that is always in the service of his survival as subject, as actor. But these transference interpretations, again, do not concern veridical reports of the past. Instead, the discovered and verbalized transference deals with patterns, with structures corresponding to, being identical with —that is, representing the *truth* of—those once experienced by the patient. Here we must demonstrate to the patient the *erroneous interpretations* that he is giving *now* to his perceptions, the *false notions* that he makes use of *now* vis-à-vis his significant *others* (ultimately his libidinal object); we do this by comparing such notions with the common reality that he is at present sharing with us and that permits a change of his interactional patterns without endangering his status as a subject.

The transference interpretations have a "mutative character"; and to me this is so precisely because of the sense and the truth that they constitute for the patient in respect to his here-and-now, and about which they enlighten him because "Seiendes 'hat Sinn' " ("Being 'has sense' "). And here I add another definition of *sense,* expanding the former one, that is, "ist in seinem Sein zugänglich geworden" ("it had been

made understandable in its being"), after and to the extent
that it was "auf sein Woraufhin entworfen" ("projected toward its where-upon") (Heidegger, 1927, p. 324). Because of
this link between sense and being,[19] I believe it is warranted
to equate sense and truth for this psychoanalytic work of ours.

Genetic History: The Vicissitudes of the Drive-Object

In forming our transference interpretations—which, we
should never forget, are presented as possibilities for the patient's consideration—we construct, as I mentioned earlier,
the *genetic history* but not the *developmental history*[20] of
his mind. This means that we give reasons to the patient that
are meant to help him gain a new reflective self-awareness,
a new critical judgment—reasons that he can live with, ren-
dering him more self-reliant. As I said, these reasons deal
with the libidinal object and its vicissitudes. At the same
time, and this is an important addition, the reasons comprise
the history of the frustrating, bad, aggressive object. As I shall
explain, it is a history no subject can escape experiencing.

The unique quality of the orgiastic experience of the libidinal drive alluded to is accompanied by "I experience pleasure, therefore I exist," creating "a conviction of absolute
truth" (Eissler, 1966, pp. 855, 856; Lichtenstein, 1964, 1970,
1971) without which the subject would psychically cease to
exist, to be. Schafer spoke of "the fates of the immortal object" (Schafer, 1968, pp. 220 ff.)—the "immortal object" being the representative and the guarantor of the orgiastic
experience.

But if the state of pure being of this specific sensual experience is to be changed into something that we possess—
that is, into a symbol of the drive object—there must be a
frustrating, bad object. Every subject would be forced to in-

19. One should realize that "being" is not understood as "static"!

20. For a lucid survey of early developmental history, see Mahler, 1974;
see also Blanck and Blanck, 1972.

vent such a bad object if they did not already exist, because one can make the step from pure being to possessing through knowledge only by the prohibition of the good drive experience. Only in this way does the object of this experience (the primary drive object) gain a status of permanence, since in itself the experience, being of an orgiastic nature, annihilates its very object by its consummatory action. It is only through the image of the bad object and its prohibitive influence that the primary drive object becomes immortal in the realm of the unconscious.

But a further step is necessary: because the representation (imago) of the gratifying drive object is endangered before long by the appearance of inevitable aggressions against it, a third person has to intervene—for example, in the case of "little Hans" it was the father (Loch and Jappe, 1974)—by introducing an ideological "reality," an order of thought that stabilizes the relationship for the benefit of future development.

In the transference we have access to these influences, and in attempting to construct them and to bring them to the attention of the patient, we reach "truth-values." But, as I said, these "truth-values" reside only in proposing, not imposing (!), a possible explanation, which makes sense if and only if its anticipatory character helps the patient to master the present by overcoming barriers. In neurotic cases, these barriers prevent the patient from realizing a wish, an up-to-now "warded-off instinctual desire"; if realized, the wish would bring about an interruption of "the analytic continuum," causing a "threat of separation from the analyst" (Hoffer, 1956, pp. 378, 377), who represents the primary object.

A somewhat different approach is necessary with the borderline personality and also with all those patients in whom environmental conditions at a very early stage of their "development" were of such an unfavorable nature that the constitution of the symbolic order was seriously hampered, which means that all the functions of the psychic apparatus that Freud still took for granted were also hampered. As Green (1975) rightly stresses, our analytic interests nowadays focus very much on such disorders. For such patients, we have to perform a "holding function" and provide a "facilitating environment" (Winnicott, 1965), and we have to behave "unobtrusively" in order to permit the patient to make use of his relationship (Balint, 1937, 1968). In this way, he can connect original, primary-drive experience with a state of "quiet well-being" before we come to represent for him the bad, frustrating object that he must attack.

By surviving these attacks without retaliating (Winnicott, 1969), the analyst creates the immortality of the good object, serving in this way to let the good object (which is primarily, in Winnicott's terms, a "subjective object") acquire a symbolic representation that becomes the basis for the further constructive and autonomous development of the individual. This positive development can fail to happen if the analyst does not provide the environment that forges links between the primary, "subjective" drive object, and the "objective" objects. Without such linking the latter would lack the "feeling of reality," not having been fused with the primary object of instinctual gratification.[21] It is by these interactions that the "continuity of being" is brought about, the counterpart of feeling "self-coherence" in the "representational world," of knowing and reasoning.

Truthfulness and Truth

Now this entire undertaking—the "holding" and the interpretations—is only successful if (and this is another important factor) *both* partners of the dialogue also derive an

21. Glover wrote in 1932: "efficient reality testing, for any subject who has passed the age of puberty, is the capacity to retain psychic contact with the objects that promote gratifications of instincts, including here both modified and residual infantile impulse" (Glover, 1956, p. 217; 1968, p. 39).

emotional satisfaction from it, because otherwise the whole process would not carry enough "sense of the real." Any experience needs this sense of reality in order to become permanent, to be acknowledged, to be mirrored in a "truthful," genuine manner by all of its participants. When such events happen in the course of psychoanalytic treatment, then we may say that "truthfulness and truth" coincide, since it is under these conditions that from *the essence* of *truthfulness*— now comprehended not just as the simple avoidance of petty lying and mean deceiving but as the full and harmonious synthesis of one's feelings, conations, and cognitions (as far as this may be attainable at all)—*ensues truth.*

It is also in this instance of a therapeutic encounter that we, the patient and the analyst, exist beyond the conflict of both "the great powers": "Truth," as seen as the "absolute goal of science," and "Love," seen as "a goal of life quite independent" of the former, a dichotomy Freud formulated in a 1910 letter to Ferenczi (Jones, 1962, p. 446). It is in this instance, also, that the difference between being and knowing—between *sentio ergo existo* and *cogito ergo sum*—is overcome in the experienced unity of the word, in a "language game" played and agreed upon by both the partners of the dialogue. This language game may perhaps in certain areas of the discussion be valid for only these two partners; to that extent, it may represent "a subgame" "created for crisis management"—that is, for the transference crisis that I referred to above (Hoffer, 1956, pp. 378, 377). One may call this function of language a "coping strategy through symbolism" (von Uexküll, 1972, pp. 421–22). From this perspective, symbols—language—may be viewed as defense strategies.[22]

The Convergence of Truth—"Aletheia" and Sense

This search for sense as truth is the main task we must fulfill. This duty of ours becomes completely evident if we look

---

22. The development of symbols by defense operations was emphasized by Melanie Klein (1930).

at our patients today and our contemporary techniques as
they are represented, for instance, by Balint, Bion, Winnicott, and others. These analysts strive to help to develop re-
gions of the personality that had previously never been conscious or had, indeed, never even existed. It is obvious that
here, in the phases of a "new beginning," in the realm of the
"true self," at first and above all, something hitherto unknown must be helped *to be,* to exist; only then is it possible
for us to succeed in transmuting it into a variable experience
(Khan, 1969), and finally into reflective self-awareness, step
by step.

It is through reflective awareness that "pure being" becomes our "possession," becomes something we are capable
of controlling—insofar as it is subjected to our "private" influences—to work with for the benefit of participating more
fully in the life of the community as well as feeling more at
ease with "oneself." The goal, then, is "providing coverage
for the patient's self-experience in the clinical situation"
(Khan, 1972, p. 305), and then to help the patient to translate this into—or better still, to substitute for it—symbols,
that is, language. At times during this process, a truth or
truths are born as "identity events of understanding" (Marten, 1972, p. 356), and words, metaphors, propositions, and
sentences are found in which interpretative work (which here
very much resembles esthetic understanding and reasoning),
at least for the time being, comes to a standstill: "There is
indeed," wrote Ferenczi, "at long last something that need not
be and must not be interpreted (transformed)" (Ferenczi,
1932, p. 275). Here we but describe or "recognize" (Balint,
1963, p. 306; 1968) something that in itself represents *sense
and truth* simultaneously.

And such an "agreed-upon truth" is simultaneously an
"agreed-upon existence," and both—and for me this is a
unique and distinguished feature of psychoanalysis—"are decided as such by the dialogical relationship" of two persons

"capable of speech . . . in so far as they" both strive to "act in a *critically* understanding way" (Marten, 1972, p. 364; my italics). This means that it is a consensus, a truth not "of language and reality," but a truth reached by "a criteriologically justified consensus in the language itself" (Zimmermann, 1973, p. 456; Schirn, 1974, p. 29). It is exactly at this point that one is fully entitled to say to oneself, "There is a language game"; and one need not worry, because one feels and knows, "You can rely on it" (Wittgenstein, 1951, p. 160). But, and this is an inevitable restriction, this truth is not an eternal one; it is time-bound. Yet the search is not.

If, under these circumstances, truth becomes an event of evidential though not of solipsistic character, then it is identical with the "aletheia" (Heidegger, 1966; 1930, pp. 14 ff.) that creates for the subject henceforth a new field for play and life. That is so because in the analyst's or in the patient's utterances it is the *sense of words, of propositions,* which *is* this *"aletheia,"* [23] and this implies that I, that the patient, can "count, calculate" with the "words" given, "transmute them into this or that image" (Wittgenstein, 1936–49, p. 439). This amounts to saying that pyschoanalytic interpretations—insofar as they are predominantly arrived at to make sense—are not so much concerned with meaning comprehended as a fixed signification [24] (truth in a scientific perspective), but are

23. "Aletheia," literally "non-concealment," is the central term in Heidegger's "truth" as the sense or truth of Being. In contrast with a correspondence or adequation theory of truth, "The 'sense' (Sinn) of anything for Heidegger is the non-concealment by which it appears as itself" (Richardson, 1963, p. 7). For the important relations between this notion and Plato's nonlogical, nonpredicative epistemology and "poetic truth," I refer the reader to the excellent work by Oehler (1962).

24. In distinguishing between sense and meaning (significance), I am following Frege (1892, pp. 40 ff.). This difference was further elaborated and radicalized by Wittgenstein, and is described and specified in Lang (1971, pp. 87 ff.; see also Zimmermann, 1973, particularly p. 384). To Wittgenstein, language and *sense* are equivalent to "calculus"! A similar distinction is made by Poland, to whom Wygotski refers (Wygotski, 1934, p. 343).

meant to open possibilities. They enable the patient to discover and construct new meanings, and they do this by free-
ing him from any fixation,[25] either by destroying an attachment to an object (destroying the "neurotic" transference) or
by releasing him from a permanent and unnecessarily re-
stricting commitment to a fixed moral system. (Both aspects
are interlocked in the superego, which also, in its primitive,
personal aspect, must be dissolved or transcended.)

Thus, a new dimension of sense is introduced, making clear
its role as the real organizer of emancipated mental life. We
would not succeed in achieving "real" sense if we merely replaced one meaning, one signification, by another. But we
should never forget that our strivings are dependent on our
constant awareness (or attitude) [26] that the patient, the *subject,* conceived of now as the *bestimmende Selbst* (determining self) and not at all as the *bestimmbare Selbst* (definable
self) (Kant, 1781, p. 402), has and must have—no, much more
correctly, *is*—a "non-communicating central self" (Winnicott, 1963).[27] He will keep his freedom by remaining uncom-
mitted in the midst of any newly won worldliness. This free-

25. This is clear from the kind of phrasing we commonly use in our
practice: "Could it be possible that . . . ?" "Isn't this as if . . . ?" And as
far as I can judge, I think that nowadays we refrain more and more from
giving definite meanings, preferring instead an "unsaturated form" of expression. For instance, we would rather say to somebody who always needs
to smoke a cigarette in the interval between negotiations with his patients,
"I guess you want to take back what you have presumably given to your
patient during the interview," instead of, "I guess you felt you have lost
your phallus (or breast) in the work with your patient and the cigarette is
meant to substitute for that imagined loss." The intention of the first
formulation is to let the person himself discover which specific meaning he
will ascribe to it.

26. "My attitude toward him," writes Wittgenstein, "is an attitude toward
a mind" ("Meine Einstellung zu ihm ist eine Einstellung zur Seele"). Wittgenstein, 1936–49, p. 489.

27. Of course, the relationship the subject has with his "subjective objects"
(Winnicott, 1963) in this secret area of his—a remnant of his narcissistic,
omnipotent realm—presupposes a "language," however primitive, which
therefore also antedates intersubjective experiences.

dom ultimately resides beyond any truth or sense, however strongly it may at present be rooted in any one here-and-now "justified identity of understanding" (Marten, 1972, p. 294). This is to acknowledge that there is always, in correlation to the "primat de l'intentionnel sur le réflexive" (Ricoeur, 1965, p. 370), an excess of being over the possibility of expressing oneself quite fully in thinking and speaking. For some people who have been aware only of their defensive aspect, the realization of the potentialities they might actualize and of the vast spaces that are being opened for further exploration produces such deep suffering that they denounce what is called sense and truth as a "lie"; like Franz Kafka, they feel: "What we are, we are incapable of expressing, because this we simply are; we cannot but communicate what we are not, the lie" (F. Kafka, 1966, p. 343).

But psychoanalysis can be understood as a method of increasing man's intelligibility to himself, by correcting errors of apperception, by lifting compulsions resulting from unrecognized object-ties and false premises, by helping him to discover new truth in the sense of the freedom to construct, to invent, new thoughts and new meanings and significations. Understood in these ways, psychoanalysis, I believe, serves and pursues an aim that opposes the pessimistic statement by Kafka quoted above. It strives to develop "the general *feeling* of *participation,* as well as the capacity to *communicate* oneself as whole-heartedly and as generally as possible," attributes that Kant described as the basic character of "humanism" ("Humanität") (Kant, 1790, A 259–60; 1793, B 263).[28] And is not humanism in that respect—namely, as a general feeling of participation and as a whole-hearted and general capacity to communicate—identical with Plato's conviction that the soul means "logistikon," that is, the capacity to speak?

28. In German: "Weil *Humanität* einerseits das allgemeine *Teilneh-mungsgefühl,* andererseits das Vermoegen, sich innigst und allgemein *mitteilen* zu können, bedeutet" (Kant's italics).

In this process of speaking, in the word, there occurs an "intimate," "general" participation and communication at the point—and precisely at that point—where *sentire* and *cogitare*, experience and thought, coincide. When the *sentio ergo existo* of the libidinal experience is mediated by the *cogito ergo sum* of substantiated insight, then real and true "self-knowledge of our limited reason" (Kern, 1975, pp. 362, 420) is indeed formed, then the "truth of the conviction of one's self" (Hegel, 1807, p. 139) occurs. And to the extent that this has been mediated by the most intimate communication and partaking of one with the other, of the patient with the doctor, the generality of communication that has now become possible is also a state in which the subject may feel united with the "general other," but without being submerged, because the subject now knows by experience that it is the search for sense, for reasons, that is the very foundation for living as an actor.

If we can realize all these connections, then I believe that we can agree with what Freud, when seventy-seven years old, told his patient H.D.: "My discoveries are not a heal-all. My discoveries are a basis for a very grave philosophy" (H.D., 1956, p. 25).

REFERENCES

Abelin, E. L. "Some Further Observations and Comments on the Earliest Role of the Father." *International Journal of Psycho-Analysis* 56 (1975) : 293–302.

Apfelbaum, B. "On Ego Psychology: A Critique of the Structural Approach to Psycho-analytic Theory." *International Journal of Psycho-Analysis* 47 (1966) : 451–75.

Balint, M. "Character Analysis and a New Beginning" (1934). "Early Developmental States of the Ego. Primary Object-Love" (1937). In M. Balint, *Primary Love and Psychoanalytic Technique.* London: Tavistock, 1965.

———. "Die drei seelischen Bereiche." *Psyche* 11 (1957) : 321–44.

———. "The Benign and the Malignant Forms of Regression" (1963). In S. Rado, *New Perspectives in Psychoanalysis*. New York: Grune & Stratton, 1965.

———. *The Basic Fault: Therapeutic Aspects of Regression*. London: Tavistock, 1968.

Balint, M., and Balint, E. *Psychotherapeutic Techniques in Medicine*. London: Tavistock, 1961.

Bartlett, F. C. *Remembering. A Study in Experimental and Social Psychology*. Cambridge: Cambridge University Press, 1932.

Bion, W. R. *Elements of Psychoanalysis*. London: Heinemann, 1963.

———. *Attention and Interpretation*. London: Tavistock, 1970.

Bird, B. "Notes on Transference: Universal Phenomenon and Hardest Part of Analysis." *Journal of the American Psychoanalytic Association* 20 (1972) : 267–301.

Birnbacher, D. *Die Logik der Kriterien*. Hamburg: F. Meiner, 1974.

Blanck, G., and Blanck, R. "Toward a Psychoanalytic Developmental Psychology." *Journal of the American Psychoanalytic Association* 20 (1972) : 668–710.

Bloch, E. *Zur Ontologie des Noch-Nicht-Seins*. Frankfurt am Main: Suhrkamp, 1961.

Blos, P. "The Epigenesis of the Adult Neurosis." *Psychoanalytic Study of the Child* 27 (1972) : 106–35.

Bollnow, O. F. *Das Doppelgesicht der Wahrheit*. Stuttgart: Kohehammer, 1975.

Eissler, K. R. "Bemerkungen zur Technik der Psychoanalytischen Behandlung Pubertierender nebst einigen Überlegungen zum Problem der Perversionen." *Psyche* 20 (1966) : 837–72.

Ferenczi, S. [Oct. 30, 1932.] *Bausteine zur Psychoanalyse*. Vol. 4. Bern: Hans Huber, 1939.

Flügel, H. *Konturen des Tragischen*. Stuttgart: Evangelischen Verlagswerk, 1965.

Frege, G. "Über Sinn und Bedeutung" (1892). In G. Frege, *Funktion, Begriff, Bedeutung*. Göttingen: Vandenhoeck u. Ruprecht, 1966.

Freud, S. *Standard Edition of the Complete Psychological Works*. London: Hogarth, 1953–66.

"The Psychotherapy of Hysteria (1895)," vol. 2.

"Extracts from the Fliess Papers (1897)," vol. 1.

"Screen Memories (1899)," vol. 3.

The Interpretation of Dreams (1900), vol. 5.

"Three Essays on the Theory of Sexuality (1905)," vol. 7.

"On the Sexual Theories of Children (1908)," vol. 9.

"Notes upon a Case of Obsessional Neurosis (1909)," vol. 10.

"Psycho-analytic Notes on an Autobiographical Account of a Case of Paranoia (1911)," vol. 12.

"Remembering, Repeating and Working-Through (1914)," vol. 12.

"Instincts and Their Vicissitudes (1915a)," vol. 14.

"The Unconscious (1915b)," vol. 14.

"A Case of Paranoia Running Counter to the Psycho-analytic Theory of the Disease (1915c)," vol. 14.

Introductory Lectures on Psychoanalysis (1916/1917), vol. 16.

"Mourning and Melancholia (1917)," vol. 14.

"From the History of an Infantile Neurosis (1918)," vol. 17.

"The Question of Lay Analysis (1926)," vol. 20.

"New Introductory Lectures on Psycho-analysis (1932)," vol. 22.

"Constructions in Analysis (1937a)," vol. 23.

"Analysis Terminable and Interminable (1937b)," vol. 23.

"Moses and Monotheism (1939)," vol. 23.

Glover, E. "The Relation of Perversion Formation to the Development of Reality-Sense" (1932). In E. Glover, *On the Early Development of Mind*, vol. 1. New York: International Universities Press, 1956.

———. *The Birth of the Ego*. New York: International Universities Press, 1968.

Goethe, J. W. "Vermächtnis." *Goethe's Werke*. Vol. 2. Leipzig: Bibliographisches Institut, 1829.

Green, A. "The Analyst, Symbolization and Absence in the Analytic Setting." *International Journal of Psycho-Analysis* 56 (1975): 1–22.

Habermas, J. "Vorbereitende Bemerkungen zu einer Theorie der

kommunikativen Kompetenz." In J. Habermas and N. Luh-
mann, *Theorie der Gesellschaft oder Sozialtechnologie*. Frankfurt am Main: Suhrkamp, 1971.

―――. "Wahrheitstheorien." In J. Habermas, *Wirklichkeit und
Reflexion*. Pfullingen: Neske, 1973.

Hampshire, S. "Spinoza and the Idea of Freedom." In S. Hampshire, *Freedom of Mind and Other Essays*. Princeton, N.J.:
Princeton University Press, 1971.

H.D. *A Tribute to Freud* [1956]. New York: Oxford University
Press, 1971.

Hegel, G. W. F. "Die Phaenomenologie des Geistes [1807]." In
Saemtliche Werke, vol. 2, edited by H. Glockner. Stuttgart-Bad
Cansatt: S. Frommann, 1964.

Heidegger, M. *Sein und Zeit* (1927). Tübingen: Niemayer, 1963.
(*Being and Time*. Translated by J. Macquarrie and E. Robinson. New York: Harper & Row, 1962.)

―――. *Vom Wesen der Wahrheit* (1930). Frankfurt am Main:
Klostermann, 1954.

―――. *Der Satz vom Grund*. Pfullingen: Neske, 1957.

―――. "Das Ende der Philosophie und die Aufgabe des
Denkens" (1966). In M. Heidegger, *Zur Sache des Denkens*.
Tübingen: Niemayer, 1969.

Hoffer, W. "Transference and Transference Neurosis." *International Journal of Psycho-Analysis* 37 (1956) : 377–79.

Jones, E. *The Life and Work of Sigmund Freud*. Vol. 2. New
York: Basic Books, 1962.

Kafka F. *Hochzeitsvorbereitungen auf dem Lande*. Frankfurt am
Main: Fischer, 1966.

Kafka, J. S. "Ambiguity for Individuation." *Archives of General
Psychiatry* 25 (1971) : 232–39.

Kamlah, W., and Lorenzen, P. *Logische Propädeutik*. Mannheim:
Bibliographisches Institut, 1967.

Kant, I. *Kritik der Urteilskraft:* 1st ed., 1790; 2d ed., 1973. *Kritik
der reinen Vernunft*, 1781. In *Kant, Werke in Zehn Bänden*,
vols. 8, 4, edited by W. Weisschädel. Darmstadt: Wissen-
schaftliche Buchgemeinschaft, 1968.

Kern, S. *Idee und Methode der Philosophie*. Berlin: de Gruyter,
1975.

Khan, M. M. R. "Vicissitudes of Being, Knowing and Experiencing in the Therapeutic Situation" (1969). "The Finding and
Becoming of Self" (1972). In M. M. R. Khan, *The Privacy of
the Self: Papers on Psychoanalytic Theory and Technique*.
New York: International Universities Press, 1974.

Klein, G. S. "Freud's Two Theories of Sexuality." In *Clinical-
Cognitive Psychology: Models and Integrations*, edited by
L. Breger. Englewood Cliffs, N.J.: Prentice-Hall, 1969.

Klein, M. "The Importance of Symbol-Formation in the Development of the Ego" (1930). In M. Klein, *Contributions to
Psychoanalysis, 1921–1945*. London: Hogarth, 1948.

Körner, S. *What Is Philosophy?* London: Penguin, 1970. (German
edition: *Grundfragen der Philosophie*. Munich: List, 1970.)

Kris, E. "The Recovery of Childhood Memories in Psycho-
analysis." *Psychoanalytic Study of the Child* 11 (1956) : 54–65.

Lichtenstein, H. "The Role of Narcissism in the Emergence and
Maintenance of a Primary Identity." *International Journal of
Psycho-Analysis* 45 (1964) : 49–56.

———. "Changing Implications of the Concept of Psychosexual
Development." *Journal of the American Psychoanalytic Association* 18 (1970) : 300–18.

———. "The Malignant No: A Hypothesis Concerning the In-
terdependence of the Sense of Self and the Instinctual Drives."
In *The Unconscious Today*, edited by M. Kanzer. New York:
International Universities Press, 1971.

Loch, W. "Über Zusammenhänge zwischen Partnerschaft, Struk-
turbildung und Mythos" (1969). In W. Loch, *Zur Theorie,
Technik u. Therapie der Psychoanalyse*. Frankfurt am Main:
Fischer, 1972.

———. "Gedanken über Gegenstand, Ziele und Methoden der
Psychoanalyse" (1971). "Der Analytiker als Gesetzgeber und
Lehrer" (1974). In W. Loch, *Über Begriffe und Methoden der
Psychoanalyse*. Bern: Hans Huber, 1975.

Loch, W., and Jappe, G. "Die Konstruktion der Wirklichkeit
und der Phantasien." *Psyche* 28 (1974) : 1–31.

Loewald, H. W. "On Motivation and Instinct Theory." *Psychoanalytic Study of the Child* 26 (1971) : 91–128.

Mahler, M. S. "Symbiosis and Individuation: The Psychological

Birth of the Human Infant." *Psychoanalytic Study of the Child* 29 (1974) : 89–106.

Marten, R. *Existieren, Wahrsein und Verstehen.* Berlin: de Gruyter, 1972.

Meltzer, D. *The Psycho-Analytical Process.* London: Heinemann, 1967.

Merleau-Ponty, M. *Phänomenologie der Wahrnehmung* (1945). Berlin: de Gruyter, 1966.

Money-Kyrle, R. "The Aims of Psycho-analysis." *International Journal of Psycho-Analysis* 52 (1971) : 103–06.

Nietzsche, F. *Umwertung aller Werte* (1884). Vol. 1. Munich: DTV, 1969.

Noy, P. "A Revision of the Psychoanalytic Theory of the Primary Process." *International Journal of Psycho-Analysis* 50 (1969 : 155–78.

Oehler, K. *Die Lehre vom noetischen Denken bei Platon und Aristoteles.* Munich: Berk, 1962.

Paul, I. H. "The Concept of Schema in Memory Theory." In *Motives and Thought: Psychoanalytic Essays in Honor of David Rapaport,* edited by R. R. Holt. New York: International Universities Press, 1967.

Racker, H. "Classical and Present Techniques in Psychoanalysis" (1958). In H. Racker, *Transference and Countertransference.* New York: International Universities Press, 1968.

Rapaport, D. "The Scientific Methodology of Psychoanalysis" (1944–48). In *The Collected Papers of David Rapaport,* edited by M. M. Gill. New York: Basic Books, 1967.

―――. "On the Psychoanalytic Theory of Motivation." In *Nebraska Symposium on Motivation,* vol. 8, edited by M. R. Jones. University of Nebraska Press, 1960.

Richardson, W. J. *Heidegger: Through Phenomenology to Thought.* The Hague: Martinus Nijhoff, 1963.

Ricoeur, P. *De l'interpretation, essai sur Freud.* Paris: Du Seuil, 1965.

Ross, M. "Some Clinical and Theoretical Aspects of Working Through." *International Journal of Psycho-Analysis* 54 (1973) : 331–43.

Sandler, J., and Rosenblatt, B. "The Concept of the Representational World." *Psychoanalytic Study of the Child* 17 (1962) : 128–35.

Schadewaldt, W. "Der 'König Ödipus' des Sophokles in neuer Deutung" (1960). In W. Schadewaldt, *Sophokles, König Ödipus.* Stuttgart: Reclam, 1973.

Schafer, R. *Aspects of Internalization.* New York: International Universities Press, 1968.

Schirn, M. "Wahrheit." In *Sprachhandlung—Existenz—Wahrheit,* edited by M. Schirn. Stuttgart: Frommann, 1974.

Toulmin, S. *Voraussicht und Verstehen, ein Versuch über die Ziele der Wissenschaft* (1961). Frankfurt am Main: Suhrkamp, 1968.

Viderman, S. *La construction de l'espace analytique.* Paris: Denoël, 1970.

Von Uexküll, T. "System and Crisis: A Psychosomatic Model of Human Development." *Psychiatry in Medicine* 3 (1972) : 417–24.

Winnicott, D. W. "Very Early Roots of Aggression" (1955). "The Antisocial Tendency" (1956). In D. W. Winnicott, *Collected Papers: Through Paediatrics to Psycho-Analysis.* New York: Basic Books, 1958.

———. "Classification: Is There a Psychoanalytic Contribution to Psychiatric Classification?" (1959). In Winnicott, 1965; see below.

———. "Communicating and Not Communicating, Leading to a Study of Opposites" (1963). In Winnicott, 1965; see below.

———. *The Maturational Processes and the Facilitating Environment.* New York: International Universities Press, 1965.

———. "The Use of an Object and Relation Through Identification" (1969). In Winnicott, 1971; see below.

———. *Playing and Reality.* New York: Basic Books, 1971.

Wittgenstein, L. *Philosophische Untersuchungen* (1936–49). Frankfurt am Main: Suhrkamp, 1967.

———. "Vorlesungen über Ästhetik" (1938). In *Wittgenstein, Vorlesungen u. Gespräche über Ästhetik, Psychologie und Religion,* edited by C. Barett. Göttingen: Vandenhoeck u. Ruprecht, 1968.

————. [1951 passage.] In L. Wittgenstein, *Über Gewissheit*. Frankfurt am Main: Suhrkamp, 1970.

Wygotski, L. S. *Denken und Sprechen* (1934). Frankfurt am Main: Fischer, 1969.

Yankelovich, D., and Barrett, W. *Ego and Instinct: The Psychoanalytic View of Human Nature*. Rev. ed. New York: Random House, 1971.

Zimmermann, J. "Von der rationalistischen Sprachkritik zur Hermeneutik der Sprachspiele." Thesis for *Erlangung des Doktorgrades im Fachbereich Philosophie der Universität Tübingen*, 1973.

9

Spinoza, Freud, and Hampshire on Psychic Freedom

ISAAC FRANCK

I

That there are interesting and suggestive resemblances and parallels between Spinoza's philosophy of mind and Freud's psychoanalytic psychology has been remarked by a number of writers in the philosophical and psychological literature of the last half-century.[1] That these resemblances and parallels are more than *curiosa* or of merely passing historical interest is reflected in the explorations of some of the substantive significance of these relationships by such writers as David Bidney (1940) and Lewis S. Feuer (1958). But no one has probed the philosophical import of these relationships more incisively or more persistently than Stuart Hampshire, first in his book on Spinoza (1951), then in his volumes entitled *Thought and Action* (1960) and *Freedom of the Individual* (1965), and also, at various times during the past fifteen years, in a succession of penetrating papers, which were eventually gathered together and published in the volume *Freedom of Mind* (1971).

The titles of these volumes are significant. They reflect Hampshire's own ongoing investigations into the philosophy

An earlier and briefer version of this paper was presented at a meeting of the Forum on Psychiatry and the Humanities, Washington School of Psychiatry.

1. See, for example, Hamblin-Smith (1925); Alexander (1927); Rathbone (1934); Brill (1940); Bernard (1946).

of mind, the nature of human action, the relationships between unconscious processes and man's reason, the meaning
and extent of psychic freedom, and thus into the conditions
of moral responsibility. A most fascinating ingredient in these
investigations is Hampshire's skillful shuttling back and forth
between the philosophico-psychological insights of Spinoza
and the psychoanalytic discoveries of Freud, as well as his
reliance on and unraveling of the philosophical implications
of both. Indeed, Hampshire's relentless and brilliant pursuit
of the problem of psychic freedom in Spinoza's deterministic
universe may well be interpreted to have as its end the con-
version of Spinoza, whom H. A. Wolfson called "the last of
the medievals" and "the first of the moderns" (p. vii), into a
contemporary, late twentieth-century philosopher.

Some of Hampshire's contributions in this still densely
overgrown territory of the philosophy of mind, and also some
difficulties entailed by his analyses and conclusions, will be
explicated in the present essay with the help of a review of
relevant portions of Spinoza's doctrine and of Freud's theories, and of their relation to Hampshire's philosophy of human thought and action.

We may utilize as our point of departure the traditional
philosophical and psychological question, "Under which conditions is a person a free and responsible agent?" and Hampshire's answer to it as formulated in *Thought and Action*.
Distinguishing between *necessary* and *sufficient* conditions,
Hampshire says:

> At least two conditions are necessary for saying of a man
> that he is a relatively free agent and responsible for his
> actions. First, that he generally know clearly what he is
> doing. . . . Secondly, there must be a comprehensively
> wide range of achievement open to him, in which he
> would succeed if he tried. . . . But are these two condi-
> tions jointly sufficient conditions for saying that a man is

> a free and responsible agent? Or is there some further
> condition required. . . . This condition is ordinarily
> taken to be the problem of free will. [pp. 180–81]

Among contemporary American philosophers who have
criticized the theory and assumptions of the doctrine of free
will, it was John Hospers, in a paper that has been widely
reprinted, who systematically and cogently marshaled some
of the evidence, based principally on psychoanalytic theory,
for a radical skepticism about the availability to men of such
conditions as are suggested by Hampshire in the above quotation. Hospers begins by directing our attention to unconscious
processes:

> I want to mention . . . a factor that I think is of enor-
> mous importance and relevance: namely, unconscious
> motivation. There are many actions . . . for which hu-
> man beings in general . . . are inclined to hold the
> doer responsible, and for which, I would say, he should
> not be held responsible. The deed may be planned, . . .
> nonetheless his behavior was brought about by uncon-
> scious conflicts developed in infancy, over which he has
> no control and of which . . . he does not even have
> knowledge. He may even *think* he knows why he acted
> as he did, he may *think* he has conscious control over his
> actions, he may even *think* he is fully responsible for
> them; but he is not. [p. 114; emphasis in the original]

Hospers then presents as additional illustrations several other
varieties of unconscious motivations. From these he proceeds
to his second point, namely, that each of us is "the product
of causes in which his volition took no part." None of us, the
"normal" person or the neurotic, is the author of his own
character.

Irrespective of whether this character is a consequence of
heredity or early environment, we cannot with justification

blame the person who is unable to overcome the defects in his character any more than we can *praise* ourselves (or others) for the ability to overcome them. Whether one is the kind of person who can exert the effort and overcome these deficiencies—hereditary or environmental—is itself a product of heredity or of early environment. "We did not give ourselves this ability; and if we lack it we cannot be blamed for not having it" (p. 126). Hospers continues:

> All this is well known to psychoanalysts. They can predict, from minimal cues that most of us don't notice, whether a person is going to turn out to be lucky or not. . . . as a physician [the psychoanalyst] can soon detect whether the patient is lucky or unlucky—and he knows that whichever it is, it *isn't the patient's fault.* [p. 126; emphasis in the original]

Thus, if Hospers is right, what Hampshire calls "a comprehensively wide range of achievement . . . in which [a person] would succeed if he tried," can hardly be open to the person. Serious doubts are thus raised about the second of Hampshire's necessary conditions for someone's being psychically free and a responsible agent.

This distillation of Hospers's skeptical scrutiny of the assumptions of psychic freedom—which he insists is not being presented as an argument *for* determinism (p. 127)—helps bring into sharp focus, in compelling contemporary terms, a central problem common to Spinoza, Freud, and Hampshire. Since man's behavior is so overwhelmingly governed or dominated by unconscious and irrational or nonrational processes and motives, since emotions, fantasies, passions, and aberrations, the nature and causes of which are unknown to us, keep us in bondage for so much of our lives, is there anything in man's constitution through the exercise of which a person can liberate himself from this bondage and attain a measure of psychic freedom? Is there any methodology, or technique, or therapy by means of which a person can achieve control over and dominate his unconsciously and irrationally motivated passions, and become a free agent responsible for his own actions?

It seems of more than historical interest that these three thinkers, writing at different times—almost three hundred years separating Hampshire from Spinoza—and launching their respective investigations from different historical and conceptual frames of reference, grappled with essentially the same problem. And it is of surpassing philosophical and psychological significance that all three converge upon what is essentially, in its paradigmatic structure, the same conclusion. The paradigm of their common conclusion, if we decide for the moment to ignore the differences and divergences among them, is that, ultimately, the only source and guarantee of the very limited portion of freedom from bondage to the passions that can be attained by man is in the exercise of *reason,* of man's fully conscious cognitive faculties, in the arduous pursuit and discovery of the *causes* of these passions; and in their modification through one's rational, cognitive *reflection* upon them.

This does not imply that, in propounding this paradigm, either Spinoza, or Freud, or Hampshire indulges in or propagates the illusion that its employment always, or even often, leads to successful results. They decidedly do not. Indeed, the differences that appear discernible in their respective assessments of the likelihood of success are among the important divergences that will be expounded for each of the three. However, a remarkable element to be noted in this paradigm of human liberation from obsessive emotions and passions, shared by these three explorers of man as a thinking being, is that the paradigm revolves around the transcendently important fact of man's *reflexive thought,* of what Spinoza so unostentatiously and yet with such stunning fecundity called *idea ideae*.[2]

But here again a caveat is in order. Reason as the antidote to the passions is far from foolproof, because of its own built-in limitations. Too often reason is impotent to deal with the passions because reason itself is subject to corruption by these passions, and often turns out to function in their service through the self-deceptive mechanism of rationalization. The differences in the degree to which Spinoza, Freud, and Hampshire, respectively, recognize this limitation make an instructive study, and I shall refer to this later. Nonetheless, their recognition of these limitations notwithstanding, it is reason—cognitive, fully conscious, reflexive thought—that is, in their view, man's only weapon for the conquest of his emotions and for his attainment of fragmentary psychic freedom. It is therefore not inaccurate to speak of Spinoza, Freud, and Hampshire, in this special sense of the term, and in this context, as "rationalists."

Now, it goes without saying that the paradigm suggested is a simplification, distilled out of the rich complexity of Spinoza's, Freud's, and Hampshire's works. It epitomizes the "ideal type construct," the "limiting case," for our understanding of the odyssey of a person from being passion-dominated to being guided by reason, or the painful, often tragic, obstacle-strewn pilgrimage of the individual from the stranglehold of the emotions to a rational understanding of their causes, and to their subsequent modification. Understandably, therefore, the formulation of the paradigm cannot but fail to reflect the person's resistances to the attainment of the aims envisioned in it, the individual's frequent regressions and reversions to the tyranny of the emotions in the course of this process, and even following the successes—often partial and limited successes—in the struggle. Of necessity, the formulation of the paradigm also fails to convey the per-

2. *Ethics,* part II, Proposition 21, Scholium.

petual state of dynamic tension—between reason and the passions—that characterizes human life, according to the image of man painted by Spinoza, Freud, and Hampshire. In what follows, an attempt will be made to sketch, for each of these men, some of the problems of liberation from our unconsciously motivated compulsions; the methodologies and therapies for the attainment of such liberation and the evidence for their availability; and the explicit or implied assessment by each thinker of the extent of psychic freedom attainable by man.

II

Part 4 of Spinoza's monumental work the *Ethics* has as its title: "Of Human Bondage, or On the Strength of the Emotions." The fifth and concluding part of the book is entitled: "Of the Power of the Intellect, or On Human Freedom." Ignoring Spinoza's important metaphysical theory at this point, even though it constitutes the indispensable matrix for his psychological and ethical doctrines, we can see from these titles that an overarching goal of Spinoza's in the *Ethics* is to outline a therapeutic method through which reason, or the intellect, can overcome the tyranny of the emotions, and through which a person can achieve a certain measure and a certain kind of psychic freedom. Man, Spinoza points out repeatedly, is dominated by his emotions and passions to such an extent that of a person so dominated "we say that he is delirious or mad." Such emotions as "avarice, ambition, lust, etc., are nothing but a kind of madness." [3] Passions "indicate our impotence," [4] and a person who is dominated by passions "is ipso facto not free." [5] "A man is necessarily always subject to passions," [6] asserts Spinoza. Man's struggle for psychic freedom is therefore perennial.

3. *Ethics,* IV, 44, Scholium.
4. Ibid., Appendix, Paragraph #2.
5. Parkinson, p. 33, n. 3.
6. *Ethics,* IV, 4, Corollary.

Are any of these emotions and passions, for Spinoza, the products of *unconscious* processes and motivations? This is a subject of dispute among commentators. Bidney, in his book *The Psychology and Ethics of Spinoza,* appears undecided (pp. 40, 391–92). First he claims that "the notion of an unconscious mind" or "the notion of an independent [unconscious] mental force determining human behavior" "did not occur to . . . Spinoza." But on the other hand, Bidney does acknowledge that the mind, according to Spinoza, is sometimes ignorant of some *mental* causes of some of its ideas. Bidney therefore concedes that "this would imply the notion of unconscious ideas"; but at the same time he persists in his view that Spinoza "nowhere makes use of the unconscious as a mental force in conflict with conscious ideas" (p. 392).

But Feuer, in his book *Spinoza and the Rise of Liberalism,* not only credits Spinoza with the "discovery of the distinction between conscious and unconscious forces in man's psychological life" (p. 210), but also argues that the conception of the unconscious "was worked out by Spinoza in order to distinguish between the free man and the slave" (p. 299, n. 55). He further suggests that "Leibnitz took over from Spinoza the hypothesis of unconscious mental states" (ibid.).

There would be little point in entering more extensively here into this textual problem except to note that, like Feuer, Hampshire's reading of Spinoza clearly ascribes to him the affirmation of unconscious processes and motivations.[7] Spinoza's language appears to me to admit of no other interpretation. One illustration is his distinction between "appetite" and "desire":

> there is no difference between appetite and desire, except that desire is generally related to men in so far as they are conscious of their appetites, and it may therefore be defined as appetite of which we are conscious.[8]

7. *Spinoza,* pp. 139–44.
8. *Ethics,* III, 9, Scholium.

> We said above . . . that desire is appetite with a con-
> sciousness of itself.[9]

Manifestly, therefore, if desires are appetites of which we are
conscious, this implies that there are appetites of which we
are not conscious, and the notion of unconscious motivation
as an element in the Spinozist psychology is clearly established.

Spinoza's method for overcoming the domination of unconsciously motivated and irrational emotions and passions,
and for liberation from them, is through the person's employment of reason in the search for and acquisition of the cognitive knowledge of the *causes* of his passions, and in the utilization of this knowledge to deprive them of their force and
modify them. This is the essence of Spinoza's therapeutic program, as announced in his preface to Book 5 of the *Ethics:*

> I pass at length to the other part of the *Ethics* which
> concerns the method or way which leads to liberty. . . .
> I shall treat of the power of reason, showing how much
> reason itself can control the emotions, and then what is
> freedom of mind or blessedness. . . . I shall occupy my-
> self here . . . with the power of the mind or of reason,
> first of all showing the extent and nature of the author-
> ity which it has over the emotions in restraining them
> and governing them. . . . We shall determine by the
> knowledge of the mind alone the remedies against the
> emotions. . . .

For man is capable of discovering and knowing the nature
of his emotions and passions and their causes: "there is no
emotion of which we cannot form some clear and distinct
conception." [10] While our knowledge of our emotions and
their causes results in only *partial* control over them, a mat-

9. Ibid., Definitions of the Emotions, #1, Explanation.
10. *Ethics,* v, 4, Corollary.

ter to which we shall return shortly, Spinoza displays no
doubt about the availability to us of this power: "every one
has the power, partly at least, if not absolutely, of understanding clearly and distinctly himself and his emotions, and
consequently of bringing it to pass that he suffers less from
them." [11]

When, through knowledge of the causes of our passions,
the passions themselves become an object of our intellectual
scrutiny and reflection, they are susceptible to change. "A passion ceases to be a passion as soon as we form a clear and
distinct idea of it." [12] Spinoza's therapeutic principle is thus
rooted in man's capacity for *reflexive* knowledge, in Spinoza's
doctrine of *idea ideae*. In Spinoza's system, the human being
is one single entity, and what we call mind and body are two
distinguishable aspects of the same single entity. What we call
the mind is "the *idea* of the body." As the *idea* of the body,
the mind has knowledge of its body. But the mind also has
knowledge of itself, it has an idea of itself. "This idea of the
mind is united to the mind in the same way as the mind itself is united to the body." [13] The very fact of knowledge entails *reflexive* knowledge, thought about thought, or *the idea
of the idea,* and this reflexiveness of thought is, to use Hampshire's phrase, "indefinitely open-ended." [14] To quote Spinoza
again:

> the idea of the mind, that is to say, the idea of the idea
> is . . . just as a person who knows anything, by that
> very fact knows that he knows it, and at the same time
> knows that he knows that he knows it, and so on *ad in-
> finitum.*[15]

11. Ibid., Scholium.
12. *Ethics,* v, 3.
13. *Ethics,* ii, 21.
14. *Freedom of the Individual,* 2d ed., "Postscript," pp. 119, 127, 129,
140–41.
15. *Ethics,* ii, 21, Scholium.

This, briefly and most inadequately sketched, is Spinoza's version of the paradigm of a person's liberation, or self-liberation, from bondage to unconsciously motivated and irrational passions. But Spinoza was fully aware of the great power of the passions, and of the resistances and difficulties in the path of overcoming them and thus becoming free. He understood the weakness of reason in its search for the causes of the emotions and passions, and its frequent failure, total or partial, to achieve their modification through the mechanism of reflexive knowledge. Forming a "clear and distinct idea" of a passion—that is, reflexive knowledge of it—is a *necessary condition* for it to cease to be a passion, but it is often, in fact, not a *sufficient condition*. He points out that "an emotion cannot be restrained nor removed unless by a contrary and stronger emotion." [16]

Accordingly, we must note that Spinoza's therapeutic strategy includes reason's utilization of the energy and power of the emotions, by employing desirable emotions to overcome spurious and undesirable ones. For the instrumental purposes of therapy, self-knowledge alone is not sufficient. For he again directs our attention to the fact that "no emotion can be restrained by the true knowledge of good and evil in so far as the knowledge is true, but only in so far as it is considered as an emotion." [17] When we succeed in transmuting true reflexive knowledge into an active emotion that is more powerful than the particular passions of which we ourselves are not the cause—which are caused by forces outside us, and to which we happen to be enslaved—only then will we possess power over the irrationally held passions—"the power, namely, by which it is possible, in so far as they are passions, if not actually to destroy them, at least to make them constitute the smallest possible part of the mind. . . ." [18] And thus

16. *Ethics,* IV, 7.
17. *Ethics,* IV, 14.
18. *Ethics,* V, 20, Scholium.

the *partial* psychic freedom we are capable of will be attained.

This exposition of Spinoza's theory of psychic liberation has left untouched the question of its relation to Spinoza's metaphysical determinism. The problem is a knotty one, and there is an understandable temptation simply to acknowledge its existence and refrain from any attempt to discuss it, on the ground that it is beyond the purview of this essay. However, a brief discussion may at least help to place the problem in perspective.

The problem can be stated, following one of Hampshire's formulations, as follows. A person, by his power and exercise of reflexive thought on his own beliefs, emotions, and passions, and through his thereby becoming conscious of their previously unconscious causes, *can* modify them—that is, he *can* do this in one sense of the word "can," namely, in the sense that he possesses the requisite instruments of thought; but does it follow that the person *can* use these instruments of self-liberation in the sense that there is no external system of causes or concatenation of forces that will prevent him from using them, and that thus makes his psychic freedom impossible? [19] Most Spinoza scholars before Hampshire ascribed to Spinoza the view that the latter *can* is not available to man, since what he does or does not do is governed by a deterministic system of universal causation. According to these interpreters, the psychic freedom Spinoza talks about is only that which is contained in the knowledge a person can achieve of the universal necessity of the causes that completely and ineluctably determine his own emotions and actions, as well as all other events.

19. Hampshire's statement of the thesis of determinism that is implicit in the above question is of value here: "The thesis of determinism is that every case of success and every case of failure in self-liberation is to be explained by some antecedent natural causes, and that, given these antecedent conditions, the outcome could not have been different from what it actually was." "Spinoza's Theory of Human Freedom," in *Spinoza: Essays in Interpretation,* p. 41.

Wolfson may provide us with an illustration. In his classic study of Spinoza's philosophy, Wolfson, on the one hand, tells us that for Spinoza, "reason, and the knowledge which springs from reason, is a means whereby man can . . . overcome the assaults of his own emotions" (vol. 2, p. 330). He speaks of reason as "an instrument of self-mastery." On the other hand, Wolfson takes Spinoza to be saying that:

> reason is the blind tool of nature, and is not an instrument wielded by man as a free agent. . . . To act according to reason . . . does not imply freedom of the will. . . . When Spinoza urges man to act according to reason . . . he does not mean thereby an exhortation to man to exercise his free will; with him it is only an exhortation to man to acquire the proper kind of knowledge upon which reason is nurtured, so that it may grow in strength and assert itself in its full power when called into action. At the challenge of the emotions reason springs into action in the same manner as our eyelids close at the sudden approach of danger to our eyes. [p. 232]

Reason, therefore, according to Wolfson's Spinoza, seems to act no less automatically than do the emotions or passions whose causes we do not know because they lie outside us and we can in no way control them. For Spinoza, whose metaphysical theory is that of a *monistic* universe, with the terms "God" or "nature" (*Deus sive natura*) signifying the totality of the universe, reason itself, as Wolfson properly points out, is a part of nature, "and it follows from the necessity of the attribute of thought" (Wolfson, p. 232). Whether or not reason will "spring into action" at the challenge of a person's emotions is not determined by the person. And all reason can do is lead us to a knowledge or understanding of the emotion and its causes, and of its inevitability as part of the universal causality of God or nature. Or, to use an illustration of essentially the same view from an essay by a contemporary American philosopher, for Spinoza

> the human affects or emotions *are* natural phenomena, continuous with all nature. . . . man is not a "kingdom within a kingdom," but rather wholly within *one* kingdom, nature. He is not a disturbance or a break in the continuity and unity of nature; and therefore, there is no realm in which man has absolute dominion, or "freedom of will," in violation of the universal determinism of the natural world. [Wartofsky, p. 342; emphasis in the original]

And yet, this honorable tradition of Spinoza interpretation fails to explain some of Spinoza's own language in the concluding pages of part 5 of the *Ethics*, when he writes about psychic freedom. He contrasts the *false* notion of freedom, which in reality is psychic bondage, with true freedom of mind. "Most persons seem to believe that they are free in so far as they may obey their lusts. . . . they would prefer to let everything be controlled by their passions, and to obey fortune *rather than themselves.*" [20] In contrast to those who passively let their passions or fortune control them *"rather than themselves,"* Spinoza ties together his fundamental enterprise in this part of the *Ethics* in the following summary:

> I have finished all I wished to explain concerning *the power of the mind over the emotions,* or the freedom of the mind.[21]

It is not knowledge alone, of the emotions and their causes, that Spinoza speaks of as he concludes the *Ethics*, but rather "the power of the mind over the emotions"—that is, a person's power to some extent *to obey himself,* and it is this that is equated with *"freedom of the mind."*

20. *Ethics*, v, 41, Scholium; emphasis added.
21. Ibid., 42, Scholium; emphasis added.

Hampshire seems to me essentially correct when he says that for Spinoza a person's knowledge of the causes of his emotions and actions is not in itself freedom, and that "knowledge of the causes of suffering" does not by itself bring liberation from suffering. For, "liberation consists in the substitution of a free activity and of self-assertion . . . for a passive reaction." [22] And, to return now to the beginning of this exposition of Spinoza's theory of psychic freedom, the "activity and self-assertion," as well as the modifications of the passions and irrational compulsions, are possible by virtue of the reflexive thought, the *idea ideae,* man's capacity to inspect and evaluate his own thoughts, beliefs, and emotions.

Does this mean a departure from, a break in, Spinoza's claimed rigorous metaphysical determinism, and a significant inconsistency in Spinoza's philosophy? I believe it does, and that its source is in Spinoza's failure to think through the full implications of the attribute of *Thought,* one of the two attributes, the other being the attribute of *Extension,* which together are the two constitutive aspects of the universe, or of nature, that are known to man. According to Spinoza, the infinite number of other attributes of the totality of nature are not known to man. There are two implications of the attribute of thought as conceived by Spinoza that make this attribute different from the attribute of extension and, theoretically, also different from any of the other hypothetical attributes. These two differences between the attribute of thought and the other attributes exhibit an inconsistency in the structure of Spinoza's system of metaphysical determinism.

The first of the two differences was noted by Spinoza's contemporary, von Tschirnhaus, in his correspondence with Spinoza,[23] and was never dealt with by Spinoza either in the

22. Hampshire, "Spinoza and the Idea of Freedom," p. 308.
23. Letters 63 and 70, *The Correspondence of Spinoza,* pp. 304–06, 336–39.

extant correspondence or in the *Ethics.* Von Tschirnhaus points out that since there are an infinite number of attributes, each of those attributes and its modifications must have, associated with them, the attribute of thought, and thus "the attribute of Thought is made to extend itself more widely than the rest of the attributes." [24] Or as Frederick Pollock said in his work on Spinoza, "in other words, Thought, instead of being co-equal with the infinity of other Attributes, is infinitely infinite, and has a pre-eminence which is nowhere explicitly accorded to it" (p. 161).[25] Now, while this difference does appear to be inconsistent with Spinoza's deterministic system as a whole, I agree with the judgment of E. M. Curley, in his book *Spinoza's Metaphysics,* that "the special status which our interpretation accords to the attribute of thought is not a difficulty. On the contrary, it is a requirement of any adequate interpretation that it account in some way for the undeniable fact that thought does have a special position among the attributes" (p. 150).

The second respect in which the attribute of thought differs from the other attributes is contained in the fact that, unlike extension (or, theoretically, any other attribute), thought can be *reflexive:* there can be thought about thought, the *idea ideae,* and it is by virtue of this special characteristic of thought that a person, reflecting on his own thoughts, emotions, and so forth, has the capacity to modify them. *Extension* is not reflexive. There is no extension about extension; there is nothing about the body that is analogous to *idea ideae.* This difference constitutes another break in the metaphysical determinism Spinoza propounded, with the result that freedom is not, in fact, foreclosed in his system, and psychic liberation, though only partial and fragmentary, becomes a genuine possibility.

24. Ibid., Letter 70.
25. Cf. also Ruth Lydia Saw, *The Vindication of Metaphysics,* p. 79.

III

The anticipations of Freudian doctrine in the Spinozist theory of mind—of man's bondage to the passions and of the road to the mind's partial liberation from them—are not difficult to perceive. It was Freud, the master cartographer of the human personality, who demonstrated empirically and clinically the presence of unconscious processes and powerful irrational, aggressive, destructive impulses and inner compulsions among the psychological constituents of man. His demonstration of their existence and pervasive power over us is, of course, one of Freud's most important and lasting contributions to our knowledge of human nature.

However, Freud also stressed the importance and forcefulness of reason and rationality in man's make-up. He depicted the individual as always in an ongoing, dynamic state of tension between unconscious, irrational impulses and the dictates of reason and rationality to control those impulses. A person's knowledge of the existence of his unconscious impulses and motivations, and his understanding of their nature, ultimately are the most important equipment for *realistically* coping with them and controlling them. Some of the unconscious and repressed elements, according to Freud, cannot be eliminated: it is part of Freudian theory that they are ineradicable.[26] But what Freud is talking about

26. *New Introductory Lectures* (1933), pp. 104, 105. Freud states here that the repressed, irrational elements in the id are "virtually immortal." He also refers to "the indisputable fact that the repressed remains unaltered by the passage of time." This has often been interpreted to mean that, subsequent to the infantile or early childhood experience that may be judged to have been the origin of a particular repression, the repressed elements remain forever *unaffected* by later experiences. I have argued elsewhere (*Human Nature in Humanistic Psychology*) that this is a misinterpretation of Freud's doctrine. The most cogent evidence against it, I believe, is implicit in the therapeutic process and experience of psychoanalysis, which, to the extent that it is at all successful, is an experience that *affects* or even modifies the particular repressed elements.

is their *control,* regulation, and partial *subjugation* through man's reason and rational processes. This, Freud believed, was now possible because a promising beginning had been made in our knowledge and understanding of man's own irrationality.

It is worth noting parenthetically that the possible, though most often only partial, victories of reason over our unconscious and irrational impulses are of fundamental significance for Freud not only in his role of descriptive psychologist and explorer of the nature of man. They are also, for Freud the moralist, as they are for Spinoza, a moral desideratum, perhaps man's highest ethical goal, the attainment of which would be impossible without a person's knowledge of, and reflexive thinking about, his unconscious motivations.

The goals of psychoanalytic therapy involve man's reason, rationality, and reflexive thought in a role of crucial and essential importance. In short, its twin goals are: first, to lead the patient, through the uncovering psychoanalytic process, to a rational, cognitive knowledge and understanding of the real, previously repressed, causes and motivations of his neuroses, irrational feelings, emotions, attitudes, and behavior; second, through his use of his own reason, through his reflection upon these previously unconscious and now uncovered causes, to make possible his overcoming and controlling them and achieving complete or partial liberation from their tyranny. Thus, the goals of therapy and the goals of ethics coincide in Freudian doctrine as they do in Spinoza's, and may, without distortion, be said to be essentially *rationalist* in character. Of course, neither for Spinoza nor for Freud, so far as psychic freedom is concerned, is the goal mere knowledge or intellectual insight alone. For Spinoza, the goal is the successful exercise of "the power of the mind over the emotions." In Freudian terms, the goal is the self-understanding that is accompanied by emotional insight achieved by the process of "working-through."

If what has been sketched here is essentially accurate, then clearly this part of Freudian theory, and the very logic of psychoanalytic therapy, reflects our previously formulated paradigm of the individual's attainment of psychic freedom. Clearly also, the affinities between the Spinozist and Freudian theories of psychic liberation are compellingly significant, and of more than casual historical interest.

The brevity and generality of this capsulated version of aspects of Freudian doctrine now make it necessary to fill in a few details, and to provide at least some references to textual sources out of the voluminous and complex corpus of Freud's writings.

However, a certain difficulty has to be cleared away in any discussion of Freud's fruitful analysis of the human personality. It is that his writing is infected by a persistent flaw—namely, his frequent and disconcerting hypostatization of the basic concepts he employs. With distracting frequency he uses such locutions as: *"The* id *knows* no values," [27] *"The* ego *has taken over* the task," [28] "from a dynamic point of view *it* [the ego] *is weak,"* [29] *"The* super-ego *seems to have made* a one-sided selection," [30] *"the* id . . . *is* totally non-moral, . . . *the* ego . . . *strives* to be moral, and . . . *the* super-ego . . . *can be* hyper-moral and thus *becomes* . . . ruthless," [31] *"the* unconscious *is a special realm with its own desires."* [32] Such hypostatizations make it seem that for Freud these concepts are *things, concrete entities,* and this opens him up to misunderstanding and misplaced interpretations of his meaning. Because of his metaphorical use of language in reference to these concepts, some critics have taken Freud to be saying that within each of us there are "subsidiary per-

27. 1933, p. 105.
28. 1933, p. 106.
29. 1933, p. 107.
30. 1933, p. 89.
31. *The Ego and the Id* (1923b), p. 79.
32. *A General Introduction to Psycho-Analysis* (1920b), pp. 101–02.

sonalities" (B. F. Skinner, pp. 78, 79)—*homunculi*, independent little men within us—who act, as it were, apart
from the total person.

This is a misreading of Freud. My own view is that his
basic concepts are what in the literature of the philosophy of
science are frequently called "theoretical constructs," and
that fundamentally Freud intended them as such, in spite
of the many, many instances in which his linguistic usage
gives the appearance of his having hypostatized or reified the
concepts. Secondly, my reading of Freud is that, for him,
these concepts essentially refer to and are shorthand symbols
for *psychic processes, dynamic* psychic processes, which much
if not most of the time are in dialectical-reciprocal tension
with each other within the individual person. These processes are distinguishable from each other only in conceptual
discourse but are actually inextricably intertwined and overlapping, often pulling the individual in opposite, apparently
contradictory directions, but often also paradoxically reinforcing each other in the total, mysterious, dialectical structure of the person.[33]

If, then, we keep in the forefront of our attention the
dynamic, process-character of such Freudian terms as "id,"
"ego," "super-ego," and others that we shall have occasion
to refer to, then manifestly it is in the interrelationships and
interactions between id-processes and ego-processes that the
Freudian version of the individual's struggle for and attainment of psychic liberation may first be discerned. Freud has
often been taken to be a psychic determinist, in part for the

33. This reading of Freud is expounded at greater length, and much more
thoroughly, in my work on human nature. Suffice it to say at this point that,
notwithstanding Freud's multiple and regrettable hypostatizations, or his
seemingly static, *spatial* depiction of id, ego, and super-ego in his famous
diagram (1933, p. 111; 1923b, p. 29), Freud does sometimes use the phrase
"unconscious *processes*," or "unconscious mental *processes*" (1933, p. 99 and
passim; *An Outline of Psycho-Analysis* [1940], pp. 37, 51, and passim), and
in at least one passage he speaks of the super-ego as a *"function* in the Ego"
(1933, pp. 86–87).

reasons implied in the essay by Hospers referred to earlier, but even more because he insisted that all human acts—even the most trivial, seemingly capricious, and apparently inexplicable ones, such as slips of the tongue, lapses of memory, and dreams—have reasons or causes, and are in fact explicable in terms of unconscious processes that give rise to them.[34] However, according to Freud, some margin of freedom from the tyranny of these deterministic inner compulsions, even though very limited indeed, is attainable through the controls that the person's ego-processes succeed in exercising over his id-processes.

The id, for Freud, "contains the passions"; [35] "it may be said of the id that it is totally non-moral." [36] "The id stands for the untamed passions," "it is the obscure inaccessible part of our personality," "a chaos, a cauldron of seething excitement," "it has no organization . . . only an impulsion to obtain satisfaction for the instinctual needs," "the id knows no values, no good and evil, no morality." [37]

The ego represents reason, and it is the function of the ego-processes to cope with and control the id and free the person from bondage to it. "The ego represents what we call reason and sanity," [38] "the ego stands for reason and circumspection," [39] "The ego develops from perceiving instincts to controlling them, from obeying instincts to curbing them." [40]

In this struggle of reason to control the "untamed pas-

34. Compare such works of Freud's as *The Psychopathology of Everyday Life* (1901), *Wit and Its Relation to the Unconscious* (1905), *The Interpretation of Dreams* (1900–01), and *A General Introduction to Psycho-Analysis* (1920b). See also Arlow, "Psycho-analysis As Scientific Method," pp. 201–11, especially pp. 204 ff.

35. 1923b, p. 30.
36. 1923b, p. 79.
37. 1933, pp. 107, 103, 104, 105.
38. 1923b, p. 30.
39. 1923, p. 107.
40. 1923b, p. 82.

sions," the contest is not an even one, according to Freud. "From a dynamic point of view [the ego] is weak." [41] Borrowing a simile from Plato, Freud describes this struggle as follows:

> One might compare the relation of the ego to the id with that between a rider and his horse. The horse provides the locomotive energy, and the rider has the prerogative of determining the goal and of guiding the movements of his powerful mount toward it. But all too often . . . we find a picture of the less ideal situation in which the rider is obliged to guide his horse in the direction in which it itself wants to go. [42]

But instructive as is Freud's realistic assessment of the weakness of reason in the struggle to curb the passions, no less instructive is his juxtaposition of this weakness and reason's ultimate and irreducible efficacy and strength:

> We may insist as much as we like that the human intellect is weak in comparison with human instincts, and be right in doing so. But nevertheless there is something peculiar about this weakness. The voice of the intellect is a soft one, but it does not rest until it has gained a hearing. Ultimately, after endlessly repeated rebuffs, it succeeds. This is one of the few points in which one may be optimistic about the future of mankind, but in itself it signifies not a little. [43]

This realistic and moderate optimism in a man who often was driven to overstating his highly pessimistic discoveries about human nature (because his contemporaries were so scandalized by them and so insistently denied their existence) is deeply anchored in Freud's faith in the liberating possi-

41. 1933, p. 107.
42. 1933, p. 108.
43. *The Future of an Illusion* (1927), p. 93.

bilities of the psychoanalytic therapy, limited though they are. "Psychoanalysis," he tells us, "is an instrument to enable the ego to push its conquest of the id further still." [44]

At one point, Freud's faith in the possibilities of psycho-analytic therapy as facilitator of reason's liberating triumph over unconscious compulsions is articulated in words that have the resonance of a manifesto: "the therapeutic efforts of psychoanalysis [have as] their object . . . to strengthen the ego . . . to widen its field of vision, and so to extend its organization that it can take over new portions of the id. Where id was there shall ego be." [45]

On what, then, is this faith based? What is it that psycho-analytic therapy does which, when it *is* successful, makes possible the psychic liberation from the "marshland of un-reason" (Allport, p. 99), the repressed and unconsciously re-membered episodes out of one's remote past, the painful and disabling fantasies that dominate the lives of all of us? A major part of Freud's answer is that, through the uncovering techniques of psychoanalysis, the person is led to an increase in his self-knowledge, to recollection of the repressed and forgotten event or events that are the focus of his fears or aversions, to rational understanding of the unconscious causes of his compulsions and of their irrational character and illegitimate origin, and to the conscious determination to eject them. The unconscious impulses, and the repressed elements to which they are related, Freud tells us, "can only be recognized as belonging to the past, deprived of their significance, and robbed of their charge of energy, after they have been made conscious by the work of analysis, and no small part of the therapeutic effect of analytic treatment rests upon this fact." [46]

A few brief illustrations of Freud's own language on the

44. 1923b, p. 82.
45. 1933, pp. 111–12.
46. 1933, p. 104.

role of reason and the intellect in the end product of success-ful analytic therapy can be found in these quotations from *An Outline of Psycho-Analysis:*

> [The therapeutic process] thus puts us in a position . . . to extend, by the information we give him [the person being analyzed], his *ego's knowledge of his unconscious.* [p. 65; emphasis added]

> The method by which we strengthen the patient's weak-ened ego has as its starting point an increase in *the ego's self-knowledge.* [p. 70; emphasis added]

> As a rule we [the analyst] put off telling him of a con-struction or explanation until he himself has so nearly arrived at it that only a single step remains to be taken. [p. 71]

> it often happens that our patient will immediately con-firm our construction and himself recollect the internal or external event which he has forgotten. . . . As re-gards this particular matter, *our* knowledge will then have become *his* knowledge as well. [p. 72; emphasis Freud's]

> The overcoming of resistances [to the therapeutic un-covering process] . . . is worthwhile, since it brings about a favorable modification of the ego. . . . And we have at the same time worked in the direction of un-doing the modification which had been brought about under the influence of the unconscious; for whenever we have been able to detect its derivatives in the ego, we have drawn attention to their illegitimate origin and have urged the ego to eject them. [p. 74]

> we induce the patient's thus enfeebled ego to take part in *the purely intellectual work of interpretation,* which aims at provisionally filling the gaps in his mental re-

> sources. . . . we restore order in his ego, by detecting
> the material and impulses which have forced their way
> in from the unconscious, and *expose them to criticism*
> *by tracing them back to their origin.* [pp. 76–77; em-
> phasis added]

There is hardly any need for additional documentation,
though it is available in abundance, to enable us to see in
bold relief the pivotal role that Freud assigns to reason, to
the intellect, to conscious self-knowledge, to reflexive knowledge by the individual himself (not by the therapist) of the
previously repressed and unremembered events that have
been functioning as the spurious causes of his problematical
behavior. The modification of that behavior is made possible
through reflexive thought about those causes. The operation
of the "rationalist" paradigm of psychic liberation is thus
evident in Freud's theory, as it is in Spinoza's. It is insightfully summarized in Philip Rieff's observation, in a chapter
entitled "Politics and the Individual," that "There remains
for Freud perhaps the highest rationality: knowledge of the
irrational" (p. 264). Rieff, who elsewhere speaks of Freud's
aseptic rationalism" (p. 370), also draws our attention to the
function of the patient's *talking* in the course of psychoanalytic therapy as part of Freud's rationalism, because talking is
a medium of communicating *conscious* thoughts:

> Talk is therapeutic in itself. By talking about the in-
> stincts, Freud says, we do not cause the instinctual de-
> mand to disappear . . . but we do accomplish a " 'tam-
> ing' of the instinct." [47] Through talking about sexuality,
> we can control it, so the healthy man can choose to ex-
> press his sexual appetite and yet not be irrationally
> driven by it. Self-mastery being a function of self-
> consciousness, by making sexual desires conscious, says

47. Rieff gives as his reference here Freud's "Analysis Terminable and Interminable" (1937), p. 326.

Freud, we gain mastery over them to a degree no system of repression can possibly equal.[48] Talk—language—is the essential medium of consciousness, and therefore the essential means of liberation. [p. 368]

However, Freud's single-mindedness in the explication and defense of psychoanalysis as a theory of, as well as a therapeutic methodology for, the individual's attainment of freedom from bondage to the id-processes goes hand in hand with a sober and realistic understanding of the paradigmatic character of the essential theory, its adumbration of what we referred to earlier as the "limiting case," or the "ideal type construct" of this species of liberation. Repeatedly Freud warns us that "it is true that we do not always succeed in winning," [49] that "the therapeutic efficiency of psycho-analysis is limited by a whole series of important factors," [50] that the patient's "resistances against our work . . . persist through the whole treatment." [51]

Moreover, there is another reason why the Freudian theory of psychic liberation is inextricably tied to the recognition that the freedom attained is most often only partial, limited, and even temporary. This theory must be understood within the matrix of Freud's larger theory of human nature. Man, as mentioned earlier, is portrayed by Freud as an inordinately complex dynamic being. Each person is host to a restless multiplicity of psychic processes in a perennial state of multidirectional tensions. Some of these processes may be understood as constantly in opposition to each other, as is most clearly illustrated in the dialectical tensions between ego-processes and id-processes, between reason and irrational inner compulsions. It is noteworthy that Freud's language about this particular relationship, in, for example,

48. Rieff's reference here is to "Psycho-Analysis" (1923a), p. 252.
49. 1940, p. 78.
50. 1933, p. 210.
51. 1940, p. 73.

An Outline of Psycho-Analysis, consistently and repeatedly
employs metaphorical words of conflict, such as *struggle,
battle, winning, losing.* But, as I indicated, even these two
psychic processes are not always to be dichotomized as mutually exclusive, because they themselves are imbedded in an
intricate network of interrelated mental processes and forces,
sometimes in dialectical opposition but shifting at times from
opposition to mutual reinforcement.

Ernest Jones claimed that "Freud was an obstinate dual-
ist" (vol. 3, pp. 266 ff.) in his view of the instincts, and of
other psychic forces as well. Though there is much evidence
to support Jones's view, I believe it to be a simplification. It
seems to me that the evidence points to an essential *pluralism*
in Freud's portrayal of the human personality. Jones's contention is based on the undisputed evidence he adduces that
Freud's analyses so often eventuate in sets of paired or twin
explanatory concepts, such as:

Primary system	versus	Secondary system
Pleasure principle	versus	Reality principle
Death instinct or		Life instinct or
Thanatos	versus	Eros
Irrational	versus	Rational
Unconscious	versus	Conscious
Id-processes	versus	Ego-processes

Jones concludes from such examples that, according to Freud,
the dynamic tensions within the person's psychic life are always bipolar. But this seems to me too mechanical and sim-
plistic an interpretation of Freud's intention, in spite of
Freud's frequently dualistic conceptual terminology, and in
spite of his own references to the notion of dualism.[52]

52. For a similar point of view with reference to Freud's alleged *dualism,*
see Roy Schafer, "An Overview of Heinz Hartmann's Contributions to
Psychoanalysis," especially pp. 426–29. I am grateful to Dr. Joseph H. Smith
for bringing Schafer's paper to my attention.

Freud's accounts of the dynamic nature of our psychic life contain both implied and direct admonitions against strict dichotomizations of mental processes, as well as references to their multiple interminglings. For example, "subtle and intricate intellectual operations . . . and the solution of a difficult mathematical problem . . . can be carried out preconsciously and without coming into consciousness . . . [or even] during sleep." [53]

In addition to pointing out this intermingling of intellectual operations of a technical type, generally assumed to be manifestations of consciousness par excellence, with states of unconsciousness, Freud mentions another kind of intermingling, this time in connection with a person's moral or social conduct: "There are people in whom the faculties of self-criticism and conscience . . . are unconscious, and unconsciously produce effects of greatest importance." Thus, both the ego and the super-ego are sometimes included in some people's unconscious processes. This leads Freud to the perhaps surprising conclusion that "we shall have to say that not only what is lowest but also what is highest in the ego can be unconscious." [54]

Other examples of intermingling include the phenomena of *ambivalence*—that is, the "clinical observation . . . that love is with unexpected regularity accompanied by hate" and "also that in many circumstances hate changes into love and love into hate"; [55] the frequent inseparability of sadism from masochism; [56] and the working of Eros and the Death-Instinct both together and against each other "to produce

53. 1923b, p. 12. Henri Poincaré, the French mathematician and philosopher of science, reports several such episodes of solutions arrived at without conscious calculation, and during sleep, in connection with complicated mathematical problems with which he had been wrestling (*The Foundations of Science*, pp. 387–94).

54. 1923b, pp. 32–33.

55. 1923b, p. 59.

56. 1933, p. 143.

the phenomena of life." [57] These and countless other illustrations can be cited in support of the assertion that the Freudian theory of man does not *dichotomize* or *fragmentize* the individual. It emphasizes the pivotal presence of continuous, unquiet, dynamic tensions of multiple mental forces and processes in opposition and interaction within the human personality, without introducing into it sharply demarcated, absolute compartments.

What is true about the interplay of these various psychic processes and propensities is also true about the interplay between our reason and our irrational inner compulsions, between the ego-processes and the id-processes. Even after successful psychic liberation, complete or partial, from passions, obsessions, fears, and neuroses through the application of reason and the employment of newly acquired self-knowledge, the person remains a commingling of the two. In the Freudian theory, reason hardly ever stands alone, either when its processes achieve some measure of victory over the id-processes, or when it ends up defeated.

Like Spinoza, Freud recognizes that emotions or passions can be overcome only with the aid of stronger emotions, and that the intellect, or rational calculation, can overcome the power of the destructive passions when it is wedded to constructive emotion. In a significant section of his *Civilization and Its Discontents* (1930), Freud emphasizes the point that "necessity alone, the advantages of common work"—that is, rational determinations of what is desirable—would not in themselves hold people together. But he asserts that there is hope for society's overcoming the destructive effects of the pleasure principle, the tendency to sexual aggression, the instinctual cravings of the id, the general instinct of aggression and self-destructiveness, and other unconscious compulsions present in the psychic structures of its individual citizens.

---

57. *An Autobiographical Study* (1925), p. 103.

This hope arises as a result only of the existence in the individual of the forces of Eros, which aim to "bind to one another libidinally" individuals, families, races, nations—that is, to bind them into a great unity of humanity.[58] In the struggle for psychic liberation, no less than in the struggle for sociopolitical freedom, the possible successes of reason depend heavily on its having attached to it a constructive emotional dimension.

Finally, the attainment of psychic liberation from irrational compulsion is often completely subverted, or substantially impaired, through the insidious collaboration of reason itself, in the form of what we call "rationalization." Among the defenses, evasions, and self-justifications in which individual humans indulge when there are guilt feelings or ambivalences about the justifiability of some of their actions, is the self-deceiving strategem of rationalization. To the best of my recollection, Freud himself used this term only once, in the *New Introductory Lectures,* and he used it there in a different sense from the meaning assigned to it today and from the sense in which it is being used here.

However, though the term "rationalization" as now understood was not used by Freud, the psychological mechanism was described by him many times. In essence, it is the process of finding some justifiable explanation or alibi to others, and especially to oneself, for doing something that is inconsistent with what is socially approved, or in good taste, or expected normal behavior. For example, a person who gives an unusual amount of money, time, and leadership to a boys' club, presenting the appearance of generosity and community-mindedness, may in fact be covering up a repressed and unconscious tendency toward a homosexual interest in young boys.

In this rationalized behavior, the intellect collaborates

58. 1930, p. 102.

with an unconscious, irrational, sexual compulsion and desire, permitting the unconscious emotion to dominate the
person's life and providing apparently rational explanations
for his actions. Thus, as Hospers characterizes the phenomenon,

> One's intelligence and reasoning power do not enable
> one to escape from unconsciously motivated behavior;
> it only gives one greater facility in rationalizing that be-
> havior; one's intelligence is simply used in the interest
> of the neurosis—it is pressed into service to justify with
> reasons what one does independently of the reasons.
> [p. 117]

Evasions and self-deceptions occur with amazing frequency
in everyday life, in interpersonal relations, in facing unpleasant imperatives in the course of one's work, and in resisting the therapeutic process when it approaches too closely
the uncovering of the real causes of neurotic behavior. I will
later comment on rationalization in connection with Hampshire, but it is sufficient to make the point here that Freud's
recognition of the mechanism of rationalization is another
explanation of his conviction that the psychic freedom attainable by an individual is only partial, temporary, and a
fragile achievement, easily fractured and destroyed.

IV

It remained for Stuart Hampshire to uncover and to exhibit instructively and cogently some further implications
for psychic freedom that are contained in Spinoza's doctrine
of *idea ideae,* of reflexive thought, and that are also contained in Freud's account of the relationships and interactions between the rational ego-processes and unconscious
id-processes in the intricate structure of the human personality, and of the methods and goals of psychoanalytic therapy.
Hampshire's own theory of psychic liberation from passions

and unconscious compulsions is deeply rooted in the theories of Spinoza and Freud. Like theirs, and perhaps even more avowedly and explicitly, his theory reflects, in its essential outlines, the "rationalist" paradigm of psychic liberation suggested at the beginning of the present discussion.

Hampshire is concerned with the broader issues of human freedom and moral responsibility, and a major part of his published work is devoted to the elaboration, in a variety of ways and with striking ingenuity, of the major thesis that the source of human freedom is knowledge, and that the exercise by man of knowledge, including self-knowledge, makes a thoroughgoing determinism untenable. Some indication of this is contained in Hampshire's adumbration of the purpose of his book, *Thought and Action:*

> To show the connection between knowledge of various degrees and freedom of various degrees is the principal purpose of this book. "Why should that which I do with full knowledge of what I am doing alone constitute that which I do with full freedom?"—this question will only be answered by the whole argument. [p. 133]

In the interest of a more thorough understanding of this thesis, as it applies to the issues that are our major concern here, it will be useful first to explicate one of Hampshire's arguments concerning human freedom—namely, that freedom of the mind cannot be denied even on the hypothesis of a metaphysical materialism, when we undertake to explain intentions, beliefs, attitudes, desires, and so forth.

Hampshire developed this argument, in two somewhat different ways, in his ingenious and provocative papers, "Freedom of Mind" and "A Kind of Materialism," presented originally as lectures in 1965 and 1969, respectively, and included in the volume *Freedom of Mind.* As Hampshire says in the earlier paper, according to one interpretation of the materialist hypothesis, when the explanation of emotions is involved, it is assumed that for every state of mind, or for every emotion, there exists a distinct physical state of the organism that is invariably correlated with it. Thus, with the emotion of anger, for example, there is an invariably correlated physiological state that can be produced or removed by certain physical stimuli, with immediate corresponding effects on the emotion. According to this hypothesis, we would find in all cases "that subjects cease to be angry with x, and to be angry with x because of y, if the appropriate physical change is made; they only consider y as a reason for being angry when they are in the appropriate physical state; and when they are in the appropriate physical state, they always find some reason for being angry with someone." [59] If this materialist hypothesis were verified, then the state which we had been calling anger would be explained as the perception of a certain physical state. Thus, when I am angry I am in fact perceiving a modification of my body, "in the same sense that we feel a bruise . . . or a heavy object on our back." [60]

Now, suppose I, who am angry at Jones, come to know about this mechanism—that is, about the physiological cause of the emotion called anger. Such knowledge would enable me to make inferences from my state of mind to a cause external to my state of mind. I would, accordingly, as a result of my quest for an explanation of my emotion of anger, now have knowledge of the physiological states involved, but I would also then have a different psychic state correlated with my new knowledge of the *explanation* for my emotion of anger. What began as my anger with Jones for something he had done would now have become an awareness of a changed physiological state, "in relation to which Jones's action was merely an inessential occasion." Because I would no longer believe that Jones's behavior was a necessary in-

59. *Freedom of Mind,* p. 16.
60. Ibid., p. 17.

gredient to my anger, it would follow that I would no longer be angry with Jones for what he had done. In this sense, my acquisition of knowledge of the (materialist) explanation has changed my emotion, or my state of mind, and the experience or phenomenon which we had first set out to explain in accordance with standard scientific procedures would vanish and remain unexplained, leaving an ambiguous and seemingly inexplicable break in the putatively universal, deterministic system of explanation. Moreover, "once convinced of the truth of the scientist's explanation," I would have to "determine [my] attitude to Jones's action all over again." [61]

For this reason, says Hampshire, there is "an unclarity, or even an ambiguity," in any claim that psychic states, or intentional states, are in principle explicable like any other natural phenomena by reference to covering laws in a deterministic system of explanation. This is especially true of intentional states, because the subject's knowledge of the explanation of his emotion by reference to a covering law within a deterministic system will by itself change the psychic state that is ostensibly being explained. Thus, "the intentional description, which incorporates the subject's thought of a cause [of the intention] will have to be changed, as the subject's beliefs change." [62]

The discovered physiological causes of the emotion—say the subject's anger—"are the causes of that independently identifiable state which the subject previously classified as anger, thereby explaining the state in a way which he now knows to have been erroneous. The causes of *that* state which he has previously classified as anger will no longer be the causes of anger." [63]

This consequence of a person's acquisition of knowledge

61. Ibid., p. 19.
62. Ibid., p. 20.
63. Ibid.

about the explanation of his own emotions, beliefs, attitudes, desires—that is, his acquisition of *reflexive knowledge*—is peculiarly true of the explanation of intentional states generally. A person's knowledge or beliefs about the explanation of his own intentional state, or a change in the person's beliefs about the explanation, "modifies the descriptions applicable to the phenomenon explained, and also modifies the explanation itself." [64] Hampshire's instructive illustration here makes the point even clearer:

> If a man comes to believe that his state of confidence in the excellence of his performance is wholly explained by a confidence-engendering pill which he has taken, he will no longer be so confident of the excellence of his performance. . . . the change in the subject's belief about its cause will constitute a change in his state of mind.[65]

Essentially these same generic complexities are entailed, as noted above, in all suggestions of hypotheses that propose causal, deterministic explanations for intentional states and processes. The difficulties, and the inescapable break they expose in the deterministic hypothesis, always become manifest when the individual reflects on proposed explanations of his own psychic processes, in this way exercising his capacity for *reflexive knowledge*. One's reflexive knowledge of an assumed causal mechanism in one's own psychic, and especially intentional, processes, constitutes a change in the effect of the mechanism. And "this is the complexity," says Hampshire, "which makes a place, as Spinoza suggested, for freedom of mind." [66]

The ingenuity of this argument in support of the principle that reflexive knowledge is the source and necessary condition

64. Ibid., pp. 15–16.
65. Ibid., p. 15.
66. Ibid.

of freedom of mind is matched in other arguments for this principle elsewhere in Hampshire's books and papers, but they cannot be developed here. The principle, of course, is predicated in the first instance on Spinoza's fertile contribution to philosophical psychology; this contribution, as reformulated in Hampshire's most recent paper, "The Explanation of Thought," says that "thoughts, whether beliefs or desires, may always be made the objects of second-order thoughts, beliefs about beliefs, desires about desires; and what a person believes about the nature and causes of his thoughts, including his beliefs, to some extent modifies the thoughts" (p. 8). In this essay he also reiterates his insistence on the fundamental differences between psychological explanations and explanations of physical phenomena:

> psychological explanation has at least one peculiarity that distinguishes it from explanation of physical states and events: that man's knowledge of, and his beliefs about, the factors determining his own states always modifies these states. . . . [p. 3]

> The causal connections are not established, as are causal connections between physical events, by referring to laws correlating independent events, but by laws referring to internal connections between thoughts, connetions that make the thoughts seem intelligible. [p. 11]

> [reflexiveness] is *one* distinguishing feature of psychological explanation, which may be a good basis for saying that deterministic conceptions cannot finally be applied without restrictions to mental events: the subject's knowledge of the cause always, in his own case, to some degree modifies the effect. [p. 3]

However, in addition to elaborating new features of the traditional *freedom versus determinism* controversy through his emphasis on the reflexiveness of mental states as opposed to physical states, Hampshire also brings his incisive analytic tools to work on the specific problem of liberation from the tyranny of unconscious motivations and compulsions. It is on this problem that Hampshire's unfolding of the Spinozist concept of *idea ideae* brings additional and revealing illumination, as well as on the concomitant problem of moral responsibility. This is helped by Hampshire's introduction of a new term, "stepping back," which in one part of its meaning is expressive of the Spinozist idea of "reflexive thought." When a person thinks about his thoughts, when he reflects on or deliberates about any strong impulse or desire that he experiences, tries to evaluate it and determine by means of his "second-order" thoughts what the causes are of the desire under his scrutiny and what his ensuing actions ought to be, it is as if his reason has *stepped back* from the experienced desire and has carried out its evaluation from a second-order position. Hampshire makes frequent use of the term,[67] and I shall have occasion to use it in the ensuing pages and to explain it more fully.

Hampshire draws on Freud for the evidence that much of the life of each of us is under the domination of unconscious policies and purposes. "We commonly do not know what we are trying to do." There are many instances in which a person "may be said to be pursuing a policy, and executing a plan, without in any sense knowing that that is what he is doing." [68] The person is powerless to control or change these policies, and his actions are often inconsistent with his sincerely professed intentions. The effects of these unconscious processes and compulsions are not limited to manifestly abnormal or neurotic behavior. According to Hampshire, their effects are observable across a wide spectrum of seemingly "normal" behavior:

67. For example, *Thought and Action*, pp. 189–90 and passim; *Freedom of the Individual*, p. 89 and passim.
68. *Thought and Action*, p. 132.

> Freudian psychology may have provided good experi-
> mental reasons for believing that sane men are in many
> situations incapable of recognizing or of controlling in-
> fluences upon their conduct that may often be evident to
> others. . . .[69]

That there is here a problem of freedom of the mind versus
psychic bondage is clearly disclosed by the fact that the meaning and direction of the subject's anomalous or seemingly
normal behavior and policies, though they are not understood
by the subject himself, often are clearly understood by others,
particularly his psychoanalyst. If I needed to be told what I
was doing, Hampshire insightfully observes, and if someone
knew and understood what I was doing better than I did,
it would follow that I was not a free and fully responsible
agent.

> Only with knowledge comes the opportunity of choice
> and therefore full responsibility. If I did not know what
> I was trying to do, no possibilities of deliberate change
> were open to me.[70]

It is therefore natural for Hampshire to assert categorically
that "the most powerful argument against the reality of
freedom is the old argument that has been given some new
basis in . . . interpretations of the work of Freud and his
followers." [71]

What then is the therapy? Essentially, for Stuart Hampshire, it is the same "rationalist" therapy that we found in
Spinoza and Freud. It is, to repeat, the individual's exercise
of reason and knowledge, especially reflexive self-knowledge,
in discovering the causes of his unconsciously propelled passions, and in achieving their ejection or modification. The
essential paradigm of psychic liberation is the same for all

69. Ibid., p. 191.
70. Ibid., p. 132.
71. Ibid., p. 178.

three. If there are any significant differences that distinguish Hampshire's doctrine from Spinoza's and Freud's, they are *first*, that Hampshire develops some rather subtle and penetrating analyses of implications of *reflexive knowledge* through an examination of the notion of *self-prediction* and of what it tells us about freedom of mind generally. The *second* difference consists in Hampshire's comparatively greater confidence about the *efficacy* of reason and reflexive knowledge in actually breaking through and eliminating or modifying a person's unconsciously motivated compulsions. This also seems to me to entail, as a consequence, Hampshire's comparatively greater confidence with respect to the moral responsibility and accountability to which a person may be held. In short, it would appear to me that Hampshire's doctrine may be said to be more "rationalist" than those of Spinoza and Freud.

Regrettably, a discussion of Hampshire's argument to show that the impossibility of *self-prediction* [72] constitutes another break in the possibility of determinism cannot be included here.

In what follows, the outlines of Hampshire's theory of psychic liberation will be presented, including a brief account of one of its moral implications. Some critical assessments of the "rationalism" of Hampshire's theory will bring the discussion to a conclusion.

Both conceptually and clinically, the *necessary* condition of psychic freedom, for Hampshire, is knowledge. One of Hampshire's difficulties is that he sometimes writes as if he believed that knowledge is also the *sufficient* condition of freedom, but to this I shall return in my concluding paragraphs. However, the therapeutic knowledge, the knowledge that eventuates in psychic freedom, is for him, as it is for Spinoza and Freud, *self-knowledge:*

72. *Thought and Action*, pp. 169–76, 187–91; *Freedom of the Individual*, pp. 73–91; Pears, pp. 80–104.

> A man becomes more and more a free and responsible agent the more he at all times knows what he is doing. . . .[73]

> The more reliable and extensive my inductive knowledge is, including self-knowledge, the less likely I am to attempt a course of action which, unknown to me [and therefore inaccessible to my free control], I cannot carry through. The more I learn of the conditions on which my passions and abilities depend, the narrower the gap between that which I set myself to do, and that which I actually achieve, will become.[74]

For Hampshire, this kind of reflexive knowledge is also a necessary condition for the improvement and freedom of thought generally, not only for freedom from the tyranny of emotions and passions:

> As self-consciousness is a necessary prelude to greater freedom of the will, so is it also a prelude to a greater freedom of thought.[75]

> The improvement of thought always requires reflection, the formation of ideas of ideas, and a critical self-consciousness; there is no other method.[76]

As to the methodology for getting hold of the reflexive knowledge required to become psychically liberated, Freudian psychoanalytic therapy is in full accord with Hampshire's theory of psychic freedom. From the standpoint of this theory, "Freudian psychology is no more than an extension of reflection in order to bring to consciousness repressed wishes and beliefs." [77] Here is a fuller statement of Hampshire's

---

73. *Thought and Action,* p. 177.
74. *Freedom of the Individual,* p. 90.
75. *Thought and Action,* p. 312.
76. "The Explanation of Thought" (p. 16).
77. Ibid.

systematic placement of psychoanalytic theory and therapy within the framework of his own theory of psychic freedom:

> The new positive science of human conduct, psycho-analysis . . . is founded upon a peculiar form of memory and a peculiar form of self-consciousness of the subject. It might even have been predicted that it must take this form, if it is to be knowledge that explains to the subject why he has the purposes he has. As an applied science, psychoanalysis identifies the increasing freedom of the agent to control his own conduct and states of mind with an extended self-consciousness, with a capacity to recognize in memory motives and purposes that he had not recognized before. Pyschoanalysis therefore provides a reflexive knowledge of the workings of the mind that fits into the philosophical definition of freedom in terms of self-knowledge.[78]

The bringing to consciousness, to self-awareness, and to the critical scrutiny of reason through second-order thoughts, of the previously unrecognized causes of one's emotions and behavior—the loosening from the grip of repression of long-forgotten memories of long-forgotten events, and their identification as the source of attitudes or compulsions—makes possible a liberation from them, and a new freedom for the subject to direct his thoughts and behavior rationally. This process, says Hampshire, inasmuch as its goal is self-conscious, deliberate action, entails as a necessary ingredient our stepping back in our thinking in order to scrutinize, via second-order thoughts, not only the causes of our previously compelled behavior but also "the possible ends that we may attempt to achieve," [79] "the new possibilities." [80] In a sense it would probably be correct to say that, from a critical point

78. *Thought and Action*, p. 255.
79. Ibid., p. 189.
80. *Freedom of the Individual*, p. 89.

of view, Hampshire's "stepping back" idea is similar to or
at least overlaps with what the psychoanalyst would call the
patient's "objectification" at a certain point in the analytic
process. But it is broader than that. Hampshire's stepping
back is unavoidable if the psychoanalytic uncovering process
does not stop at only identifying and understanding the causes
of the problematic behavior but endeavors to bring about
changes from the earlier situation. As Hampshire explains:

> About the "stepping back" and secondary decisions; any
> inductive knowledge that a man acquires of the deter-
> minants of his behavior, which are other than his own
> decisions, changes the situation as he confronts it; he
> sees that certain possibilities which he had believed to
> be open, are closed. But he now has to decide what he
> is to try to do in the new situation. He is not absolved
> from further decision, just because he now realizes that
> the primary decision would have been inoperative. This
> is the "stepping back," which opens new possibilities of
> things that he might now do. . . .[81]

Whether Hampshire's "rationalist" implication that the
uncovering process of psychoanalytic therapy, and its liberation of the subject from his compulsions, must in fact "inevitably" result in either a "change" in the subject's behavior
or in an inescapably *deliberate* decision on his part to leave
the situation as is, constitutes an interesting problem. Is it
truly "necessary" or "inevitable" that the subject will make
a new decision? In what sense is the subject "not absolved
from further decision" because he now realizes "that the
primary decision would have been inoperative"? Is it not possible that the subject will neither take any new action nor
rationally and deliberately decide to commit himself to the
old situation, but rather will simply and will-lessly and pas-

81. In Pears, p. 98.

sively continue as before? This possibility is neither contradictory to Freudian theory nor unfamiliar to clinical psychoanalytic experience, though it of course seems repugnant to Hampshire's deeply ingrained "rationalism."

Hampshire's doctrine here is most tempting and provides a suggestive antidote to one phase of Hospers's antilibertarian argument. It was Hospers's contention that since none of us is the author of his own character, the person guilty of immoral or criminal behavior can justifiably claim that he cannot be held responsible for his criminal acts because, he might argue, "I am that kind of person as a result of heredity or environment, and I could not help doing what I did; it was impossible for me—I was not free—not to do it." Hampshire's argument against this kind of position is a provocative one. If I have acquired reflexive knowledge about the kind of person I am,

> I cannot have this last kind of knowledge without a policy, a strategy, being required of me as my response to the situation now recognized. . . . I can always be asked when I first recognized these features of my situation. From this moment onwards, I am responsible for changing or not changing my policies in one direction rather than another. . . . It is unalterably impossible that we should either explain or excuse our present or future voluntary and deliberate action by referring to the influences bearing upon us, unless we are explaining or excusing in advance an unexpected failure to achieve that which we shall genuinely try to achieve.[82]

> [Therefore] my character is still something for which I am responsible. . . . If I had thought that my history, and the external causes influencing me, were . . . bad in their effects, I at least could have tried to find the means to prevent or minimize their effect. . . . I am

82. *Thought and Action*, pp. 188–89.

faced with the choice of acquiescing or of trying to find the means of diverting or minimizing their effects.[83]

This is Hampshire's "stepping back," and his confidence that the reflexive knowledge that is part of it will unavoidably result in a free choice. But it does not always happen, and Hampshire's phenomenological description of the stepping-back process, with its features of required moral responsibility, fails to demonstrate that the subject, having become aware of these features, was not still bound by some compulsion to repeat the crime, did indeed have the freedom to change, and was disingenuous in his self-prediction that he would inevitably repeat the crime.

Perhaps, in this dispute between Hospers and Hampshire, one might be driven to support an unpopular separation— namely, between being held morally responsible and being subject to punishment. Perhaps, if *ex hypothesi* the subject did phenomenologically experience the stepping back and the moral features of the situation but nevertheless did not change, we would hold him *morally* blameworthy for not changing; but on the basis of the Hospers-Clarence Darrow hypothesis that the subject, in spite of his rational, reflexive awareness of the moral features of the situation, was nonetheless under psychic compulsion and not free to refrain, he should not be subjected to severe punishment.

The purpose of this discussion of Hampshire versus Hospers was to help focus on what I earlier called Hampshire's greater confidence (compared to Spinoza and Freud) in the "rationalist" paradigm of psychic liberation. Not that Hampshire is oblivious to the failures of reason to prevail: he is not, as is evident in numerous passages in his writings. But an extract from his most recent paper illustrates his relative sanguinity. Hampshire points out that a person, when asked

83. Ibid., p. 187.

about his belief or desire or any other kind of thought, "may be self-deceived, or he may make a mistake," but in the self-same passage he goes on to claim categorically that "he is at least privileged in respect to conscious thought. He will modify his beliefs and desires, and they will change, as he reflects on their causal connections. He will even on occasion be ashamed of the causal dependences when he reflects on them, and he will consequently disavow and change what he has discovered to be his previous thinking." [84]

One carries away an impression from this and other passages that too often, for Hampshire, self-conscious thought and reflection on the causes of desires and passions automatically result in the subject's triumph over and liberation from these desires and passions. Such a doctrine would suggest that he holds the exercise of reason and reflexive thought to be the *sufficient* condition for psychic freedom, and would be provocative of many doubts, as we shall see below.

This brings us back to the thesis that knowledge is the *necessary* condition of freedom. We can take it to be part of Hampshire's thesis, as it is of Spinoza's and Freud's that every person's achievement of psychic freedom from unconsciously caused compulsions is a case of the person's having exercised his reason, his reflexive knowledge, and the resulting self-modifying power of his thought—that without this kind of knowledge and thinking the liberation could not have taken place. But is the converse of this statement also and always true? Is every case of a person's self-knowledge, of reflexive thinking, of his having become conscious of predictions of his behavior, also *necessarily* a case of his becoming liberated from the tyranny of a passion, or of modification of his behavior? Are there not many cases of the subject's ignoring the acquired reflexive knowledge, even defying it, or resisting and evading any modification of his behavior by various

84. "The Explanation of Thought," p. 9.

strategies of self-deception and rationalization? Are knowledge and intention identical? Are all intentions conscious? What of *unconscious* purposes? Hampshire says:

> I cannot escape the burden of intention, and therefore of responsibility, which is bestowed upon me by knowledge of what I am doing, that is, by recognition of the situation confronting me and of the difference that my action is making. As soon as I realize what I am doing, I am no longer doing it unintentionally.[85]

Strictly speaking, all Hampshire is entitled to say here is that as soon as I realize what I am doing, "I am no longer doing it *unknowingly.*" I may be doing it knowingly, but at the same time be governed by some *unconscious purpose,* the existence of which Freud demonstrated most persuasively and Hampshire would of course not deny.

Another observation forces itself upon the student of Hampshire's work, especially when it is seen through the Spinozist and Freudian perspectives—namely, that he attributes to *reason,* which is so significant in his doctrines, a central and strange exclusivity in relation to psychic liberation. There is in his texts insufficient evidence of his recognizing, as Spinoza did, that an emotion can be overcome only by a contrary and stronger emotion, and that therefore reason is in need of the collaboration of emotion. Except for a brief reference to a person's first-order desire for alcohol being eliminated "because other desires were being frustrated by alcoholism," [86] no other outstanding illustration comes to mind of any attention being given to this important psychologico-philosophical point for any theory of psychic liberation. Absent also is any noteworthy attention to the intricate interminglings, in man's complex and dynamic structure, of reason and unreason, ego and id, Eros and Thanatos, love and hate, sadism and masochism. For the most part

85. *Thought and Action,* p. 175.
86. *Freedom of the Individual,* p. 134.

Hampshire does not comment on the ambivalences and tensions that characterize human existence and are so compellingly relevant to the understanding of both the strong resistances to and the hoped-for triumphs of psychic liberation.

It is perhaps this overemphasis on the role of reason, not as a moral desideratum but as a force in man's psychological structure, that may account for Hampshire's unsatisfactory treatment of the phenomenon of *Akrasia*,[87] a term that is discussed at some length by Aristotle [88] and is variously translated as "Incontinence," "Imperfect Self-control," "Moral Weakness," or "Weakness of Will." Aristotle's problem was to try to explain how it was possible for a person to display the puzzling moral weakness implicit in his asserting that he knows that to do X would be a mistake or evil, and his proceeding at the same time to *do* the very act called X. Aristotle pointed out that Socrates had denied the existence of the problem on the ground that such a person did not really have the "knowledge" that doing X was evil; he was obviously ignorant or mistaken about this.

Aristotle's attempt to resolve this paradox need not detain us here. But Hampshire's explanation simply does not have the ring of reality:

> a man cannot be sincere in accepting the conclusion that some course of action is entirely mistaken, if he at the same time deliberately commits himself to this course of action. . . . a man cannot without absurdity *say* of himself that he is convinced . . . [that the action would be a mistake but that] he will do exactly this . . . mistaken thing.[89]

Human beings often display precisely this kind of moral weakness. We may recall, for example, the familiar case of Saint Paul, who in his Epistle to the Romans (7 : 19), made

87. Ibid., pp. 71 ff.
88. *The Nicomachean Ethics,* book 7, especially chap. 3.
89. *Freedom of the Individual,* p. 71; Hampshire's emphasis.

just such a public confession, "I do not do the good I want, but the evil I do not want to do is what I do," without either insincerity or absurdity *necessarily* characterizing his declaration. Hampshire's judgment here seems obviously predicated on the assumption of total or overwhelmingly great *rationality* in man, and consequently of the impossibility of self-contradiction—or of the coexistence of two mutually opposed intentional states—infecting the human psyche; but men are obviously self-contradictory with disconcerting frequency.

And finally, a brief comment must be made about the relationship between reason and rationalization. Hampshire does take cognizance of the phenomenon of rationalization as one of the impediments that lie in the way of a person's efforts to know what he is doing, to act freely, with full self-consciousness and rational, reflexive self-knowledge. However, here too his overemphasized rationalism gets in his way. He suggests that if one reflexively becomes convinced that in his "rationalized" situation his "regret, shame, discouragement, disapproval, hope, confidence, admiration [are] utterly inappropriate to their subjects, *the state of mind must disappear*," and further, that "when the subject recognizes that the object does not have the properties that are required . . . [he] cannot still regret *that which he now knows not to be regrettable*." [90] But this does not always happen. The state of mind in which the "rationalization" prevails often does not disappear, and we often do precisely continue to regret that which we know "not to be regrettable."

For it is a well-known feature of rationalization that the intellect collaborates with the process, and that reason in fact often helps find spurious self-justifications for continuing the self-deception. Reason itself may turn out to be fickle and may permit itself to be used in the service of the unconsciously motivated purpose. In the process of rationalization,

90. Ibid., pp. 94 ff.; emphasis added.

reason may in fact conspire to circumvent itself, furthering conclusions or actions that are really advancing the unconscious passion or compulsion or delusion. The subject thus maintains the illusion that cognition and reason have triumphed immaculately, whereas in actuality they have not. Since Hampshire's texts do not always remark on these dangers inherent in the rigid reliance on reason as the ultimate arbiter of truth, goodness, and right, residual questions about this frequently exclusivist "rationalism" are unavoidably raised.

However, even after these deviations from the rationalistic paradigm have been noted, and man's resistances to its guidance are seen in their naked force, and even after the extreme narrowness and fragility of the margin of psychic freedom that can be achieved have been recognized, the ultimate fact still remains that such psychic freedom is always a product of, or a function of, the exercise of reason, of reflexive thought. Ultimately, it is only by the employment of reason that we can detect, identify, penetrate, expose, or explode rationalizations, so that the self-deceptions may be made transparent, the falsity held up to one's own and perhaps to public scrutiny, and the mask of rationalization torn off.

In the final analysis, therefore, it is only reason, imperfect and open to misuse though it is, that remains the ultimate guide and tribunal to which man must repair in order to distingiush between freedom and servitude, good and evil, right and wrong, truth and falsehood. Hampshire's seemingly overstated emphasis apart, it is only true knowledge, reflexive thought—especially when we succeed in imparting to it an emotional dimension—that is able to overcome or at least to restrain our damaging or pathogenic emotions or compulsions. Psychic freedom, to the limited extent that it is attainable—whether we pursue the quest for it via Spinoza's insights, or via Freud's clinical discoveries, or via Hampshire's penetrating inquiries—is shown to be attainable only when the necessary condition is present, namely, *the exercise of reason*. In this sense, a theory of psychic freedom must rest on the bedrock of the fundamental and indispensable rationalism shared by these three seminal thinkers.

REFERENCES

Alexander, B. "Spinoza und die Psychoanalyse." *Chronicon Spinozanum* 5 (1927) : 196–203.

Allport, G. W. *Becoming: Basic Considerations for a Psychology of Personality.* New Haven, Conn.: Yale University Press, 1955.

Aristotle. *The Nicomachean Ethics.*

Arlow, J. A. "Psychoanalysis as Scientific Method." In *Psychoanalysis, Scientific Method, and Philosophy,* edited by S. Hook. New York: Grove Press, 1960.

Bernard, W. "Freud and Spinoza." *Psychiatry* 9 (1946) : 99–108.

Bidney, D. *The Psychology and Ethics of Spinoza.* New Haven, Conn.: Yale University Press, 1940.

Brill, A. A. "Reminiscences of Freud." *Psychoanalytic Quarterly* 9 (1940) : 177–83.

Curley, E. M. *Spinoza's Metaphysics: An Essay in Interpretation.* Cambridge, Mass.: Harvard University Press, 1969.

Feuer, L. S. *Spinoza and the Rise of Liberalism.* Boston: Beacon Press, 1958.

Franck, I. *Human Nature in Humanistic Psychology.* Unpublished.

Freud, S. *The Interpretation of Dreams (1900–01); The Psychopathology of Everyday Life (1901); Wit and Its Relation to the Unconscious (1905).* In *The Basic Writings of Sigmund Freud,* translated and edited by A. A. Brill. New York: Modern Library, Random House, 1938.

———. *Beyond the Pleasure Principle (1920).* Translated by C. J. M. Hubback. London: Hogarth Press and Institute of Psycho-Analysis, 1948a.

———. *A General Introduction to Psycho-Analysis (1920).* Translated by J. Riviere. Garden City, N.Y.: Garden City Publishing Co., 1938b.

———. "Psycho-Analysis (1923)." In *Standard Edition of the Complete Psychological Works,* vol. 18. London: Hogarth, 1955a.

———. *The Ego and the Id (1923).* Translated by J. Riviere. London: Hogarth Press and Institute of Psycho-Analysis, 1947b.

———. *An Autobiographical Study (1925).* Translated by J. Strachey. London: Hogarth Press and Institute of Psycho-Analysis, 1948.

———. *The Future of an Illusion (1927).* Horace Liveright and Institute of Psycho-Analysis, 1928.

———. *Civilization and Its Discontents (1930).* Translated by J. Riviere. New York: Jonathan Cape & Harrison Smith, 1930.

———. *New Introductory Lectures on Psycho-Analysis (1933).* Translated by W. H. J. Sprott. New York: Norton, 1933.

———. *Collected Papers.* New York: Basic Books, 1959. Vol. 5, "Analysis Terminable and Interminable," edited by J. Strachey, 1937.

———. *An Outline of Psycho-Analysis (1940).* Translated by J. Strachey. New York: Norton, 1963.

Hamblin-Smith, W. "Spinoza's Anticipation of Recent Psychological Developments." *British Journal of Medical Psychology* 5 (1925) : 257–78.

Hampshire, S. *Spinoza.* Baltimore: Penguin Books, 1951.

———. *Thought and Action.* New York: Viking Press, 1960.

———. *Freedom of the Individual.* 2d ed., with postscript. New York: Harper & Row, 1965.

———. *Freedom of Mind.* Princeton, N.J.: Princeton University Press, 1971.

———. "Spinoza and the Idea of Freedom." In *Spinoza: A Collection of Critical Essays,* edited by M. Grene. Garden City, N.Y.: Anchor Books, Doubleday, 1973.

———. "Spinoza's Theory of Human Freedom." In *Spinoza: Essays in Interpretation,* edited by E. Freeman and M. Mandelbaum. LaSalle, Ill.: Open Court Publishing Co., 1975.

———. "The Explanation of Thought." In *Psychiatry and the*

Humanities, vol. 2, edited by J. H. Smith. New Haven, Conn.: Yale University Press, 1977.

Hospers, J. "What Means This Freedom?" In *Determinism and Freedom in the Age of Modern Science,* edited by S. Hook. New York: New York University Press, 1958.

Jones, E. *The Life and Work of Sigmund Freud.* 3 vols. New York: Basic Books, 1953.

Nelson, B., ed. *Freud and the 20th Century.* New York: Meridian Books, 1957.

Parkinson, G. H. R. "Spinoza on the Power and Freedom of Man." In *Spinoza: Essays in Interpretation,* edited by E. Freeman and M. Mandelbaum. LaSalle, Ill.: Open Court Publishing Co., 1975.

Pears, D. F., ed. Dialogue, "Freedom and Knowledge," by I. Murdoch, S. Hampshire, P. L. Gardiner, and D. F. Pears. In *Freedom and the Will.* New York: St. Martin's Press, 1963.

Poincaré, H. *The Foundations of Science.* Translated by G. B. Halsted. Lancaster, Pa.: Science Press, 1946.

Pollock, F. *Spinoza: His Life and Philosophy* (1899). 2d ed. New York: American Scholar Publications, 1966.

Rathbun, C. "On Certain Similarities Between Spinoza and Psychoanalysis." *Psychoanalytic Review* 21 (1934): 1–14.

Rieff, P. *Freud: The Mind of the Moralist.* Garden City, N.Y.: Anchor Books, Doubleday, 1961.

Saw, R. L. *The Vindication of Metaphysics: A Study in the Philosophy of Spinoza.* London: Macmillan, 1951.

Schafer, R. "An Overview of Heinz Hartmann's Contributions to Psychoanalysis." *International Journal of Psycho-Analysis* 51 (1970): 425–46.

Skinner, B. F. "Critique of Psychoanalytic Concepts and Theories." *Minnesota Studies in the Philosophy of Science.* Vol. 1, *The Foundations of Science and the Concepts of Psychology and Psychoanalysis,* edited by H. Feigl and M. Scriven. Minneapolis: University of Minnesota Press, 1956.

Spinoza, B. *Ethics.*

———. *The Correspondence of Spinoza.* Translated and edited by A. Wolf. London: George Allen & Unwin, 1928.

Wartofsky, M. "Action and Passion: Spinoza's Construction of a

Scientific Psychology." In *Spinoza: A Collection of Critical Essays,* edited by M. Grene. Garden City, N.Y.: Anchor Books, Doubleday, 1973.

Wolfson, H. A. *The Philosophy of Spinoza: Unfolding the Latent Processes of His Reasoning.* Cambridge, Mass.: Harvard University Press, 1948.

Index

Action, 117, 161–63; practices as, 87; vs. state, 32; and will, 34–36, 161–63

Adaptive mechanisms, 79, 81; in dreams, 51, 54-55, 56, 65, 72, 75, 76–77; and reality, 203–04

Affects, 288–90, 302; and dreams, 64–65; and memory, 61–62; and subjective experience, 192. *See also* Passions

Akrasia, 303

Aletheia, 245

Alienness. *See* Otherness

Ambiguity, 114, 135, 142–43, 155; in speech, 42–43; and synesthesia, 137; in thinking, 43

Ambivalence, 284–85

Anderson, J. R., 54

Animals, thinking by, 25–27

Anthony (saint), 31

Anxiety, 20, 23, 182–83

Aristotelian Society, 126, 127

Aristotle, 30, 303

Arlow, J., 141–42

Art, 91–92, 107

Association: of ideas, 6–8, 11–13, 16, 19; and memory, 52. *See also* Free association

Attitudes, and thought, 12–13

Augustine (saint), 47

Austin, J. L., 113, 116

Ayer, A. J., 127

Balint, M., 236

Bartlett, F. C., 229–30

Bateson, G., 145, 146–47

Behaviorism, 127

Being, 118; and clarity, 113–17; and consciousness, 119, 120; and language, 122; pure, 244

Belief: vs. feeling, 7; systems of, 209–11; and thought, 10, 13

Beres, D., 206

Berkeley, George, 30

"Beyond the Pleasure Principle" (S. Freud), 64

Bidney, David, 257, 264

Bion, W. R., 222, 236

Bodily states. *See* Physical states

Bonaparte, M., 148

Borges, Jorge Luis, 149–50

Bower, G. H., 54

Brain, physical aspect of, 17–18

Breger, L., 54

Bridgman, P. W., 149

Brodey, W. M., 197

Brunswik, E., 204

Cameron, N., 176

Cartesianism, 19, 113–14, 128, 161, 162. *See also* Descartes, René

Change, in thought, 10, 18, 21–22, 296

Civilization and Its Discontents (S. Freud), 285

Clarity, and Being, 113–17

Cognition, 185–211, 212. *See also* Thought

Coherence, and truth, 231–32

Colby, K. M., 51

Communication, 47–48, 147, 247–48

Computer simulations of memory, 53–54

Conceptualization, 208–11

Condensation, dream, 56–59, 78

Connectedness. *See* Association

Consciousness, 86, 111–12, 119–21; and dreaming, 61–64, 65, 78; and enownment, 99–100; and intentionality, 125–30; and language, 113–14; and self-organization, 192; thinking as, 86–87, 88–89, 93, 96; of thoughts, 5–6, 8, 11, 13, 31, 32, 46, 79–80

Consensus, and truth, 233–35, 245

Construction, and truth, 227, 238–39

"Constructions in Analysis" (S. Freud), 227

Conviction, and truth, 227

Copernicus, Nicholas, 232

Corrections: in dreams, 65–75. *See also* Improvement

Correlations, in thinking, 9, 12–13, 14

Culture, and philosophy, 130

Curley, E. M., 272

Deaf-mutes, thinking by, 46–47

Decisions, and talking, 38

Defensive mechanisms, 59, 65, 72, 76–77; in infant development, 183; in paranoid process, 168–69, 174; and superego, 228–29

Déjà vu, 138, 141–42, 143, 150

Descartes, René, 6, 27–28, 30, 31. *See also* Cartesianism

Determinism, 15, 22, 268, 271, 272, 276–77, 291

Development: infant, 178–84, 193–94; and paranoid process, 168–69, 178–85, 200

Dewan, E. M., 54

Dialectics, 94–97, 102, 112–13, 114, 124

Double-bind theory, 135, 144, 145–47

Dreams, 49–50; condensation in, 56–59, 78; corrections in, 65–75; information-processing in, 50, 54–55, 56, 60–61, 62–65, 75, 76–79; and memories, 51, 60, 63, 65, 74, 75, 79

Drives, 137, 155, 218–20, 222–23, 240–42. *See also* Motivation

Dualism, in Freud, 283

Dufrenne, M., 118, 119, 121

Ego, 284; fictitious normal, 237–38; vs. id, 276–78, 282–83, 285; in psychoanalysis, 280–81; and reality, 200–01, 236; and self-organization, 189–90

Einstein, Albert, 92

Elation, 13–14

Emotions, 288–90, 302. *See also* Affect; Passions

Empathy, 186

Empiricists, 30, 80

Enownment, 97–102, 103–08

Errors: in speech, 43–44; in thought, 44

Ethics (Spinoza), 263, 265, 270, 272

"Explanation of Thought, The" (Hampshire), 3–23, 292

Extension, and thought, 271–72

External experience: vs. internal, 159–66, 178–79, 180–81; and phobias, 173–74. *See also* Realities

Fantasies, 159–61, 225, 226–27. *See also* Internal experience

"Fausse Reconnaissance in Treatment" (S. Freud), 143

Fear, 13–14

Federn, P., 153

Feeling, vs. belief, 7

Ferenczi, S., 141, 243, 244

Feuer, Lewis S., 257, 264

Fliess, Wilhelm, 224

Food, and enownment, 100–02

Free association, 6–7, 16, 51, 186, 223–24

Freedom, 305–06; and enownment, 105; Freud on, 260–61, 275, 277, 282, 286, 287, 301; Hampshire on, 258–59, 260–61, 268, 271, 287–88, 291–92, 294, 295–97, 301, 302–03, 305; Hospers on, 259–60; and sense, 246–47; Spinoza on, 260–61, 268, 270–71, 272, 291–92

Freedom of Mind (Hampshire), 257, 288

Freedom of the Individual (Hampshire), 257

Free will, 259, 269

Frege, G., 121

Freud, Anna, 135, 169

Freud, Sigmund, 242, 248, 275–77; and ambiguity, 144, 145, 147; and causal agents, 231; and continuity, 148; and déjà vu, 141, 143; and dreams, 49, 50, 51, 55, 56–59, 60, 63, 64, 65, 75, 78; and drives, 218–19; and fantasy, 159–60, 225, 226–27; and freedom, 260–61, 275, 277, 282, 286, 287, 301; Hampshire and, 258, 260, 261, 293–94; and memories, 224, 226; and narcissism, 167; and phobias, 174; pluralism of, 283–85; and rationalization, 286–87; and reality, 159–60, 199, 224–25; and reason, 262, 273–74, 277–81, 285–86; and repression, 80–81; and Spinoza, 257, 258, 260, 261, 274; and superego, 167, 223; and truth, 223, 228, 243; and the unconscious, 147, 273, 279, 284, 293–94, 302

Fry, William, 149

Fugue states, 138, 140

Gill, M. M., 190

Gödel, K., 146, 147, 148, 149

Goethe, J. W., 232

Green, A., 242

Greenberg, R., 54, 56, 66

Guntrip, H., 189

Habermas, J., 238

Hampshire, Stuart, 80, 257–58; and action, 161–63; and emotions, 288–90; and freedom, 258–59, 260–61, 268, 271, 287–88, 291–92, 294, 295–97, 301, 302–03, 305; and psychoanalysis, 296–99; and reason, 262, 302, 303, 304, 305; and reflexive knowledge, 291, 294–96, 299–300, 301; and reflexive thought, 3, 8–23, 77, 266, 287, 292–93; and Spinoza,

6, 7, 17–22 passim, 258–71 passim, 293; and the unconscious, 293–94, 302

Hartmann, Heinz, 133–34, 163–64, 199, 200

Hawkins, D. R., 54–55

Hegel, G. W. F., 94, 95–96, 99

Heidegger, M., 99, 114, 115, 118, 221

Heisenberg, Werner, 148–49

Heraclitean Fragment *123*, 115

History, 121–22, 124; developmental, 230, 240; genetic, 230, 240; and truth, 220–21, 224, 227, 228, 231, 239

Hitler, Adolf, 88

Hobbes, Thomas, 30

Hospers, John, 259–60, 277, 287, 299, 300

Human Associative Memory program, 54

Humanism, 247

Hume, David, 16

Husserl, Edmund, 121, 126, 238

Id, vs. ego, 276–78, 282–83, 285

Ideologies, political, 210

Illusion, 193, 195–96

Imagination: and perception, 205–06; and thinking, 34, 40, 45–46

Improvement: in thought, 18, 21–22, 296. *See also* Corrections

Individuation, in infant development, 181–82

Infant development, 178–84, 193–94

Information-processing, 51; in dreams, 50, 54–55, 56, 60–61, 65–65, 75, 76–79

"Instincts and Their Vicissitudes" (S. Freud), 218

Intention, 34–37

Intentionality, 125–30

Internal experience, vs. external, 159–66, 178–79, 180–81. *See also* Fantasy; Subjective experience

International Psycho-Analytic Congress (*1971*), 135

Interpretation of Dreams, The (S. Freud), 49 56–59
Introjection: in infant development, 181–82, 194; in paranoid process, 167–72, 173–75, 176–77; and subjective experience, 187–88 191–92
Introspection, 186–87, 189
Isolation, thought in, 7–8

Jacobson, E., 167, 172
Jones, Ernest, 283
Judgments, in cognition, 209
Jurisprudence, as thinking, 90–91

Kafka, Franz, 247
Kant, Immanuel, 161, 247
Kinship, 105–06
Klüver, Heinrich, 133, 136
Knowledge: of animals, 25; and reality, 201–02; reflexive, 288, 291–92, 294–96, 299–300, 301; vs. thought, 25
Kohut, H., 169, 186, 188, 191, 198
Kuhn, T. S., 210–11

Language, 121–25; and clarity, 115–16; and consciousness, 113–14, 119–21; ontology of, 118, 120; and thought, 12, 29–30, 31, 44, 108; and truth, 234–36, 243, 244, 245
Laws: in association of ideas, 16; in physical sciences, 3, 14–15, 17
Learning theory, 16
Leiderman, P. M., 54
Lenin, V. I., 88
Lichtenstein, H., 134, 136
Life forms, 102–03, 105
Lindsay, R. K., 52
Little Hans (*1909*), 174, 241
Loewald, H. W., 134, 149, 156, 170, 171, 201
Logic, in thoughts, 12
Love, 243

Mahler, Margaret S., 178–79, 181, 182
Manipulation, of insights, 15–16
Marcovitz, E., 141–42

Materialism, 288–90
Medical knowledge, 18, 22
Memories, 51–56, 60–61, 62, 64, 76; and dreams, 51, 60, 63, 65, 74, 75, 79; in infant development, 180–81; screen, 224, 226
Mental acts: vs. mental states, 32; and saying, 37–38
Mental states, 3, 18–21, 32
Merleau-Ponty, M., 114, 221
Metacommunication, 147
Metaphysics, 117
Miller, G. A., 204
Milner, B., 55
Mind: philosophy of, 17, 111, 119–21, 257–58, 273; as time, 149, 156
Modell, A. H., 184, 197–98
Money-Kyrle, R. E., 207
Motivation, 137; unconscious, 217, 259, 264–65, 273. *See also* Drives; Passions
"Mourning and Melancholia" (S. Freud), 219
"Mystic Writing Pad" (S. Freud), 55

Narcissism: and illusion, 197; in infant development, 179, 180, 183; and introjection, 167, 168–69; and self-organization, 188, 190–91
New Introductory Lectures (S. Freud), 286
"New Refutation of Time, A" (Borges), 149–50
Newtonian science of thought, 16
Novey, S., 134

Oberndorf, C. P., 141
Object constancy, 133, 135–42, 150, 155, 156, 184–85
Objective experience. *See* Realities
Objects: drive, 218–20, 240–42; transitional, 193–98, 201–02
Oedipus complex, 217–19, 221–23, 238
Ontology, 117–18, 120
Orderliness, of thoughts, 6–8
Ornstein, R. E., 151

Otherness, 87, 93, 94; in art, 92; and consciousness, 86, 89, 96; and en-ownment, 97–98

Outline of Psycho-Analysis, An (S. Freud), 280–81, 283

Ownness, 94, 97–99, 106

Paradigm, scientific, 211

Paradox, 135, 144–48, 149, 150, 155

Paranoid construction, 176–78, 208, 210

Paranoid process, 166–78, 207–08, 210, 212, 213; and development, 160–69, 178–85

Passions, 21–22; and reason, 261–68, 277–78, 285. *See also* Drives; Emotions

Pattern, and realities, 141, 156

Paul (saint), 303–04

Pearlman, C., 56, 66

Perception, 155–56, 205–08

Personality, theory of, 19, 275

Peterfreund, E., 51

Phenomenology, 114–16, 117–20, 124, 125–30

Philosophy, 80, 256–57; analytic, 114–16, 117–24, 125, 129–30; of mind, 17, 111, 119–21, 257–58

Phobias, 173–74. *See also* Paranoid process

Physical sciences: belief systems in, 210–11; explanations about, 3, 4, 14–16, 17; knowledge in, 201; and passions, 22

Physical states: and emotions, 288–90; and thought, 17–21, 22, 292

Picasso, Pablo, 92

Plato, 28–29, 34, 247, 278

Platonism: on thinking, 30–31, 36, 37, 38–39, 44, 48; on understanding, 15–16

Pluralism, in Freud, 283–85

Polanyi, M., 201

Politics, 106–07, 210

Pollock, Frederick, 272

Port Royal Grammar, 30

Practice, 87–93, 103–04

Pragmatics of Human Communica-tion (Watzlawick et al.), 145

Primal scene, 160

Principia Mathematica (Whitehead and Russell), 145

Projection, 172–77, 181–82, 194, 207

Propositions, 33

Psychoanalysis, 80, 147–48, 212, 257, 274, 279–82, 296–99; and informa-tion-processing, 51; and internal vs. external experience, 159–60, 164–66; and object constancy, 133, 135; and realities, 198–99, 213; and time, 148, 150–51, 152–55; and transi-tional experience, 196–97; and truth, 221–23, 228–48

"Psychoanalytic Notes on an Auto-biographical Account of a Case of Paranoia" (S. Freud), 219

Psychology, 16, 19, 133, 136; vs. physi-cal sciences, 3, 4, 14–17

Psychology and Ethics of Spinoza, The (Bidney), 264

Quanta, 148–49

Rapaport, David, 190, 212, 218

Rationalism: Freud and, 262, 274, 281, 288, 294–95, 306; Hampshire and, 262, 288, 294–95, 304, 306; and language, 30; Spinoza and, 262, 274, 288, 294–95, 306

Rationalization, 286–87, 304–05

Realities, 133–35, 144–45, 155–56; and development, 185; experience of, 198–211, 212, 213; and fantasy, 159–61, 225; psychical, 224–26. *See also* External experience; Internal expe-rience; Truth

Realizing, and talking, 37–38, 39–40

Reason: and freedom, 305–06; Freud and, 262, 273–74, 277–81, 285–86; Hampshire and, 262, 302, 303, 304, 305; and passions, 261–68, 277–78, 285; and rationalization, 304–05; Spinoza and, 269–70

Recoding, 153
Reconstruction, vs. construction, 227
Referring devices, 40–42
Reflection, 6, 8. *See also* Knowledge, reflexive; Thought, reflexive
Religion, 107–08, 210
"Remembering, Repeating and Working-Through" (S. Freud), 226
Rieff, Philip, 281
Romanticism, 80
Ross, M., 228
Rousseau, Jean Jacques, 80
Russell, Bertrand, 145, 146
Ryle, Gilbert, 29, 40, 126–27, 129

Saint Anthony, 31
Saint Augustine, 47
Saint Paul, 303–04
Sandler, J., 188
Sartre, Jean-Paul, 120
Saying: vs. showing, 116; and talking, 33–36; and will, 34–37. *See also* Speech
Schachtel, E. G., 143
Schafer, Roy, 163, 164, 170–71, 172, 187, 188, 240
Schilder, P., 153
Schönberg, Arnold, 92
Schopenhauer, Arthur, 80
Science, 87. *See also* Physical sciences
Self-prediction, 295
Sense, truth as, 220–21, 227, 231–40, 241, 242–48
Sensory data, 17; cognition of, 202–05, 206; in dreams, 52, 59, 61, 62, 63, 75, 77–78; and synesthesia, 137
Separation, in infant development, 181–84, 193–94
Showing, vs. saying, 116
Socrates, 303
Speech, and thought, 27–31, 33–48, 281–82. *See also* Language
Spinoza, B.: and determinism, 268–70, 271, 272; and freedom, 260–61, 268, 270–71, 272, 291–92; and Freud, 257, 258, 260, 261, 274; Hampshire and, 6, 7, 17–22 passim, 258–71 passim, 293; and passions, 21, 22, 263–67, 302; and reflexive thought, 261–62, 272, 287, 293
Spinoza and the Rise of Liberalism (Feuer), 264
Spinoza's Metaphysics (Curley), 272
Stepping back, 293, 297–98, 300
Street cleaning, as thinking, 92–93
Subjective equivalence, 133, 136–37, 155, 156
Subjective experience, 185–92. *See also* Internal experience
Superego, 167, 190, 223, 228–29
Symbols, 236, 243, 244. *See also* Language
Synesthesia, 137–41, 143

Talking, and thinking, 33–39, 281–82. *See also* Speech
Taylor, Charles, 127
Theaetetus (Plato), 28–29
Therapy: as practice, 88; rationalist, 294–95. *See also* Psychoanalysis
Thought, 4, 32, 86; by animals, 25–27; as consciousness, 86–87, 88–89, 93, 96; dialectic, 94–97; and enownment, 100, 101–02, 104, 105–08; and extension, 271–72; first-person, 4–8; and memory, 51, 77–79; as practice, 88–93, 104; propositional, 33–34, 39; reflexive, 3, 8–23, 77–81, 261–62, 266–68, 271, 272, 287, 292–93, 305; and speech, 12, 27–31, 33–48, 281–82
Thought and Action (Hampshire), 257, 258, 288
Time, experience of, 148–56
Transcendence, 121, 124
Transference, 196, 228, 239–40, 241
Transitional experience, 193–98, 201–02
Translating, 45
Truth: and fantasies, 226; and free association, 223–24; historical, 220–

Truth (*continued*)
23, 224, 227, 228, 231, 239; as sense, 220–23, 227, 231–40, 241, 242–48
Truthfulness, and truth, 242–43
Tugendhat, E., 238

" 'Uncanny,' The" (S. Freud), 144
Unconscious, the, 96; Freud on, 147, 273, 279, 284, 293–94, 302; Gödel on, 147, 148, 149; Hampshire on, 293–94, 302; and motivation, 217, 259, 264–65, 273; and Spinoza, 264
"Unconscious, The" (S. Freud), 219
Understanding: Platonism on, 15–16; and thinking, 37, 44; and truth, 235

Visible and the Invisible, The (Merleau-Ponty), 114
von Tschirnhaus, Ehrenfried W., 271–72

Wallerstein, R. S., 134, 199
Watzlawick, P., 145
Whitehead, Alfred North, 92, 145, 146
Will, and saying, 34–37. *See also* Free will
Winnicott, Donald W.: and ambiguity, 143, 144–45, 147; and environment, 181, 236; and objects, 143, 193, 194–95, 198, 242
Wittgenstein, L., 5, 29, 116, 234
Wolf Man (*1918*), 160, 174, 225
Wolfson, H. A., 258, 269